FIGURE DRAWING

in proportion

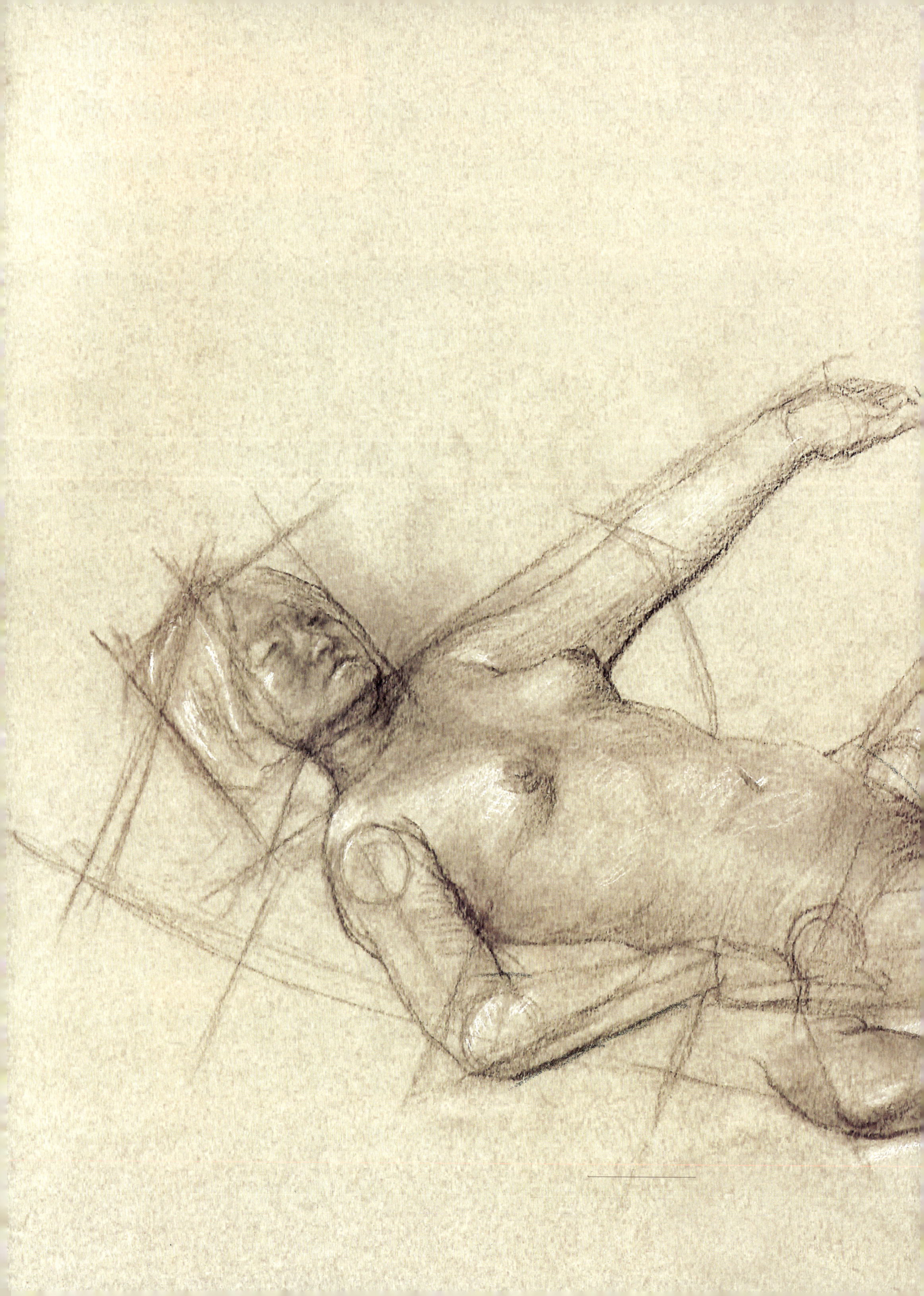

FIGURE DRAWING
in proportion

Easy to Remember, Accurate Anatomy for Artists

Michael Massen

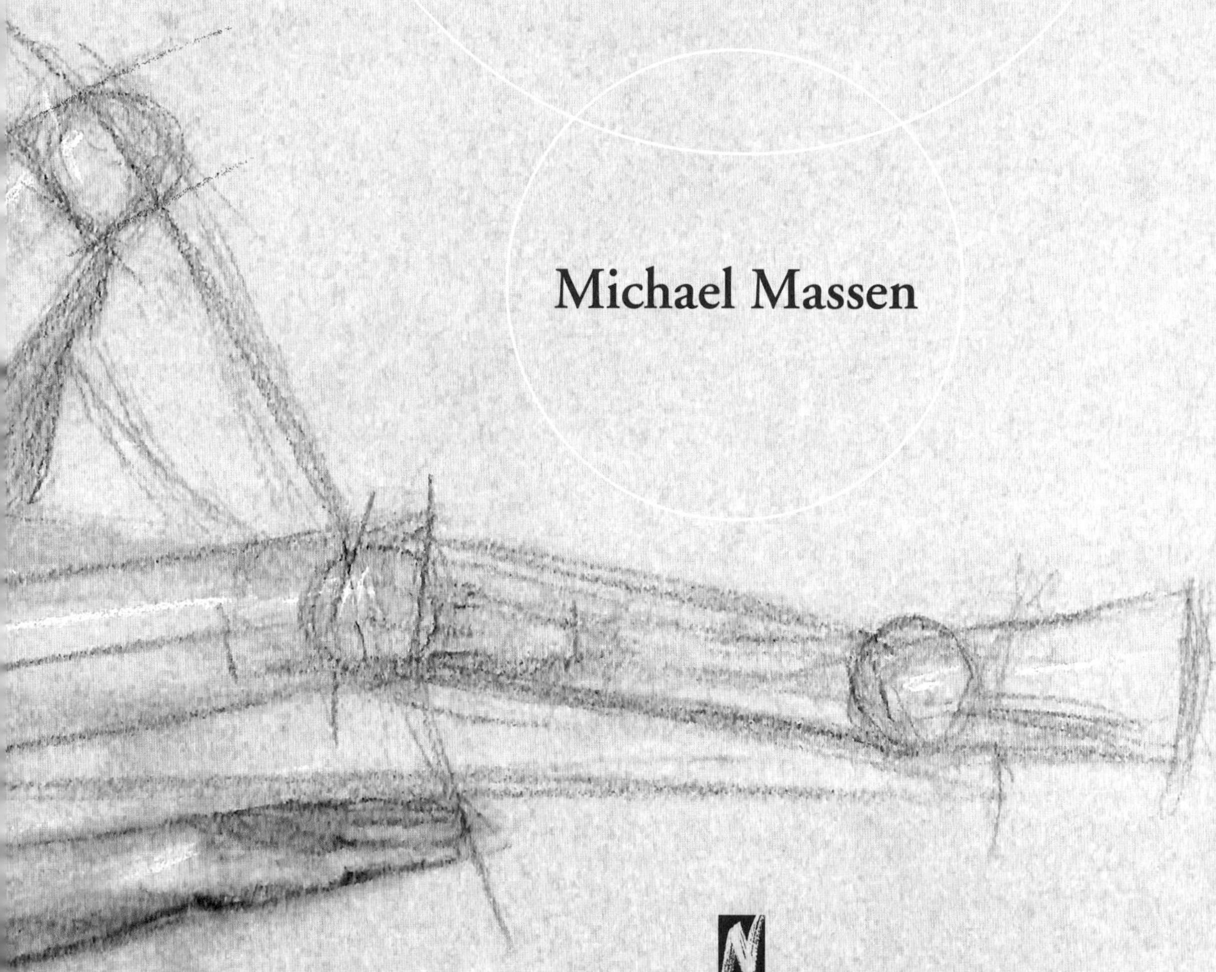

NORTH LIGHT BOOKS
CINCINNATI, OHIO
artistsnetwork.com

CONTENTS

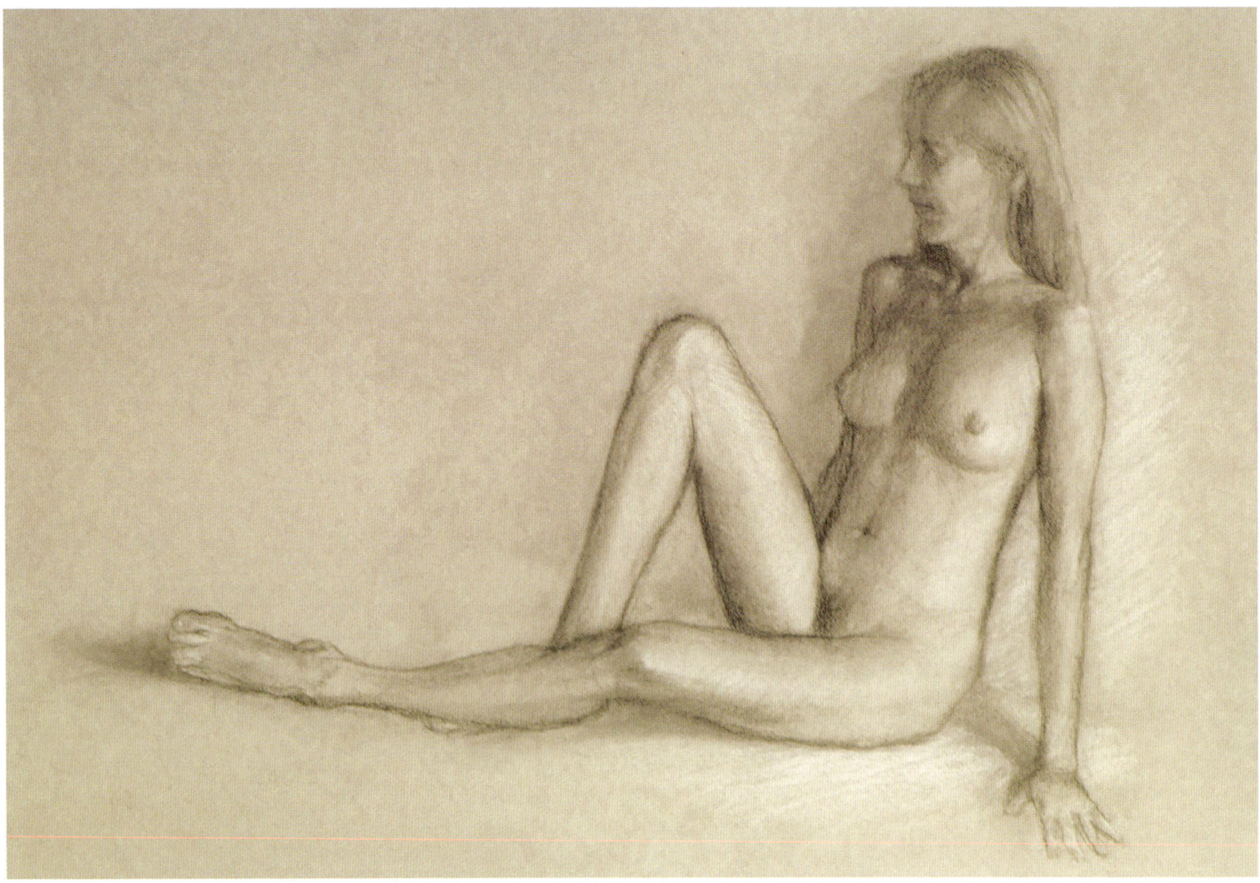

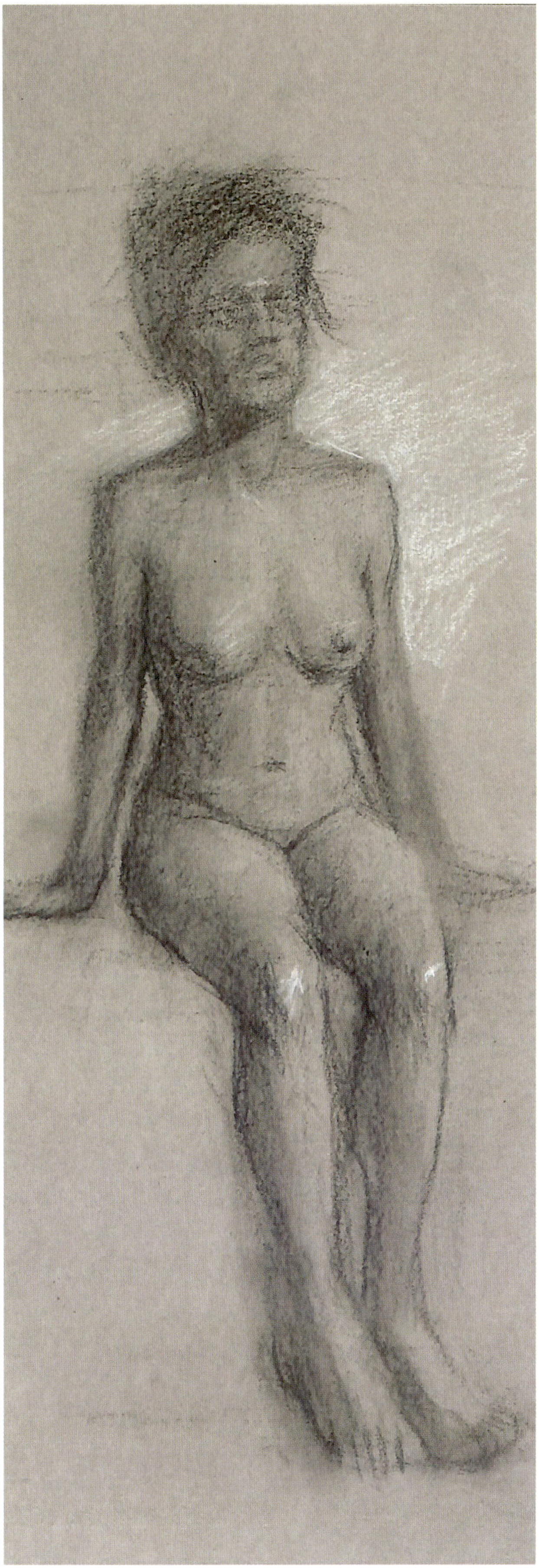

WHAT YOU NEED

Surface

Canson Mi-Teintes 98-lb. (160gsm): gray, green, light blue, orange, pink, purple, tan, white

semi-translucent graphics paper

Pencils

charcoal pencils: B, HB, 2B, 4B, white

Conté pencils: HB, 2B, 4B, white

graphite pencils: HB, 2B, 4B

sepia Conté pencils: HB, 2B, darker color or black

Other Supplies

chamois cloth (or rag or paper towel)

dividers

kneaded eraser

pencil sharpener or knife and sanding block

tortillion

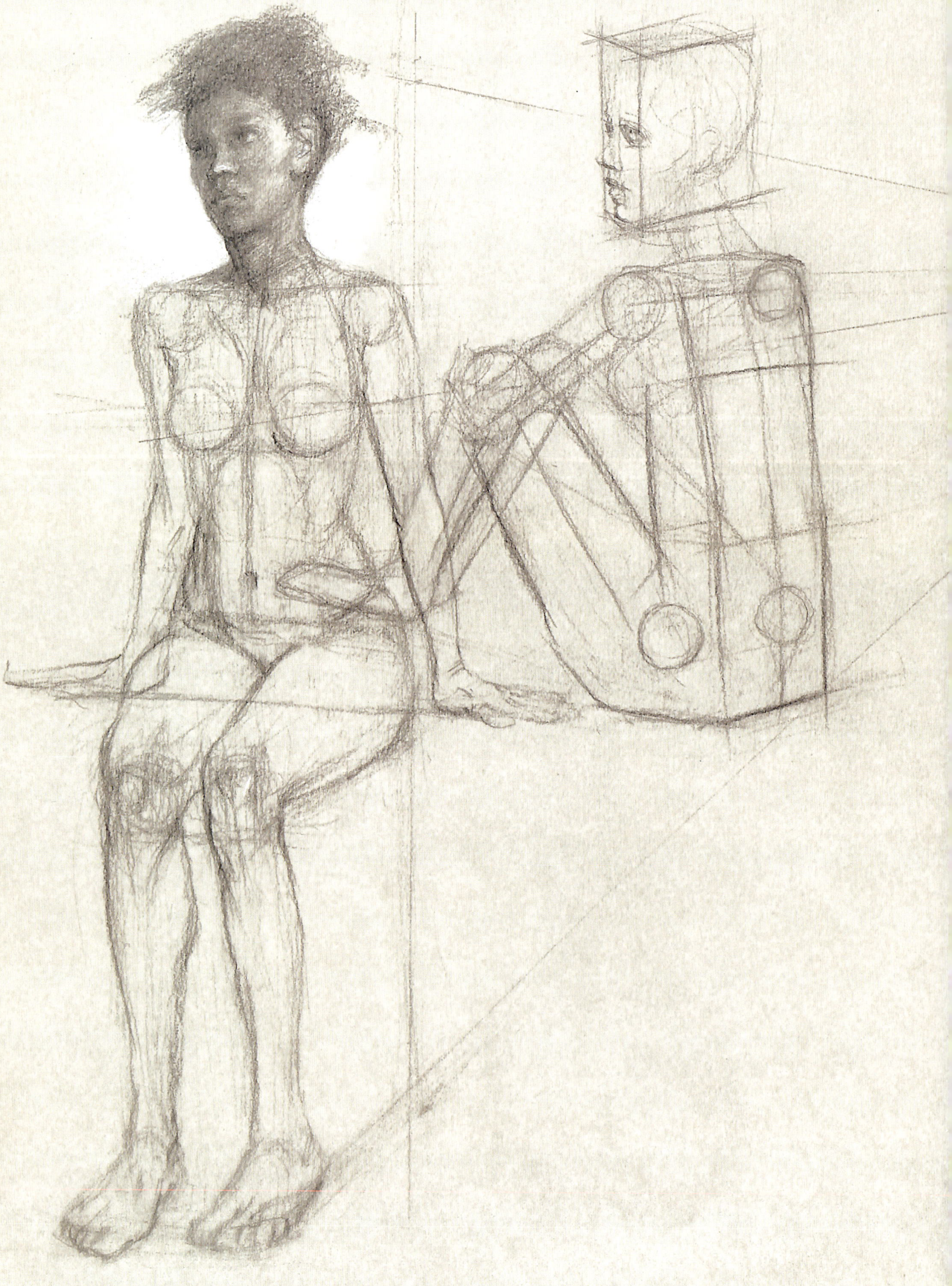

INTRODUCTION

This is a book about proportion. More specifically, it's a book on figure proportion for visual artists. Just what is proportion anyway? Let's define it as "a relationship between measurements."

For example, we could talk about the proportion (or the relationship between measurements) between two lines or two sticks. And from there, we could make interesting observations, such as "those two lines are of equal length" or "the second stick is shorter than the first stick" or "the first line is twice as long as the second line." Having such information makes it a lot easier for us to draw representations of the same objects on paper, whether they be lines, sticks or whatever.

Proportions can also consist of comparisons between the different dimensions of the same object. For example, we could say something like, "That box is twice as long as it is wide." Or "That box is as wide as it is high." If you are drawing a cube or sphere, both of these sayings would be true.

Simple Proportions

Certainly, some proportions are easier for us to make quick sense of than others. If we want to draw a cube, for example, we know that we have to make its width equal to both its length and its height. Similarly, if we know that something is spherical, then we know that it is also of equal width, length and height. (And we can easily envision it as being described within a cube.) So cubes and spheres, having a common measurement for width, height and depth, are relatively simple constructs for us to understand and to draw.

Complicated Proportions

Other forms are not as simple to figure out. Thanks to the ancient Greek philosopher Pythagoras, we know that side "a" of the Pythagorean right triangle (see illustration) is equal to the square root of $c^2 - b^2$. Knowing this complicated relationship between "a" and the other two sides of the triangle can be useful and important. But it may not be very easy to figure out right off the cuff.

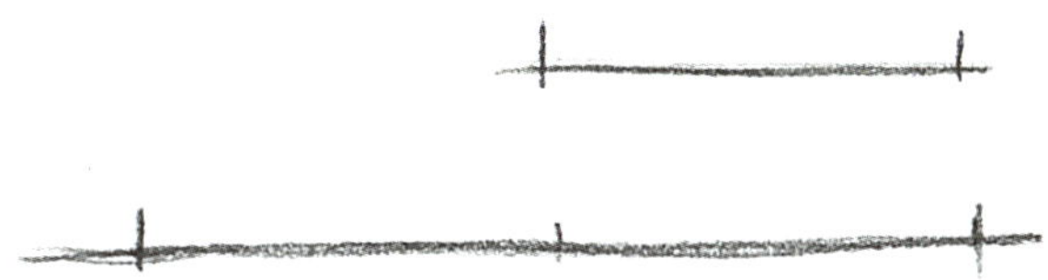

The Relationship Between Measurements

The second line is twice the length of the first.

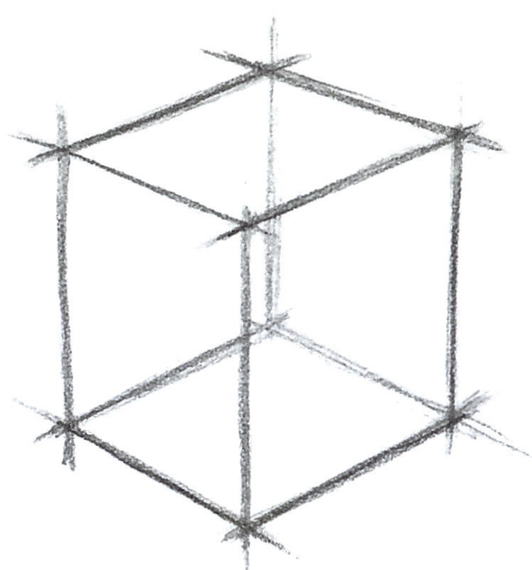

Simple Proportions

A cube has an equal height, width and depth. Its proportions are easy to understand.

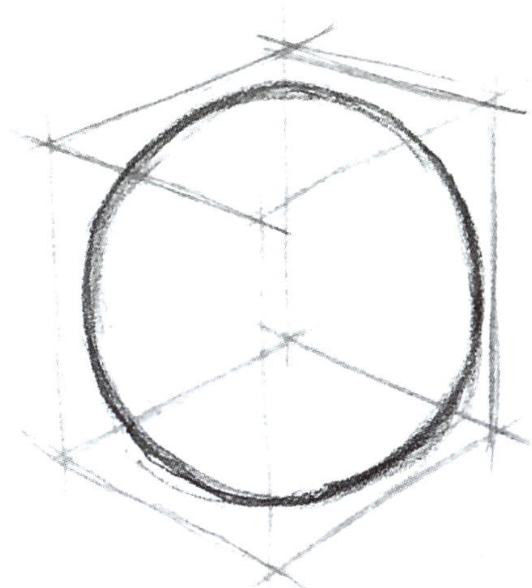

Deducing Proportions

Knowing the proportions of a cube, for example, can help us draw a sphere, which also has the same width, height and depth.

Easy Proportions for Artists

As artists, we want to have a system of proportions that is easy to figure out, because when we draw or paint or sculpt, there are many other factors in addition to comparative length that we have to deal with at the same time, such as light, composition and texture.

The human body is difficult to draw to begin with. It has oddly shaped parts and varies in color and texture across its surface. And because any figure in any artwork can be understood, at least to some degree, as a stand-in for ourselves, it is freighted with psychological and sociological significances, which would not be found in a tree or a rabbit or a wagon.

One chief difficulty in depicting the human body is that it doesn't for the most part divide into proportions that are simple to understand. Unlike a cube, for example, humans are not of the same height, width and depth. They're not even twice as deep as they are high, or of some other easy proportion like our imaginary box was.

Thankfully, some easy proportions do regularly exist within the human figure, if not 1:1, then at least 2:1 or even 3:1. If you know that the collarbone is the same width as the head, it makes it much easier to draw the head in proper relationship to the shoulders. Or knowing that the figure's palm should be the same width as its knee makes it easier to set down the correct relationships when doing a seated portrait.

This book tries to find and exploit these relatively simple size relationships wherever they are found. If you find others that are useful to you, then you should remember and use those as well.

Now let's consider another riddle regarding bodily proportions: Just whose body are we talking about?

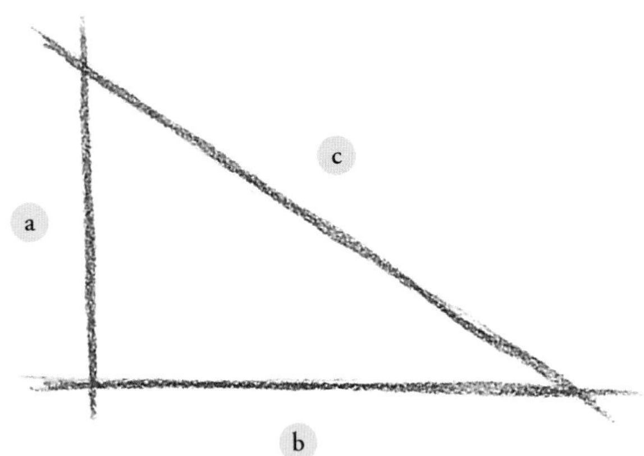

Pythagorean Triangle

We can find the relative length of any side of this triangle, but it's not easy to do.

Human Proportions

Just as no two people look exactly alike (not even identical twins), no two people have exactly the same proportions. Or, it might be better put that no two people look exactly alike *because* no two people have exactly the same proportions.

So how and why should we endeavor to establish a system of figure proportion when we know that proportions change from person to person?

It is important to keep in mind that the guidelines set in this book, as well as the rules that appear in most artistic anatomy or drawing books, are based on average human measurements, either by sampling a number of individuals and computing their average measurements, or by observing a smaller number of people with averagely proportioned bodies.

There do exist canons of proportion that are decidedly not average. Books on how to draw fashion figures or comic book superheroes present a special set of comparative measurements to construct figures of a very specialized appearance. While you can use many of the ideas in this book to help you to draw those special types, these guidelines are to help you represent more regular-looking figures.

Humans for the most part don't vary that greatly in their proportion from one to another, not even from male to female. It is generally the accumulation of relatively small differences in proportion among people that gives them their character and makes them recognizable to us as distinct persons. The purpose of this book is to get the figures in your drawing "in the ballpark."

Once you have the ability to draw a reasonably well-proportioned, convincing figure, you can then modify your drawing to align better with either the physical model you see before you or with your expressive artistic purpose. And you should!

But here is something well worth remembering. Few people who look at your artwork will know what your model looked like at the time that he or she posed for you. However, they may well notice if something is badly proportioned about your rendering, since we are able to pick up on even slight deviations in proportion from the average.

This brings us another main undercurrent of the methodology outlined in this book: If we accept that we all share a relatively similar set of proportions, then the figure in your artwork should not only resemble the model, it should resemble the viewer, and it should also resemble you. Any proportional relationship in your model's body should be present in your figure drawing as well as in your own body.

Use Your Body as a Guide

Knowing this methodology can make the study and practice of figure proportion significantly easier. If you find yourself unsure about any proportional relationship in your artwork, you can always use your own body as a guide. If you don't know, for example, how wide the thickest part of the forearm should be drawn, you can lay your palm upon your own forearm, and see that it is about the same thickness. If you don't know how long the thumb is, lay your own crosswise upon your palm, and you will see that the length of the thumb is the same as the width of the palm. While you work, establishing the proportions in your drawing, constantly ask yourself, "Could I do what the model is doing?" "Could the model do what my drawing is doing?" and "Could my drawing do what I'm doing?"

Essentially, that is what anyone viewing your artwork will be asking himself or herself, too. "Does this look like a reasonable construction of a human figure?" "Would its bodily parts align as mine or any other person's would?"

The answer to all the above questions should be "Yes" (within reason). And so you never need to go further than your own body to find a trustworthy guide to constructing a standard figure.

The following pages help to introduce and make more memorable what some of those relationships might be.

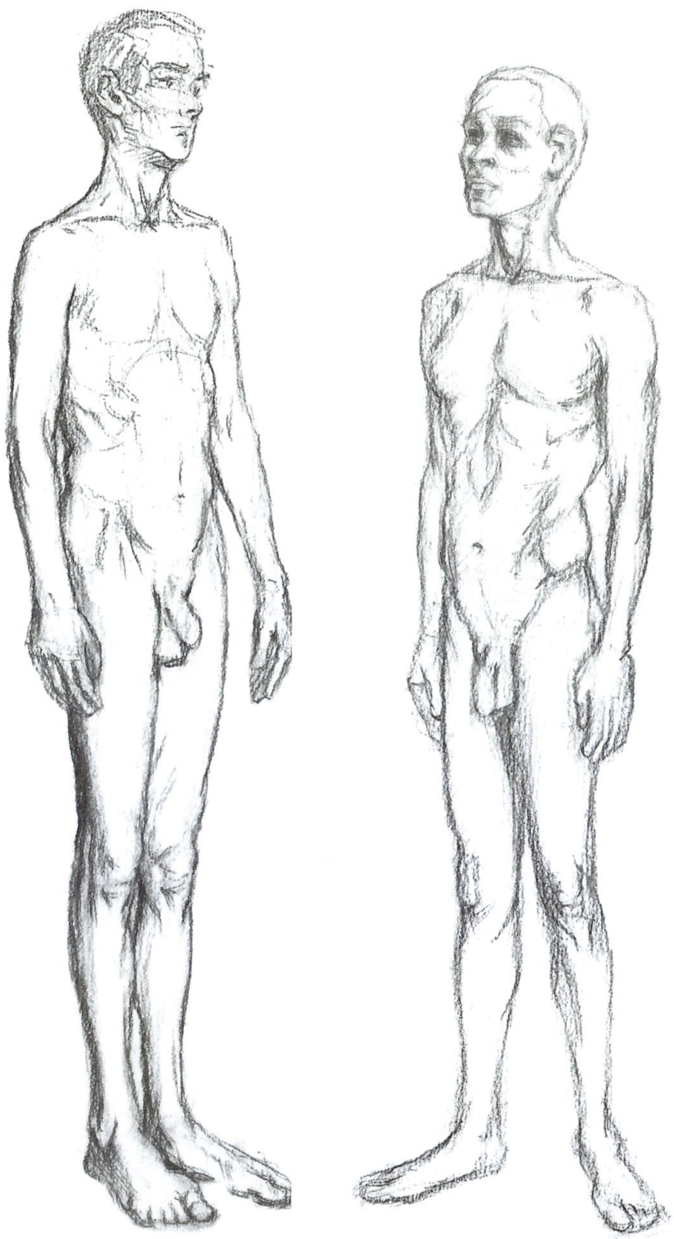

Whose Proportions are Correct?
They both are. Use the proportions in this book as a general guide.

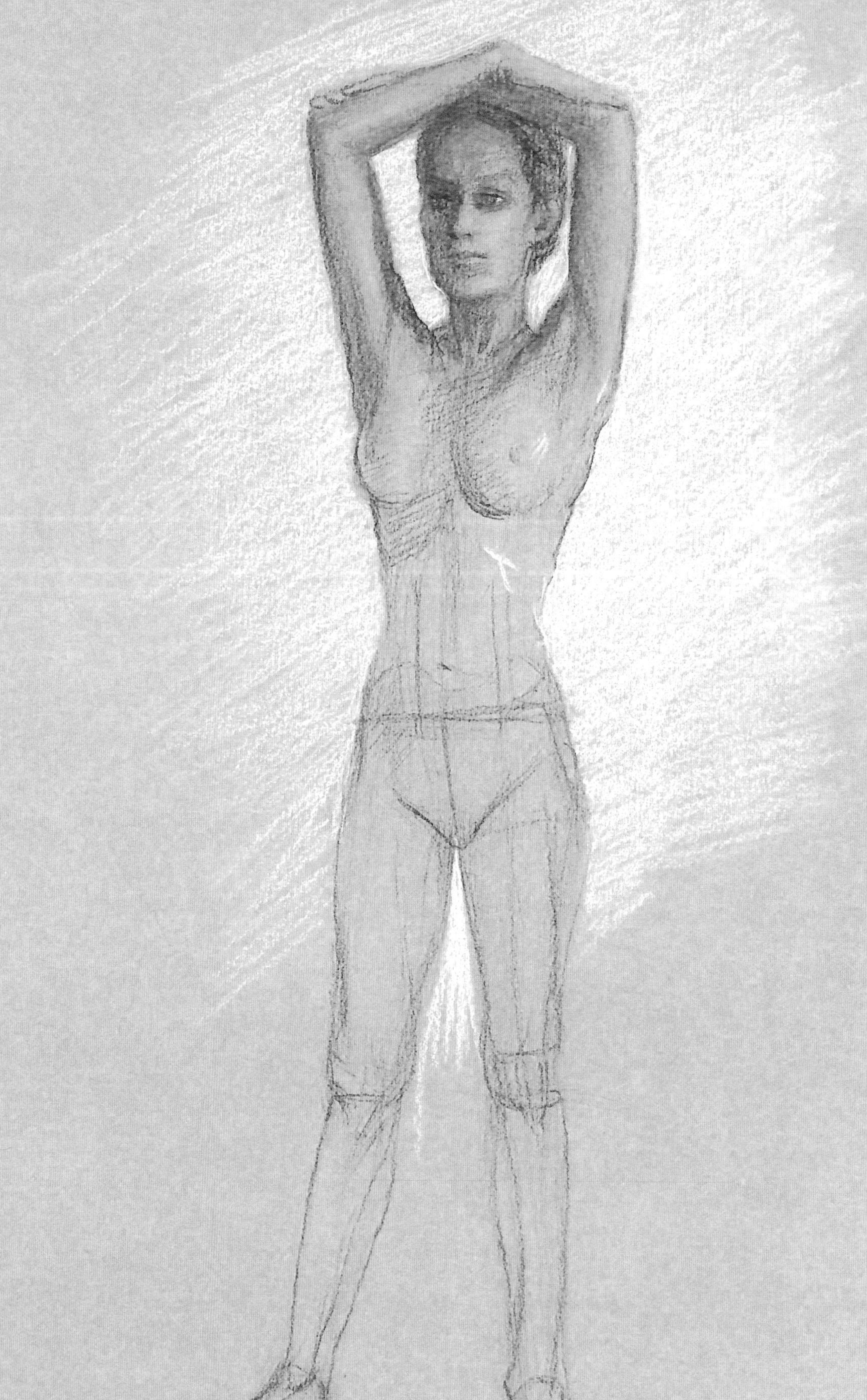

1

DRAWING BASICS

Drawing the figure correctly has traditionally been considered one of the greatest challenges for an artist. Although this book concentrates on figure proportion, you will need to integrate this knowledge with a host of other skills: mark-making, perspective, foreshortening, anatomy, rendering basic forms, and the proper measure of distances and of lights and darks.

None of those topics will be covered in depth here, but the better you learn them, the stronger your drawing will be. Likewise, the better you understand proportion, the more concentration you can devote to other areas of drawing.

Even more important than all the above are the aesthetic choices you will make: the composition, subject and treatment or style of rendering that will carry your feelings and artistic ideas to the viewer.

MATERIALS

This book is filled with drawings. But you can use the principles they illustrate to help you portray the figure in any medium you wish, including paint, clay or even computer animations.

Pencils

I drew the illustrations in the first three chapters of the book in charcoal pencil on semi-translucent graphics paper. The graphics paper makes it easy to trace over previously worked images, allowing you to keep the graphics clean and to select and enhance the lines and forms that you like best.

An easy trick I use is to keep each grade of pencil lead (2H, HB and 2B) consistently in three differently colored pencil lead holders. That way, I can easily grab for the grade of pencil I want without having to search the back of the lead for the tiny print that indicates what grade the lead is.

In the demonstrations chapter I mostly used charcoal pencil, staying in a medium range (HB and 2B), using a 4B grade for my darkest accents and a white pencil for highlights. I used the same grades for those drawings done in Conté pencil.

Essential Tools

Draw using any materials you like. My favorites are graphite pencils, Conté pencils or charcoal pencils. A chamois is great for blending. I find a kneaded eraser to be indispensable.

Sharpeners

To sharpen my graphite pencil leads, I use a rotary sharpener. These are simple to use and available in any art supply shop.

Sharpening charcoal or Conté pencils involves a little more of a process. Using a pocket knife (you can also, very carefully, use a box cutter or single-edged industrial razor blade), gently whittle away at the wood surrounding the lead until a good ¾–1" (19–25mm) of lead is exposed. Then sharpen the tip to a point by dragging the lead across a sanding block or a piece of sandpaper, rotating the pencil evenly as you drag it.

Erasers

In addition to mark-making tools, make sure to take advantage of a good eraser that you like. Kneaded erasers allow you to shape the eraser into any form you wish and to remove a varying degree of dark from the page, depending on whether you use a cleaner or dirtier section of the eraser. They also don't leave any grit on the page. Best of all, they give your hands something to toy with as you draw!

Other Supplies

To blend tones, you can use a chamois cloth or a paper tortillion (available in art supply stores) or even just a rag or a paper towel.

You may also want to get yourself a pair of dividers to help mark equal spacings on your drawings. A divider looks like a compass except that it has points on both of its arms. You can find one online or at any store that sells graphic supplies.

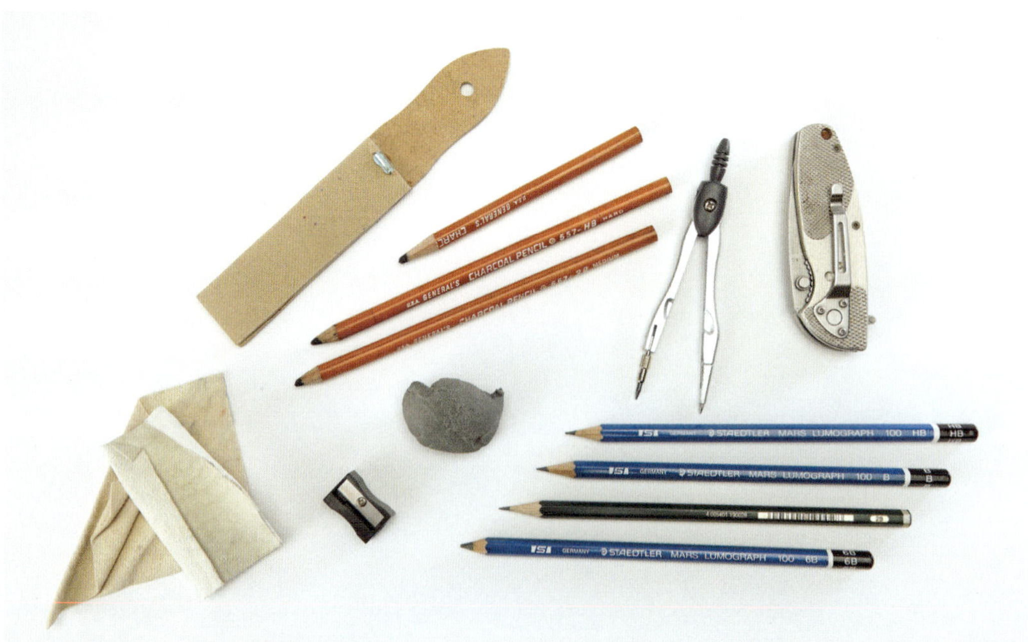

PERSPECTIVE

Unless you're drawing a cartoon or in some other graphic style that's meant to look absolutely flat on the page, you have to consider linear perspective when you think about proportions.

Simply put, linear perspective is the representation of the way that objects appear smaller as they get farther away from a viewer. This is not only true of objects but of distances within the same object. The far end of a building will look smaller to you even though it's actually the same size as the side closer to you. Similarly, the more distant portion of a figure you're drawing will look smaller than it actually is compared to the closest area.

Therefore, because proportion is all about comparing relative sizes, we have to always keep in mind how linear perspective will affect it.

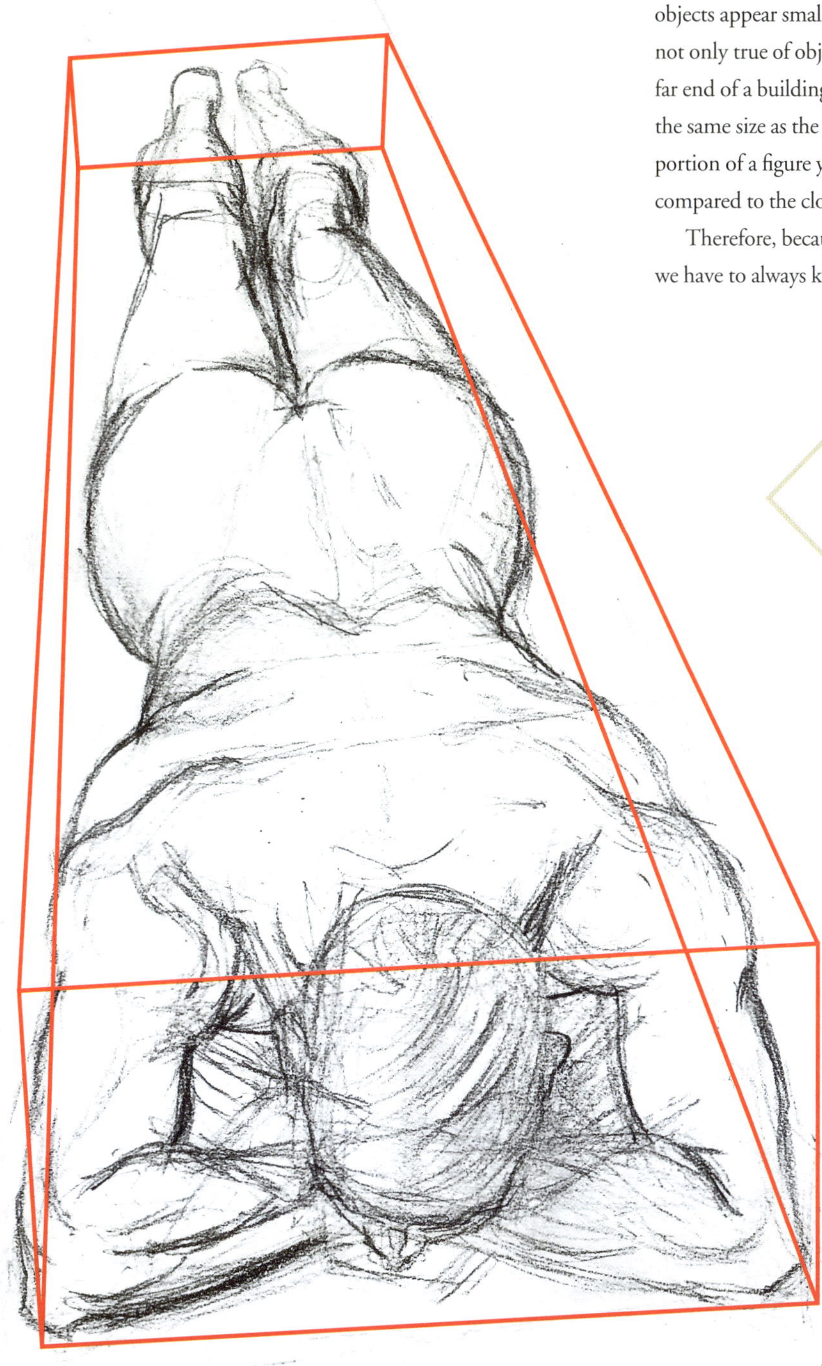

Proportion in Perspective

Any proportion you use must make sense in your drawing's perspective. We live in a three-dimensional world. Linear perspective helps to represent that sense of space on the flat two-dimensional plane of our drawings. Treat the figure or any of its parts as a box, and use guidelines to help convey the sense of those boxes getting smaller in the distance.

FORESHORTENING

Closely related to linear perspective is the concept of foreshortening. Basically, foreshortening refers to the appearance of something when it's pointed toward you. It appears to look shorter than it would look if it were held at an angle perpendicular to your point of view. If you're looking at a body or a limb end-on, it does not appear as lengthy as it would if you looked at it from the side.

In practice you'll find it very rare that any part of the figure you're drawing will be at a perpendicular angle to you, that is to say "flat on the plane." Most everything you draw will be held at some degree of an angle to your point of view. So, just as you should always be conscious of perspective in your drawing, you should also be conscious of foreshortening.

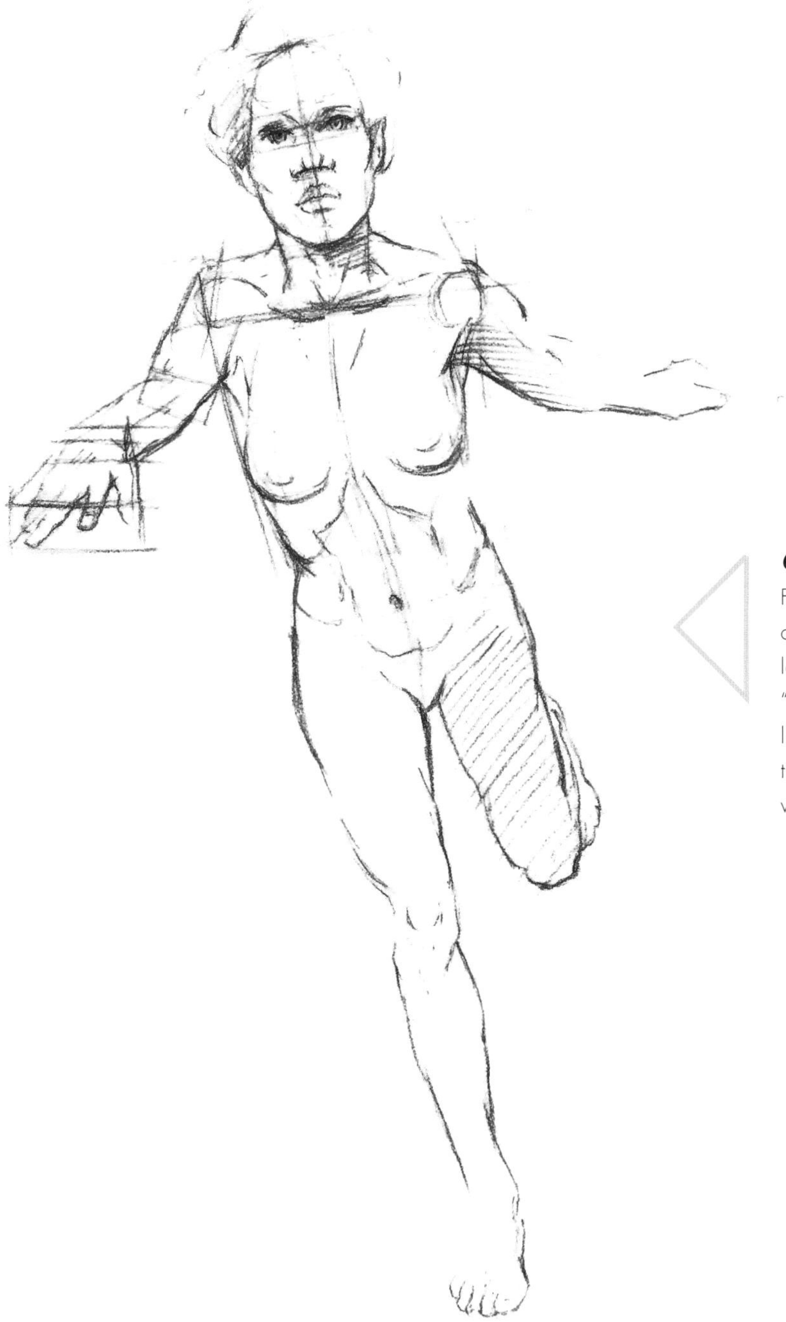

Construction Lines

Foreshortening occurs when you see an object end-on, rather than by one of its lengthier sides. Use construction lines to "house" and describe the position of a limb for your viewer and to help you find the boundaries for that body part's height, width or depth.

WORKING DEDUCTIVELY

No one system of drawing will work for everybody. In time, you will find the one that works best for you. Or even better, you may have several methods of working so that you can use whatever method or methods are best for creating a particular artwork.

Some people like to start their drawing at one particular spot on the page and then work out from there. It's an exciting and creative way of working, precisely because you never know where you'll end up.

But it's also important to be able to work the opposite way, i.e., working deductively. Working deductively means that you work from the biggest concept to the smallest. For example, if you want to fill your page with a group of figures, first determine where on the page your group will fall and how much area it will take. Then you can start working on the individual figures within the group.

Likewise, if you want to fill your page with a lone figure, start by deciding what part of the page you want the figure to occupy. Mark off the topmost part of the figure and the bottommost. Mark the left and the right. Now you know that all the parts of the figure must fall within those points. Now you can draw a gesture within the area that you have created or a midpoint or any of the other helpful markings that you may find in this book.

Within this large blocking of the figure, you can find smaller and more subtle points.

Working this way may not lead to any great surprises because you know from the outset exactly how the figure will end up. On the other hand, you won't find yourself halfway through a beautiful figure drawing with the sudden realization that you haven't left enough room for the feet!

First Find the Largest Limits of the Figure
Working deductively means that you consider the largest concerns of your artwork first. Here, a gesture drawing is used to quickly find where the largest limits of the figure will appear on the page.

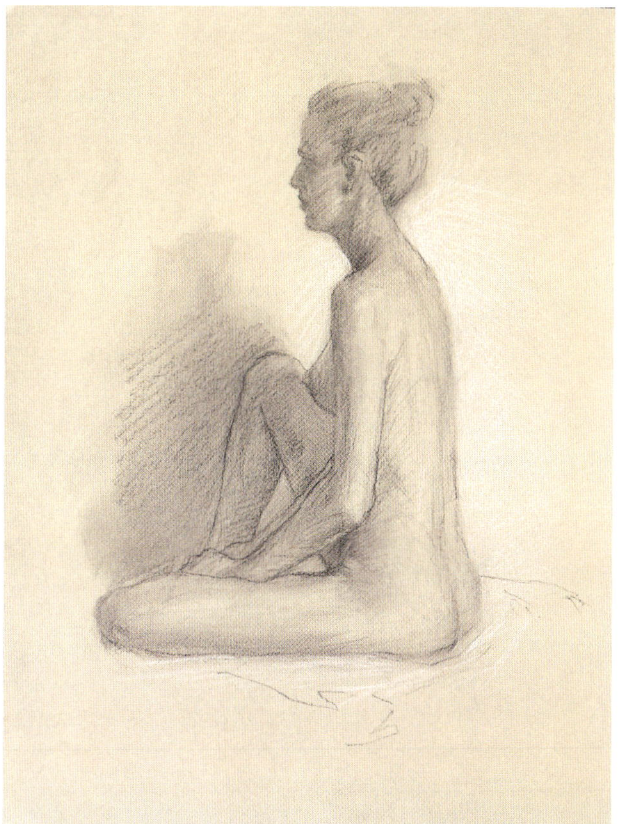

Then Complete the Mapped-Out Figure
After you have the large concerns of your artwork mapped out, it becomes easier to complete the rest without the fear of ending up with any gross mistakes.

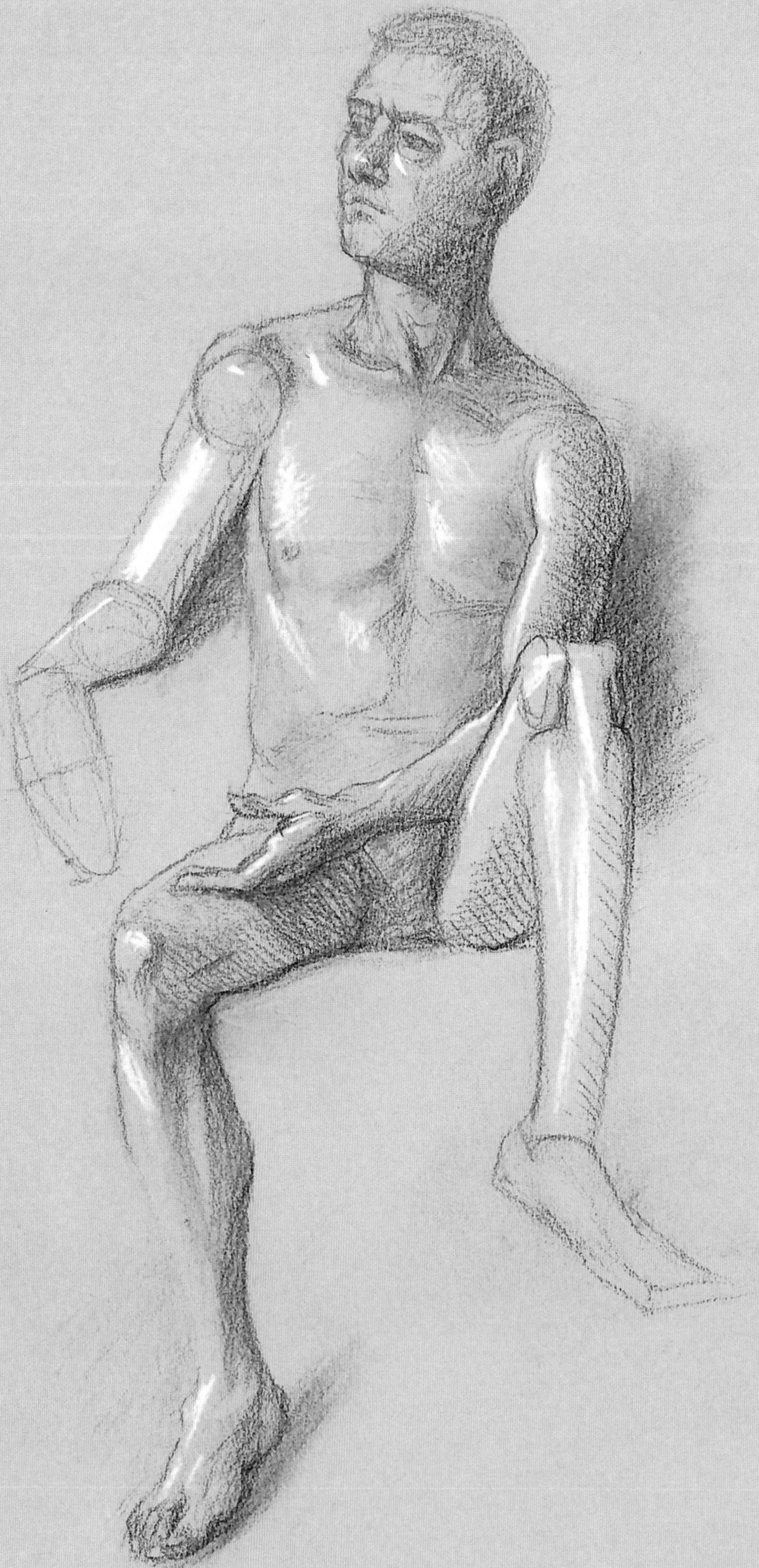

2

ANATOMY BASICS

If we want to keep a consistent set of rules to help us with bodily proportions, then we need to establish some rules to define the parts of the body that we are comparing (for example, what exactly do we mean by the width of the hand or the length of the thigh?).

Anatomy is the science that teaches us how to split up the body. This is not a book on anatomy, but we still need to borrow some basic rules from it to create a proportional system that will make sense among the body's various parts. And, as a general rule, the better you know anatomy, the stronger your drawing will be.

One of the first things to know is that the body is bilaterally symmetrical. That means that all the parts on the left hand of the body should have the same heights, widths and depths as their partners on the right.

In real life, you will find that that is not precisely true; most people's left sides differ a tiny bit from their right sides. For some people, this difference can be very marked.

But unless you have some artistic reason for stating otherwise, most people will assume that any figure in one of your drawings will have a right side that measures the same as its left. So you should take care to draw your figures that way.

In the rules that are presented later in this book, you can use this to your advantage. If, for example, you want to equate the width of the knee with the width of the palm, you will find that you can measure the left knee against the right palm as well as against the left palm.

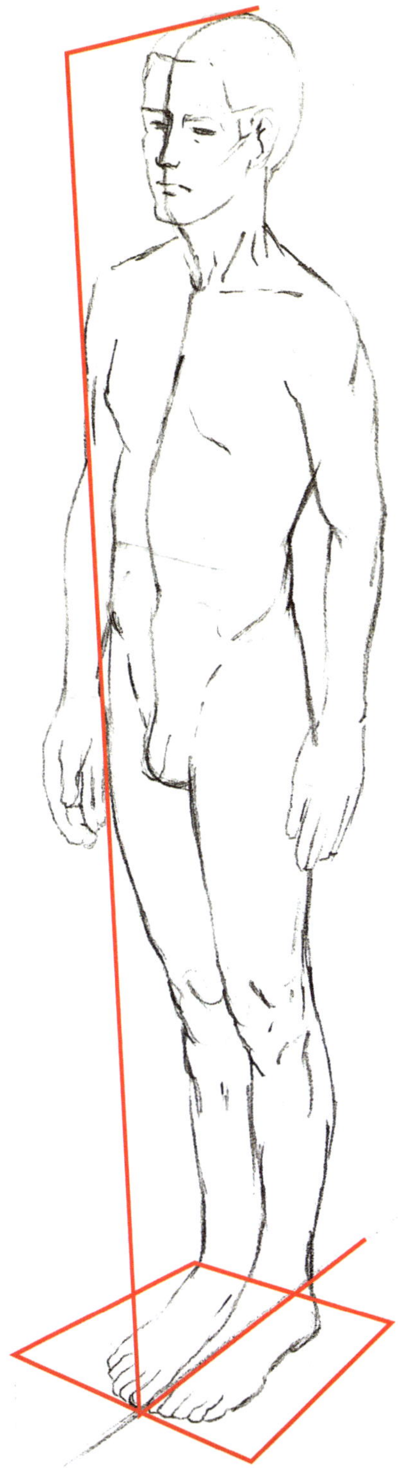

Bilateral Symmetry

The parts on the left and right sides of the human body should be the same height, width and depth.

ANATOMY MEASUREMENT PARAMETERS

When we are talking about the length, width or height of any particular body part, it is essential that we know where it is that we're measuring. If, for example, we were to say the "length of the foot," most people would probably assume we mean the distance from the tip of the toes to the back of the heel. In other parts of the body, however, especially where the limbs join the trunk, these measurements are a little more difficult to gauge.

The illustrations on these pages are meant to clarify what is meant by each height, width or depth that is referred to in the rest of the book.

Front of the Body Measurements

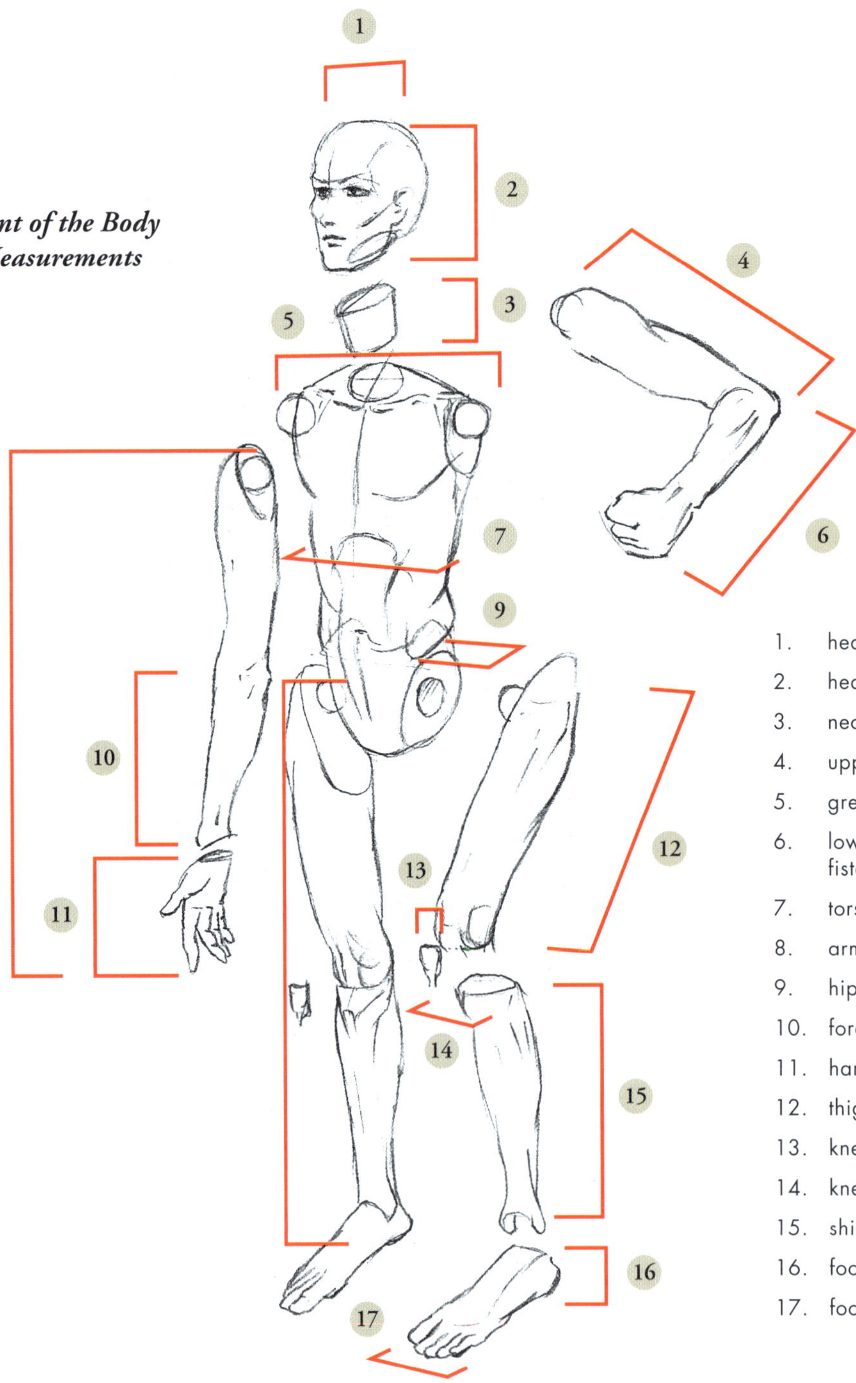

1. head width
2. head height
3. neck height
4. upper arm length
5. greatest width of the body
6. lower arm length (with fisted hand)
7. torso width
8. arm length
9. hip depth
10. forearm length
11. hand length
12. thigh length
13. kneecap width
14. knee joint width
15. shin length
16. foot height
17. foot width

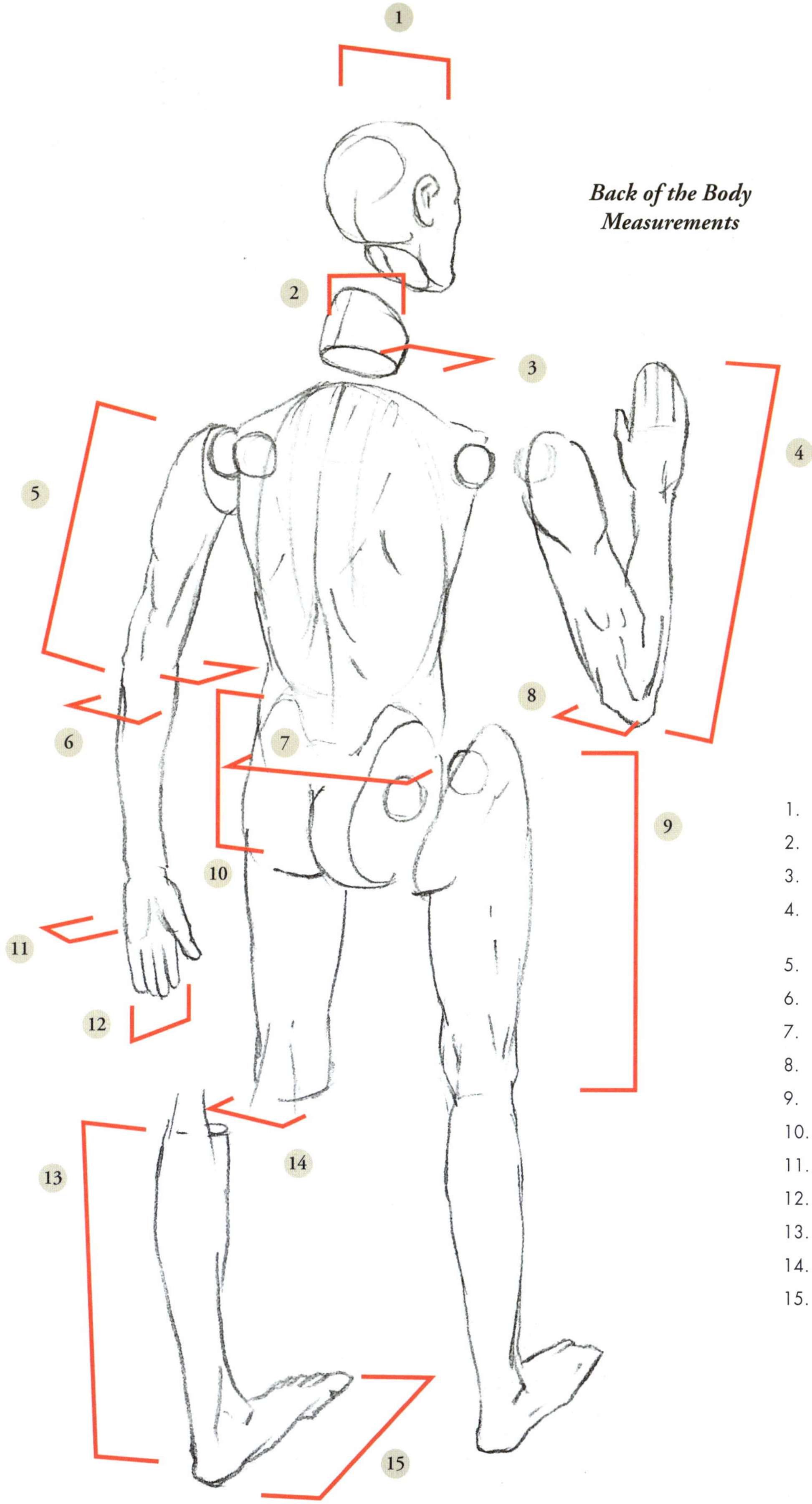

Back of the Body Measurements

1. head width
2. neck width
3. neck depth
4. lower arm length (with fingers outstretched)
5. upper arm length
6. elbow joint width
7. hip width
8. elbow joint width
9. thigh length
10. hip height
11. hand depth
12. hand width
13. lower leg height
14. knee joint width
15. foot length

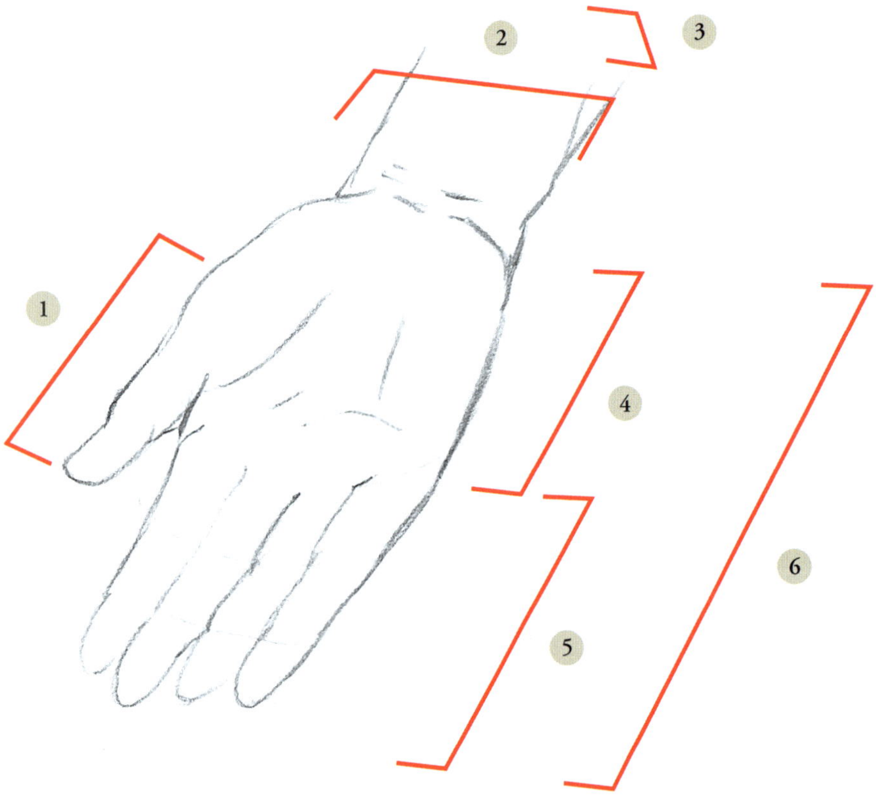

Hand Measurements

1. thumb length
2. palm width
3. palm depth
4. palm length
5. length of the fingers
6. hand length

Foot Measurements

1. foot height
2. foot width
3. length of the toes
4. foot length

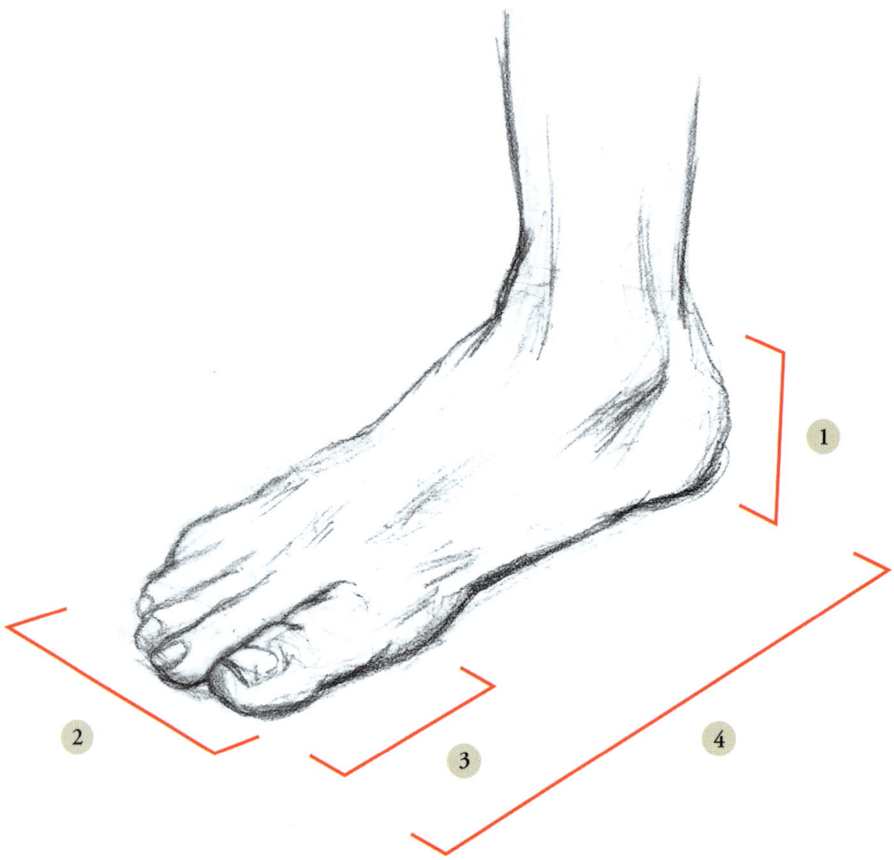

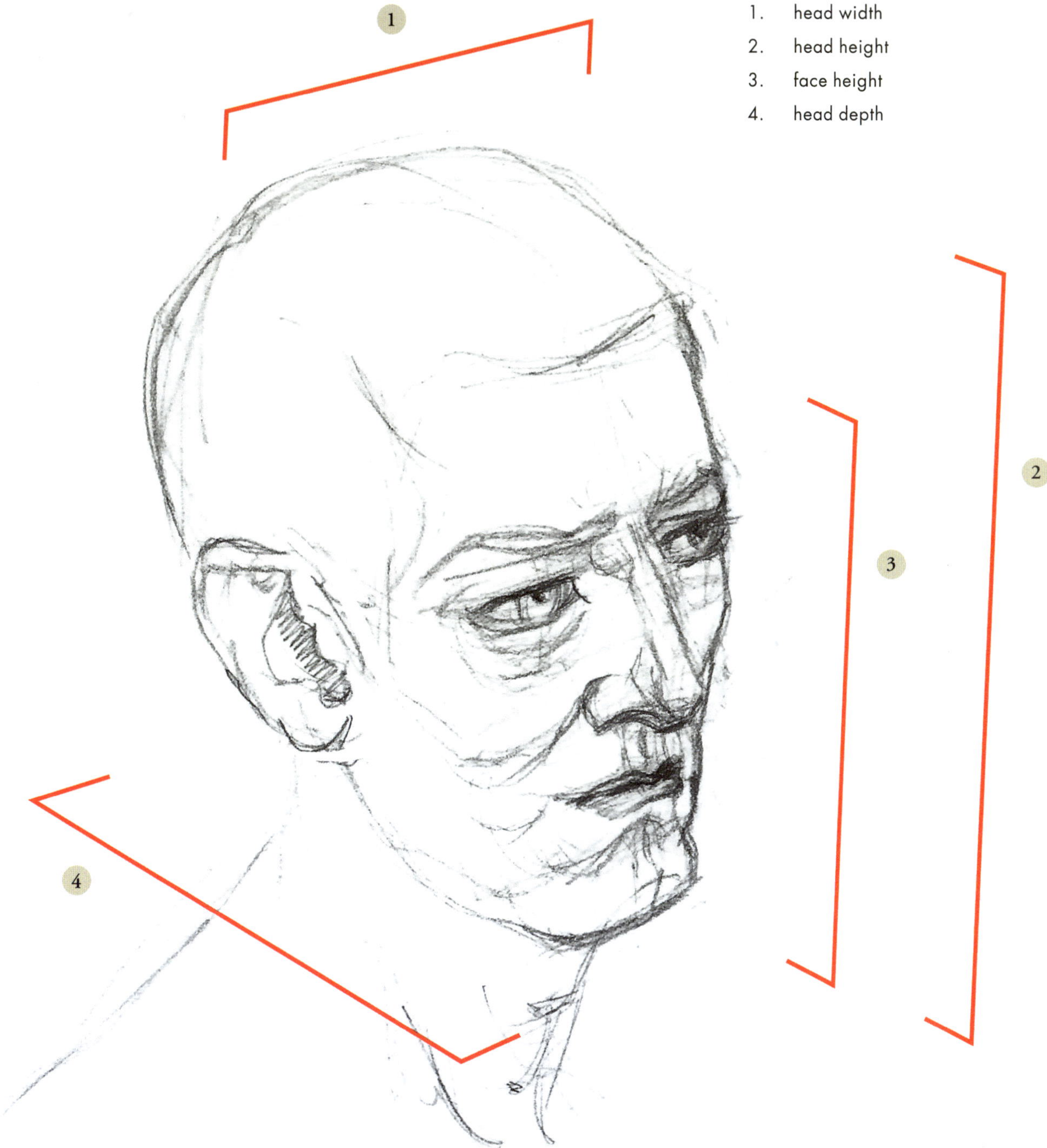

Head Measurements

1. head width
2. head height
3. face height
4. head depth

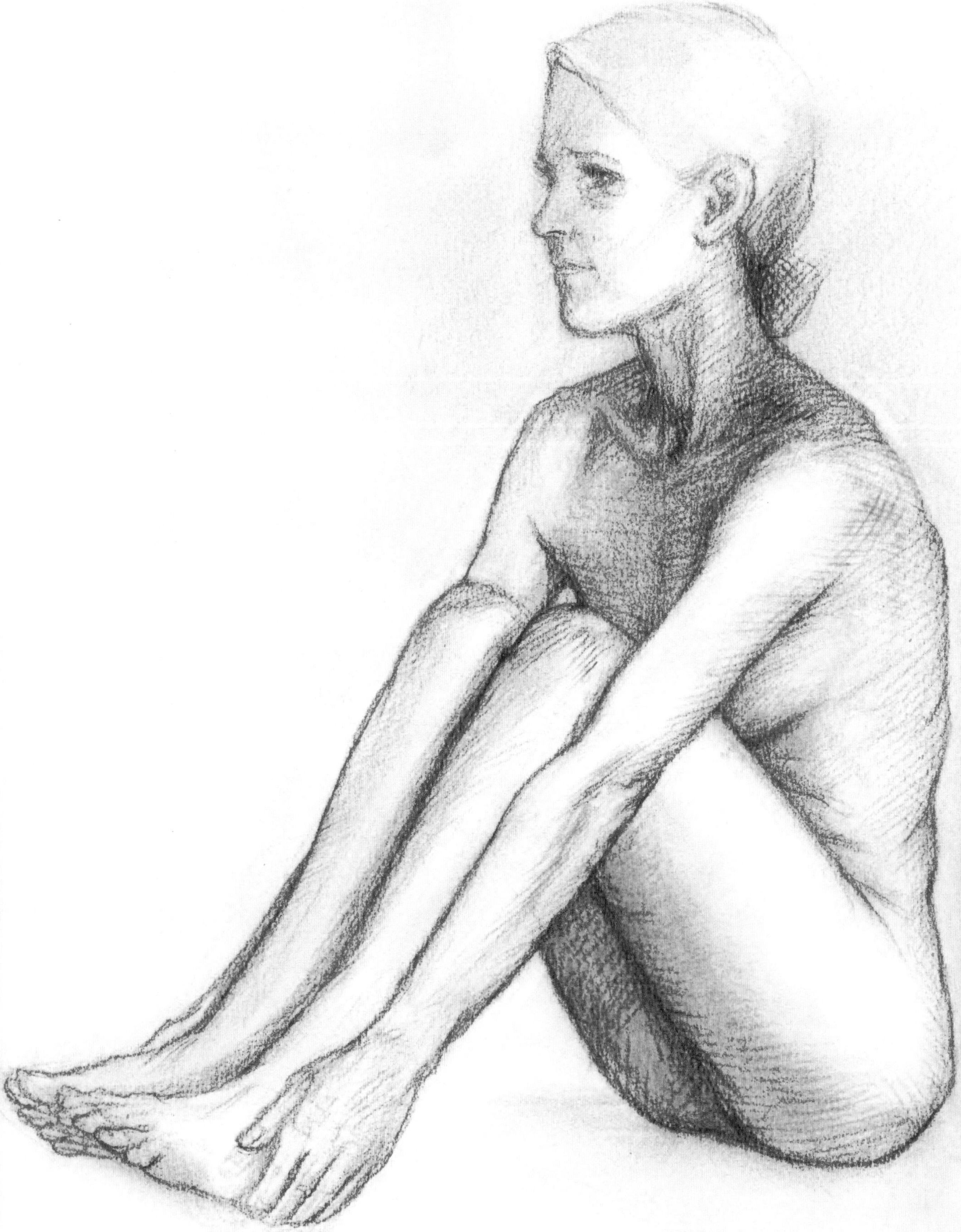

3

THE BODY'S INTERNAL PROPORTIONS

In the next chapter we will compare various parts of the body to other body parts, for example, the hand to the face or the lower leg to the forearm. But we will start by comparing the *internal* proportions of the parts of the body—how one dimension of a particular part relates to another dimension.

These relationships will not be as easy to remember as those listed in the next chapter. You can't, for example, hold the upper quarter of your arm next to the lower quarter for comparison. But they are very useful as general guides, so it may be helpful to simply memorize them.

CENTERLINE

In Chapter 1 we looked at the benefits of working deductively from the biggest artistic concepts to the smallest. Let's do the same here, starting by finding the midpoint of the figure from the top of the head to the soles of the feet.

From the front of the figure, the midpoint is found at the pubic symphysis, the hard prominence of bone found right above the genital area on a male or female. From the back, the midpoint is a bit more difficult to pinpoint . It's at the level of the second coccyx bone, right below the top of the cleft of the buttocks.

If you're drawing an averagely proportioned person and you know how tall you want the figure to be on the page, you can find the halfway mark from top to bottom. There you know that you can set the symphysis pubis or the coccyx.

To draw a person with longer legs, it's an easy matter to move the position of the symphysis pubis above this middle mark. For a person with a longer torso, do the opposite.

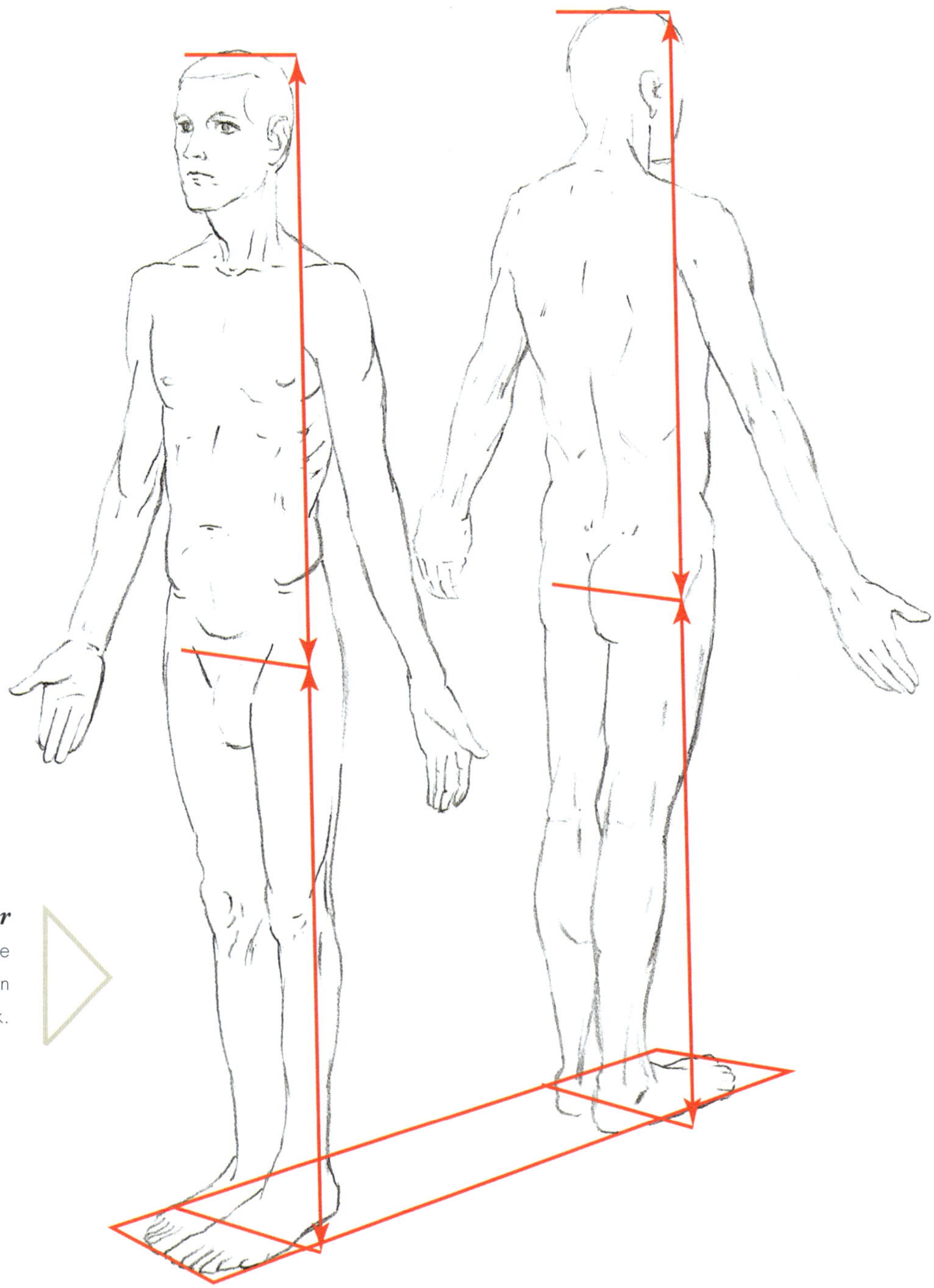

The Body's Center

It is somewhat easier to find the midpoint on the front of the figure than on the back.

FRONT BRACKETS

Although we said we were going to address only the internal divisions of the body in this chapter, we have to make an exception. In drawing the average figure, you will find that the length of the upper body equals that of the lower body. (In the pages immediately following, we will explore the internal proportions of these two parts.)

The upper body is measured from the top of the head to the bottom of the pelvis. The lower body is measured from the top of the thighbone to the sole of the foot. Of course, the upper and lower body do not simply hinge together along a straight line. The legs socket into the pelvic area and vice versa.

Therefore if we draw a bracket demarcating the length of the upper body, along with another bracket denoting the length of the lower body or legs, you will see that they are of equal length. The height of the upper body equals that of the lower body.

However, the upper and lower body overlap each other a bit. This overlap is about one-eighth the length of either the upper or the lower bracket (either one because they're both of the same length).

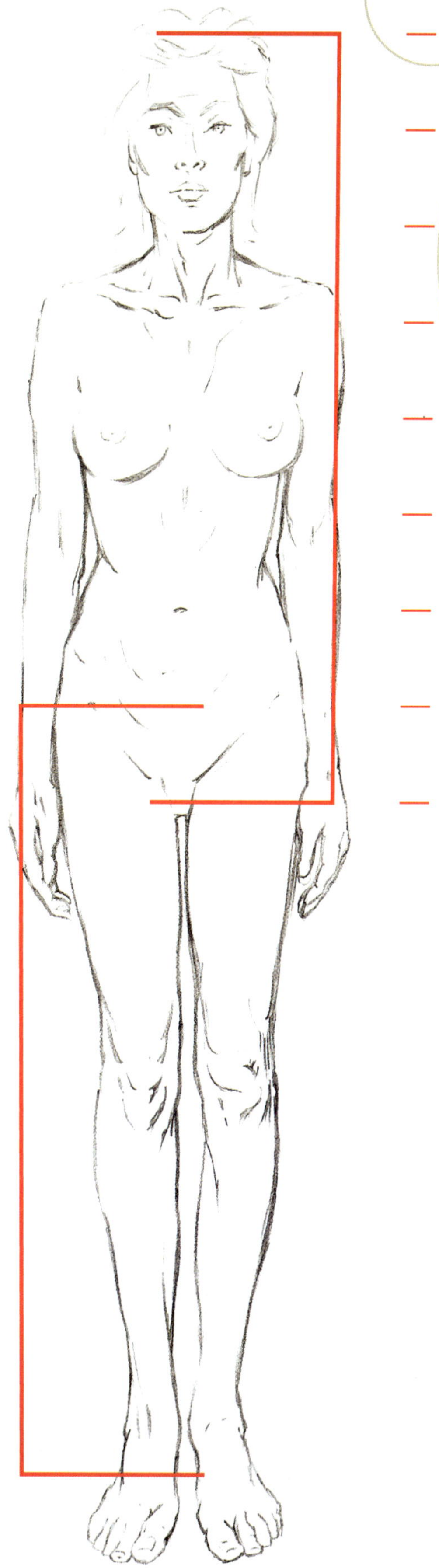

Upper and Lower Brackets

The upper and lower brackets are the same length and overlap slightly.

WIDENED STANCE BRACKETS

As long as your figure is keeping its leg straight, the leg should be equal in height to the upper body.

In the drawing on this page, the figure has widened her stance so you would compare the length of the upper body to the length of the angled leg from the top of the leg to the bottom of the foot. Do not compare the length of the upper body with a line dropping straight down from the top of the leg to the ground plane.

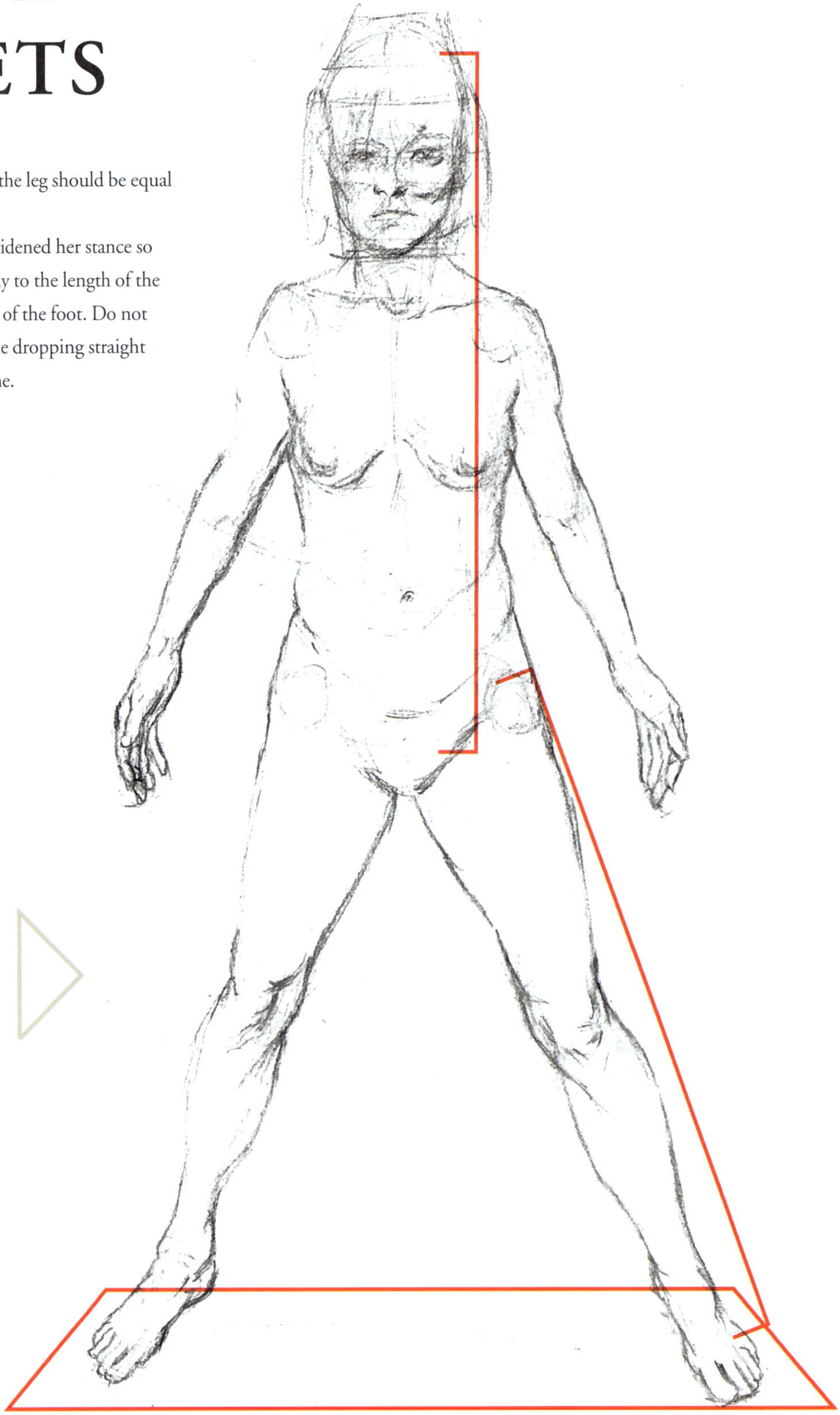

Brackets for a Widened Stance
For a widened stance, measure the length of the leg for the lower bracket.

BRACKETS IN PERSPECTIVE

As discussed in Chapter 1, you always need to keep the effects of perspective and foreshortening in mind. So when you show the upper and lower brackets to be the same length, they must appear to be so in the perspective scheme of your drawing, not as lines drawn flat on the page.

In this drawing, you can see how useful it is to have two measurements that you know are equal to each other.

Bent Figure Brackets

Because the upper body's length equals that of the legs, this half bent over figure will form two adjacent sides of a square. (Drawn in perspective, of course.)

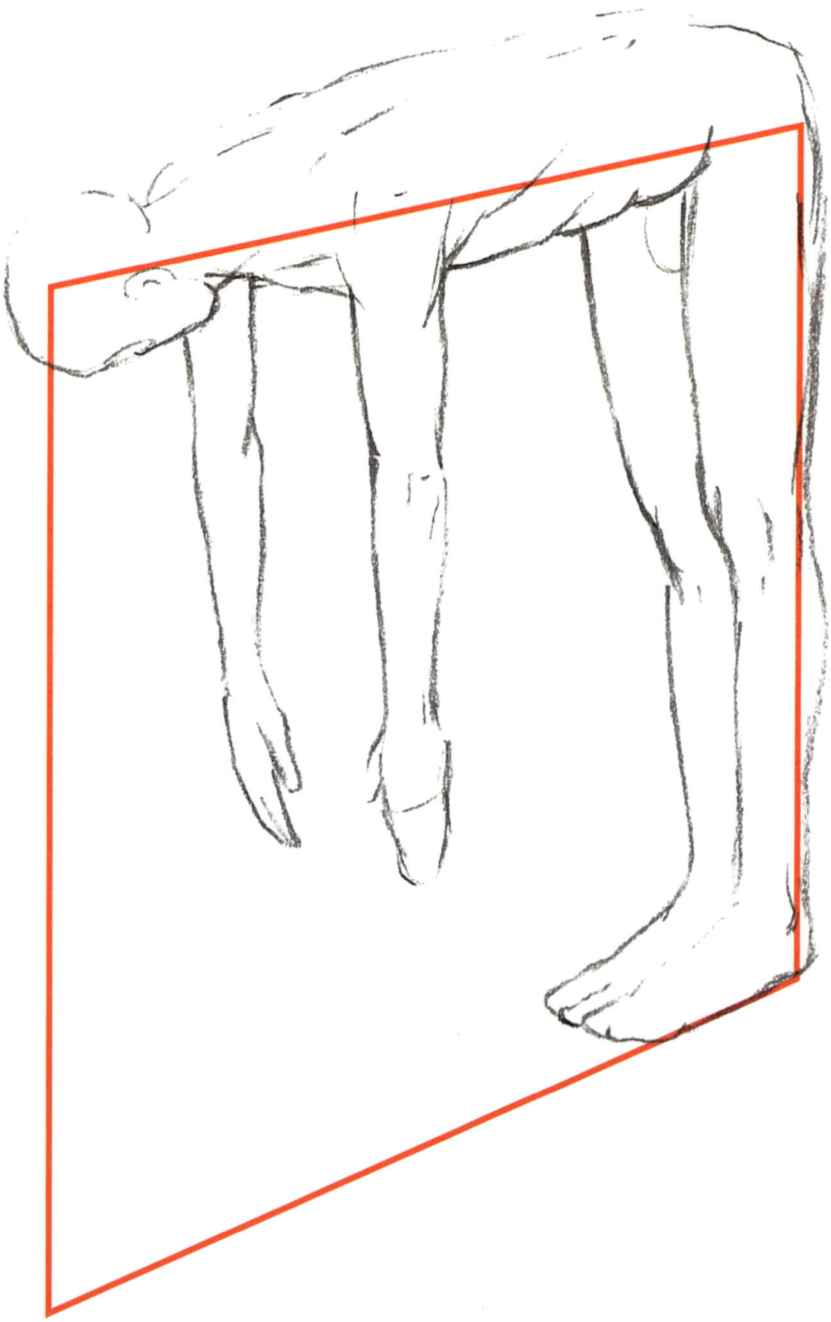

UPPER BRACKET DIVISION

Let's divide the bracket we've created to represent the length of the upper body. Unfortunately, drawing a midline in this bracket doesn't yield very helpful landmarks. At its most helpful, it falls at the point where the tips of the shoulder blades start to move off the plane of the rib cage. The mark also indicates the general area where the deltoid muscle inserts into the upper arm when the arm is resting at the model's side.

Upper Body Division
The midline of the upper body isn't as useful a landmark as some of the other divisions.

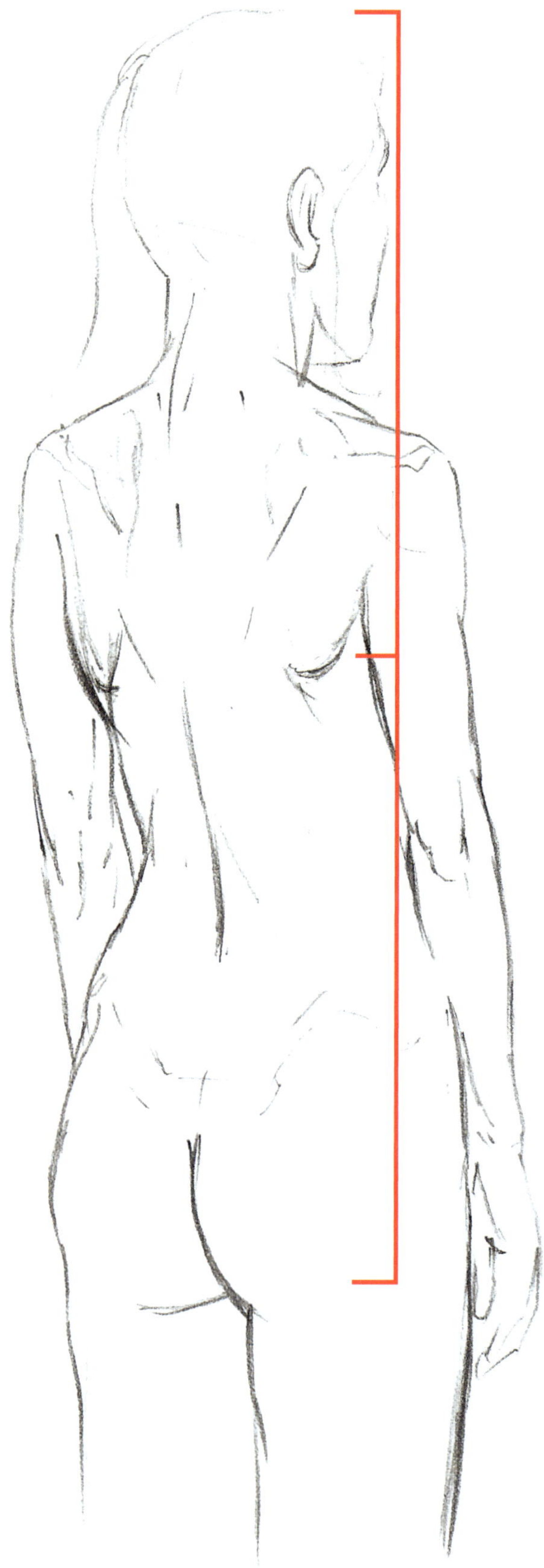

UPPER BRACKET QUARTER SUBDIVISIONS

If we continue to divide the upper bracket into quarters, then we get some very useful results. The top of the bottom quarter of the bracket is marked by the navel on the front of the figure and the highest point of the pelvis on the back of the figure. (The top of the pelvis is certainly not as distinguishable as the navel, but if you study your anatomy and continue to look for it, you'll be able to find it readily.) The topmost fourth of the upper bracket gives us the length of the head.

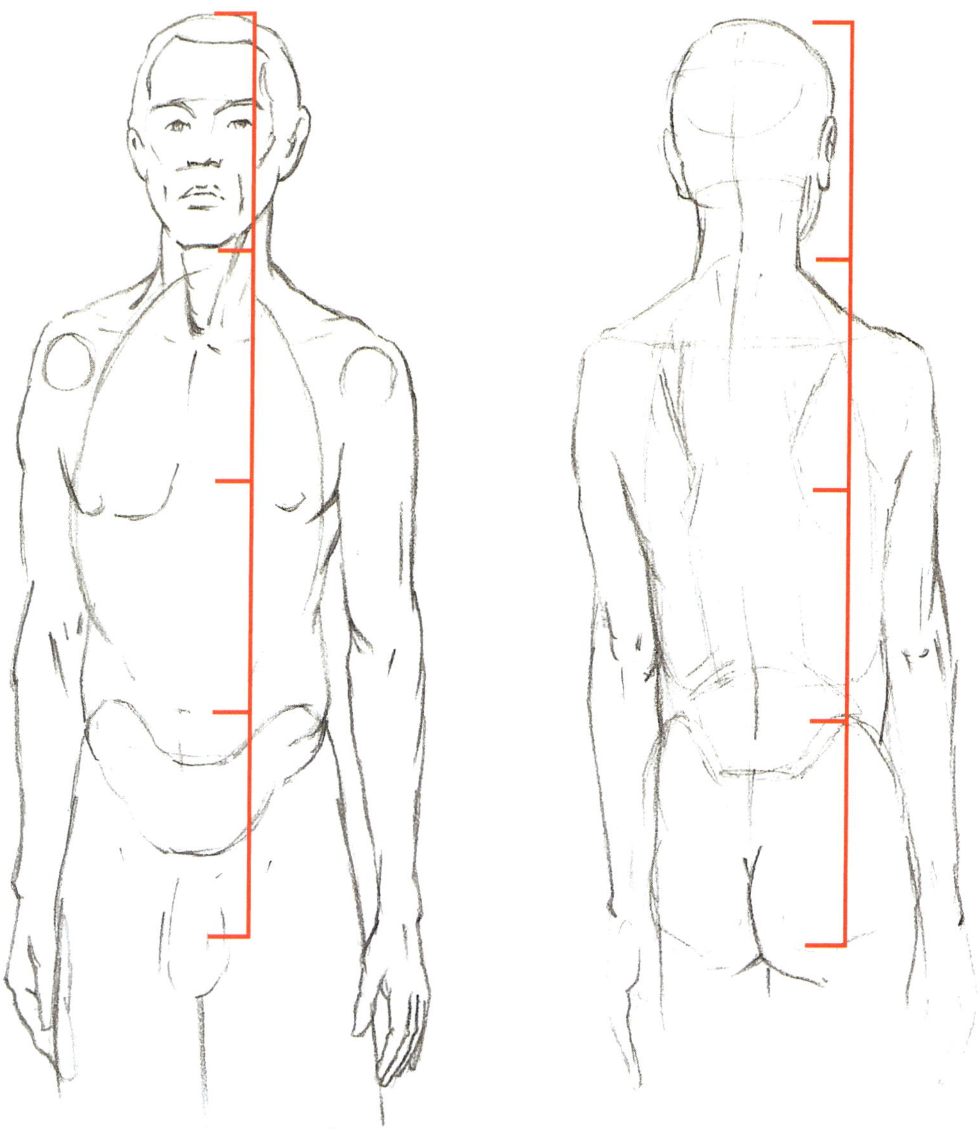

Upper Body Subdivisions

The quarter divisions in the upper bracket have more distinguishable landmarks.

UPPER BRACKET EIGHTH SUBDIVISIONS

If we divide the quarters of the upper bracket one more time (now into eighths), we get another important set of construction lines on which to build our figure.

The line that divides the topmost quadrant (where the head is) is the standard placement for the eyes. The irises should rest just on this line.

The line that divides the next quadrant down is the line of the shoulders. It is on this axis that the upper arm bones rotate in the shoulder socket. You can draw a sphere on this axis to stand for the ball of the shoulder. Although the ball of the shoulder will be referred to many times in this book, it is not a true anatomical feature of the body. It is more of a conceptual construct, suggesting the head of the humerus and the muscles around it, which helps in drawing this area of the body.

And as we previously discovered, the bottom eighth line (the subdivision of the lowest quarter) gives us the top of the lower leg.

Upper Body Eighth Subdivisions
Continue dividing the upper bracket to find more useful landmarks.

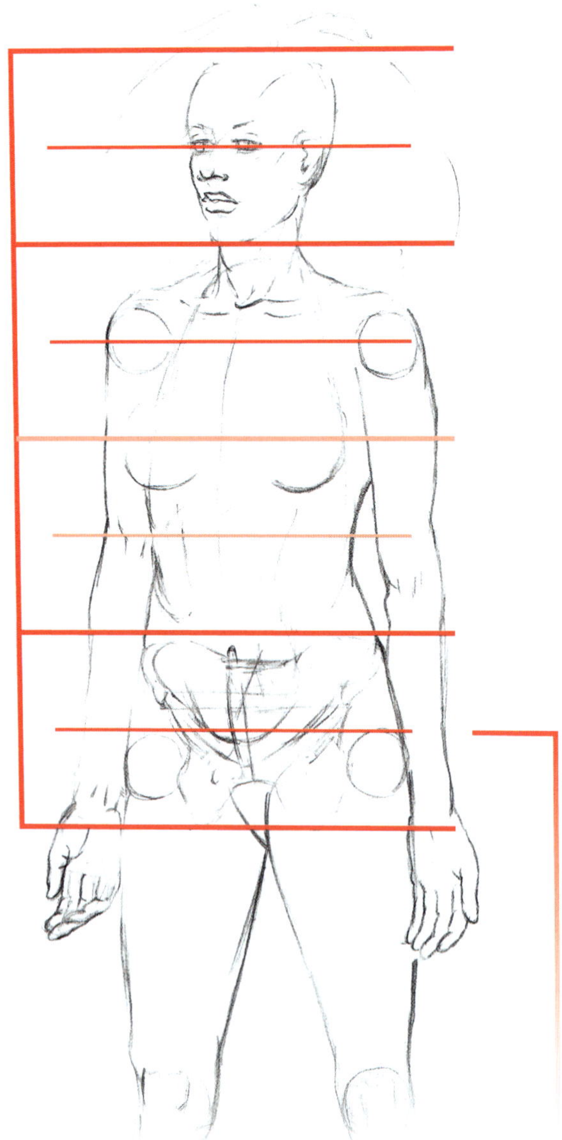

TORSO DEPTH

Seen in profile, the upper body makes a kind of zigzag. Starting from the head downward, the shoulder blade projects to the rear at its lowest point. Then the lower back comes forward along with the abdomen. Finally, the buttocks project backward as the lower abdomen recedes from the front.

In a way, the whole upper body retains the same front-to-back thickness along this path. And that path is about the same depth as the head itself.

Imagine that the figure you're drawing swallows its own head. As it passes down through the body, it will move backward, forward and backward again. By keeping this front-to-back measurement consistent, you can construct a good general thickness for the torso.

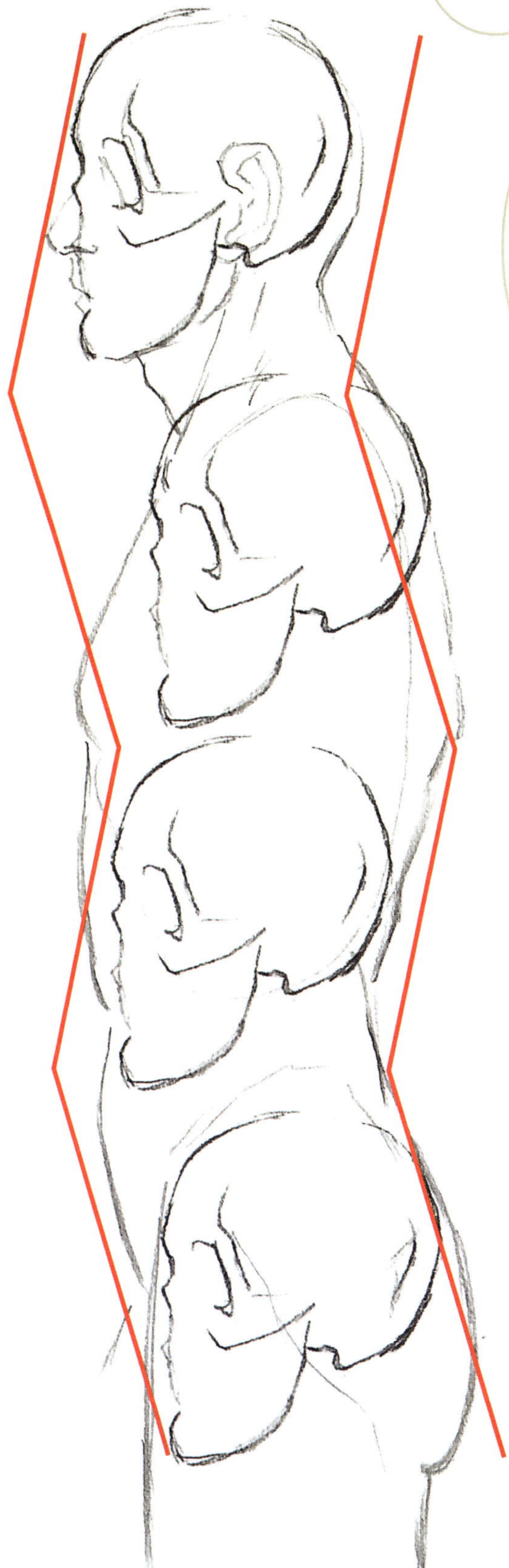

Torso Zigzag

The torso is about the same depth as the head and zigzags back and forth, front to back.

HIP AND SHOULDER WIDTH

How wide should the upper body be? After we've divided the upper bracket into quarters, finding the body's width becomes relatively simple.

Square off the lowest quarter division (draw a box as wide as that quarter division is high). When drawing a male figure, you can set the balls of the hips so that they are halfway sunken into the sides of the box. (Similar to the balls of the shoulders, the balls of the hips are not anatomical constructs. They are created visually by the great trochanters of the upper leg bones and the muscles that attach to them.)

For a female figure, draw the balls of the hips so that they sit to the outside of the box. In other words, set them a little wider apart.

If you extend this width up the full extent of the upper bracket, you can use it to find the width of the shoulders, too. For a male figure, set the balls of the shoulders to the outside of the box. You can set them just outside or farther outside, depending on how broad the shoulders are.

For a female figure, you can set the balls of the shoulders just to the outside of the box or even within the box's sides, depending on how broad-shouldered the figure is.

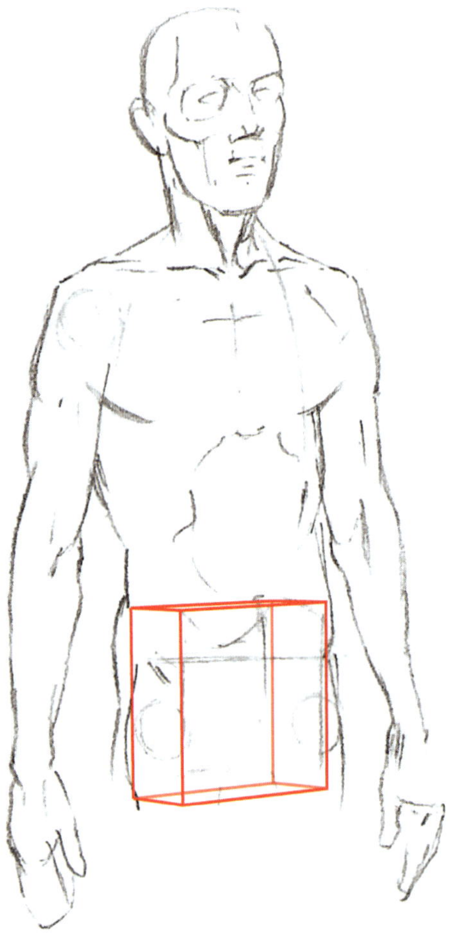

Hip Width
For male figures, draw the balls of the hips inside the box. For female figures, draw them just outside the box.

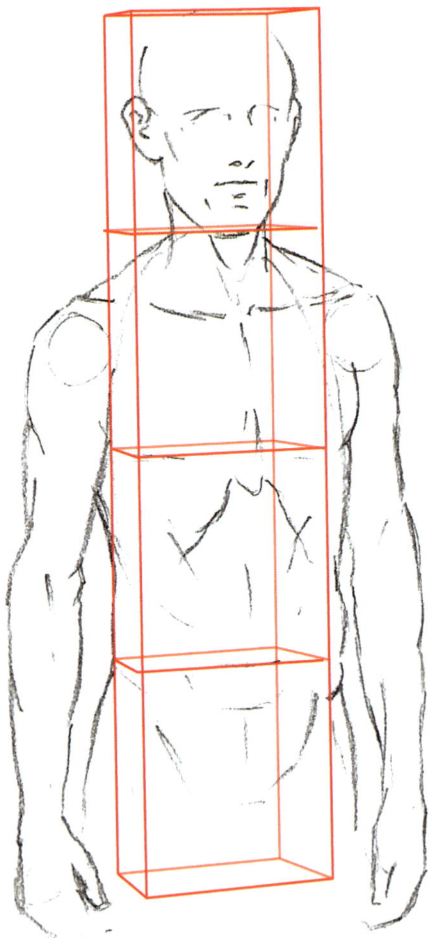

Shoulder Width
For male figures, draw the balls of the shoulders outside the box. For female figures, they may be just outside the box or even inside the box.

HEAD PROPORTIONS

As we saw in the section on eighth subdivisions, dividing the head in two, top to bottom, gives us the proper height on which to set the eyes. Dividing the head, top to bottom, into thirds gives us another set of useful markers.

The brow ridge falls on the upper third plane. On the lower third sit the base of the nose, the base of the skull (in back of the face) and the site where the earlobe connects to the head. This plane also marks the lowest point of the arches of the cheekbones.

If you divide the head into two halves, front to back, you will find that the ear sits to the back of this line, while the jawline descends from in front of it.

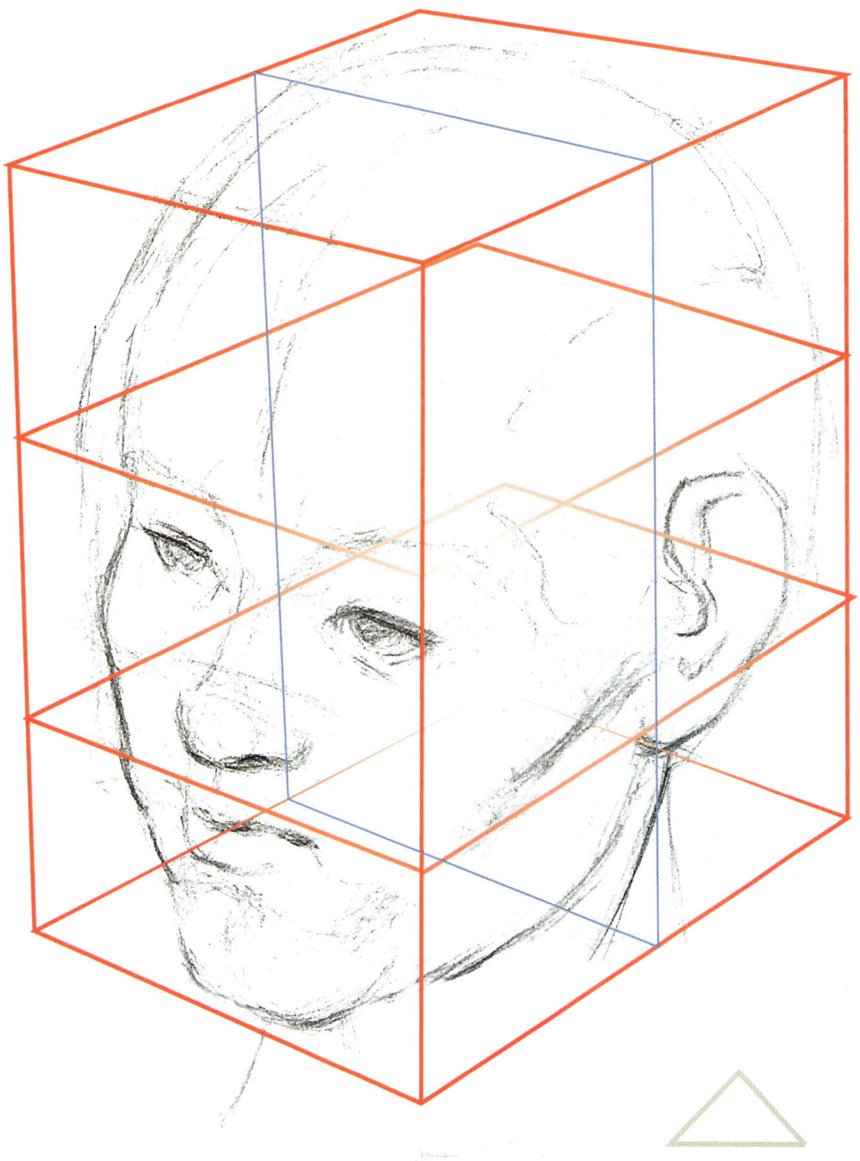

Head Subdivisions

Divide the head into thirds, top to bottom, and in half, back to front, to find more useful markers.

LOWER BRACKET DIVISION

Our lower bracket divides top to bottom in a very useful way: The distance from the top of the upper leg bone to the middle of the knee joint is the same distance as from the middle of the knee joint to the bottom of the foot.

As with all the proportions in this book, you will have to compensate for the effects of perspective and watch for bends in the leg. But merely knowing that the upper leg is equal in length to the lower leg can help establish a good portion of your drawing from the outset.

Because the upper bracket that we drew is the same size as the lower bracket, you can already begin to make some correlations between the halves of the upper bracket and these divisions.

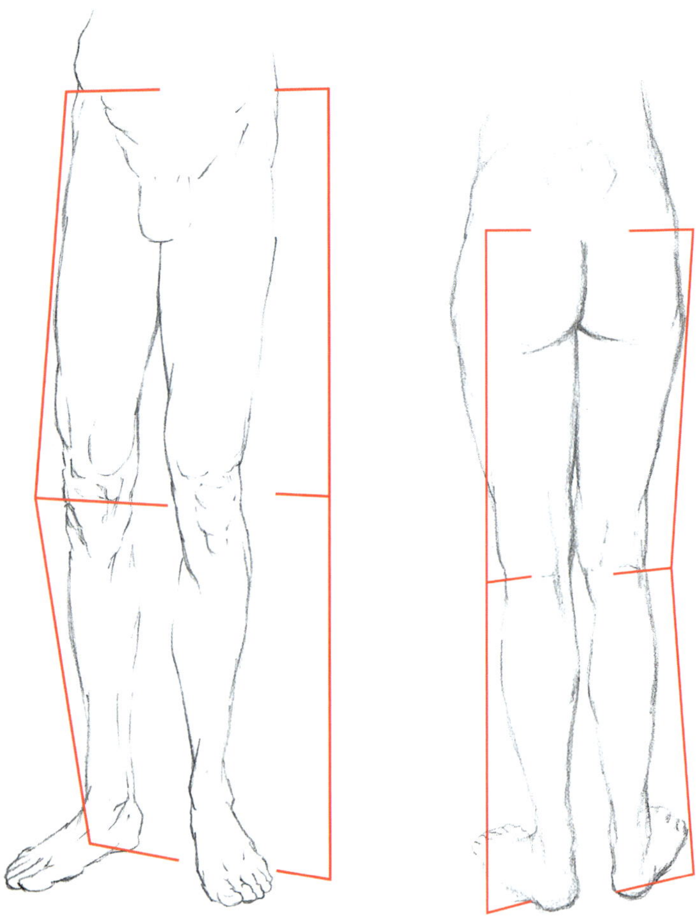

Lower Body Division

The lower body bracket divides at the knee. It is the same for both the front and the back of the figure.

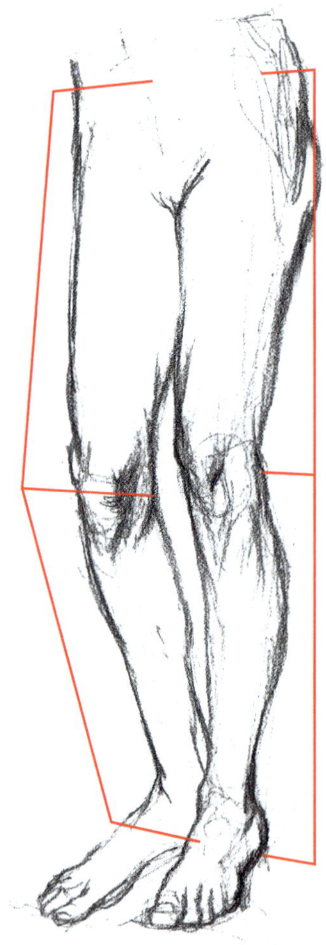

Lower Bracket in Perspective

Take perspective into account when you divide the lower bracket in half at the knee.

ARM PROPORTIONS

The distance from the very top of the upper arm (just under the collarbone when the arm is in a vertical position) to the elbow joint is the same from the elbow joint to the knuckle line of the hand. If the hand is fisted, that will define the end of the lower arm.

If we divide this measurement from the elbow to the knuckle line into four and add one of these quarters onto the end of the forearm, it will bring us to the end of the little finger.

Notice how this measurement (one-quarter of the distance from the elbow to the knuckles or one-fifth of the distance from the elbow to the end of the little finger) can be squared off to find the width of the bony parts of the hand. It is the same width as the bony part of the elbow, and generally it describes the width and depth of the fleshy portion of the upper arm where the biceps and triceps lie.

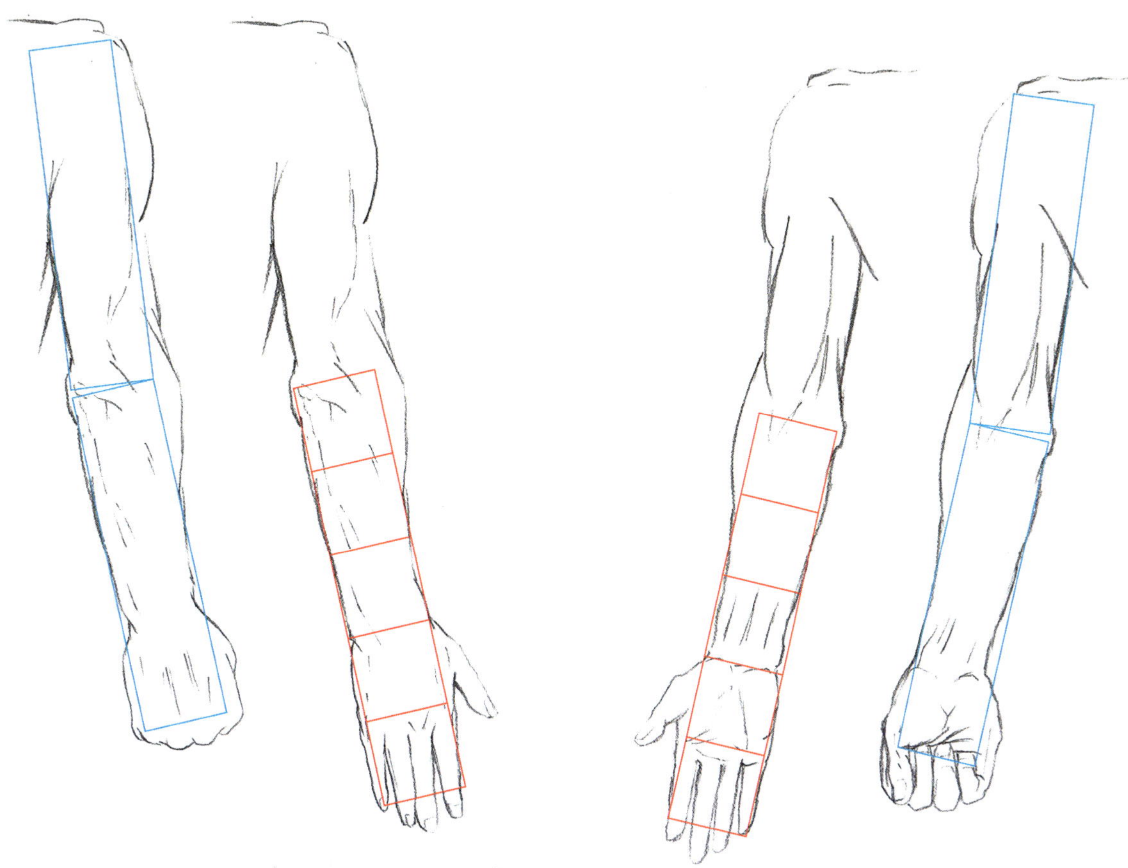

Arm Division

The distance from the top of the upper arm to the elbow is equal to the distance from the elbow to the knuckle line of the hand.

Arm Subdivision

Divide the lower arm into four sections between the elbow and knuckle line and add one additional section of the same size to find the tip of the little finger.

HAND PROPORTIONS

The hand is a complex, very movable part of the body. It is divided into three sections: the palm, the fingers (as a group) and the thumb.

Each finger is a slightly different length. However, by focusing on the smallest finger, we can establish some useful guidelines for ourselves in the form of a double square. You will find that the width of the palm is equal to its length. You will also find that the length of the little finger from the tip to the knuckle is equal to the length of the palm. So, accordingly, the length of the little finger will be equal to the width of the palm.

We will have more fun with these relationships later in the book, especially when we note the equivalence in length between the little finger and the thumb.

The four fingers, while they vary in length, are generally of the same width and depth. If you divide the square of the fingers into four parts, you can easily find the general size of any finger. You can adjust the individual contours from there.

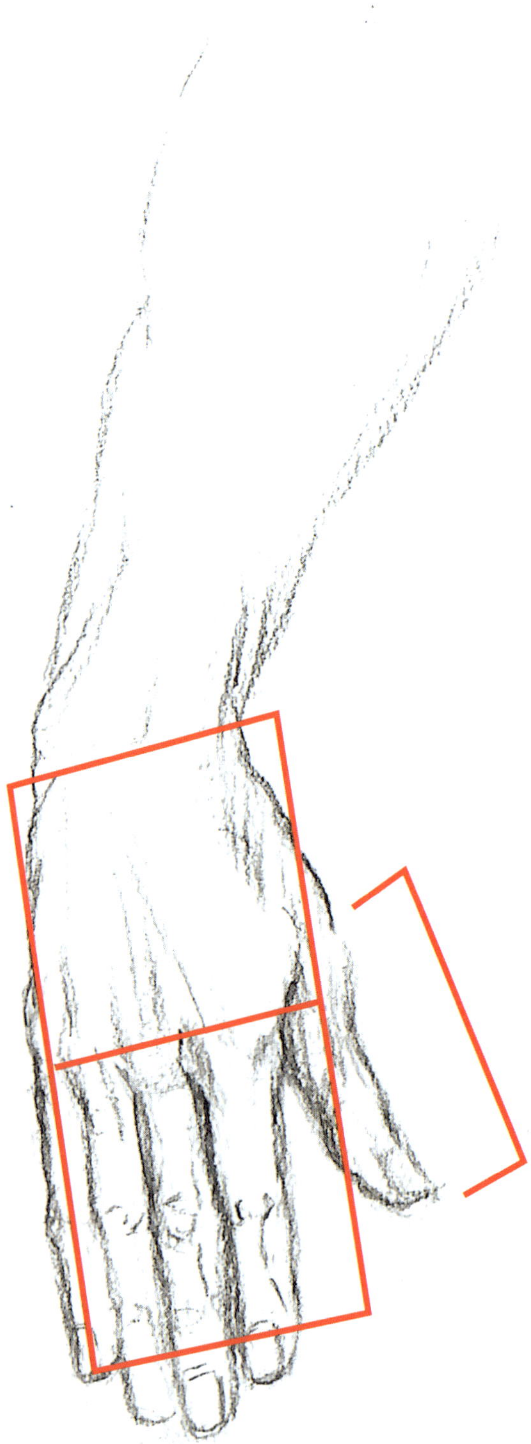

Palm and Little Finger Proportions

The width and length of the palm and the length of the little finger are all equal and form two squares.

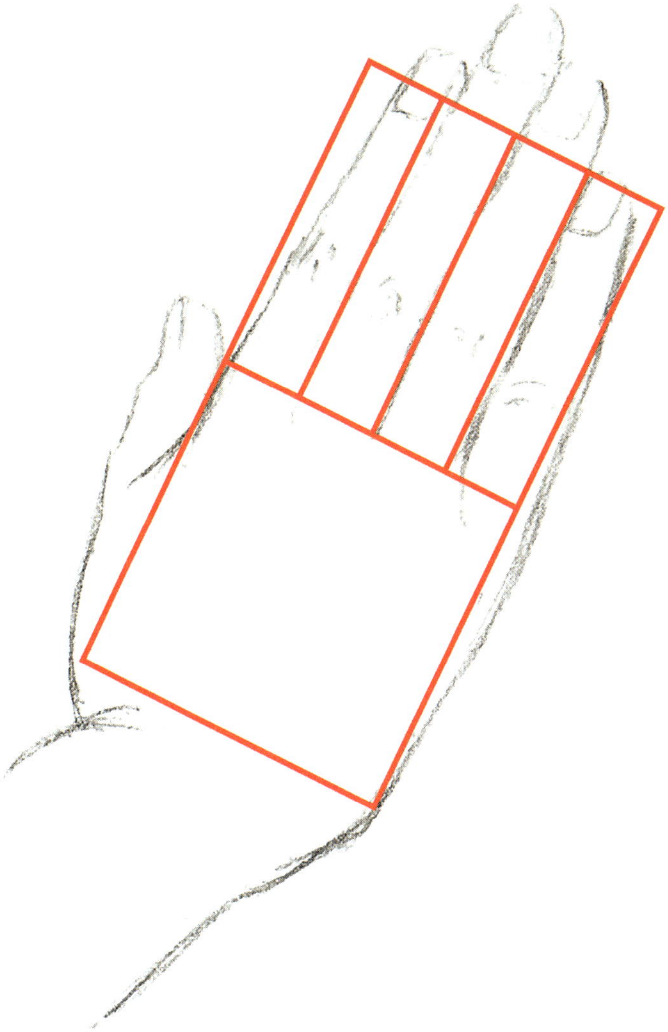

Divide the Four Fingers

To divide the square into four parts, you will find it easier to divide the box in half, and then each half into half again, rather than trying to estimate what a quarter of the box looks like at the outset.

Finger Depth

The fingers, where they meet the palm of the hand, are generally as deep as they are wide. They gradually narrow and flatten as they move toward the fingertips, but you can create helpful guidelines for the fingers by squaring off each of the quarter-width boxes drawn in the previous illustration.

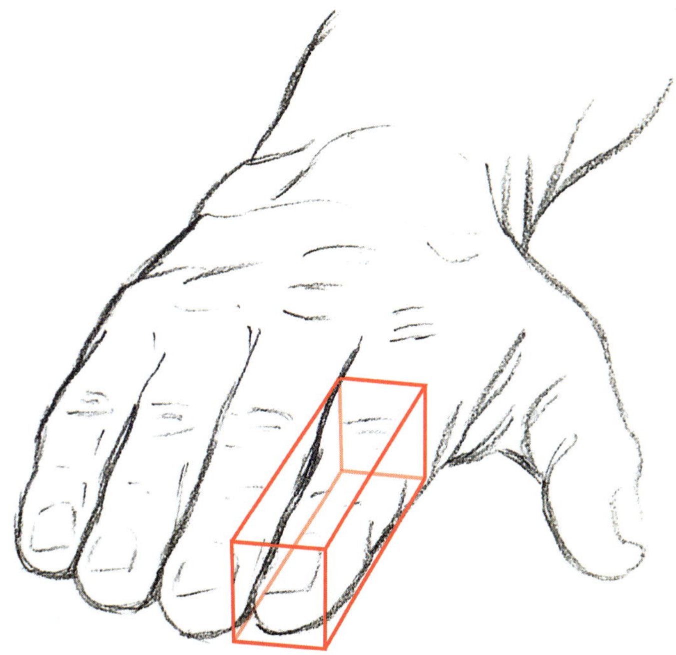

KNEE PROPORTIONS

The knee (the full bony portion, not just the kneecap) is as wide as it is deep (front to back). It is also roughly speaking the same measurement in height.

The measurements depend, of course, on what we mean by the knee's top and bottom. But if we consider them to be the thicker bony ends of the femur bone, above, and the tibia, below, then we can describe the entire knee joint within a cube or with a sphere if that's easier.

Finding the Point of the Knee

At the bottom level of this cube or sphere, we find the "point" of the knee, an important landmark for drawing the lower leg properly.

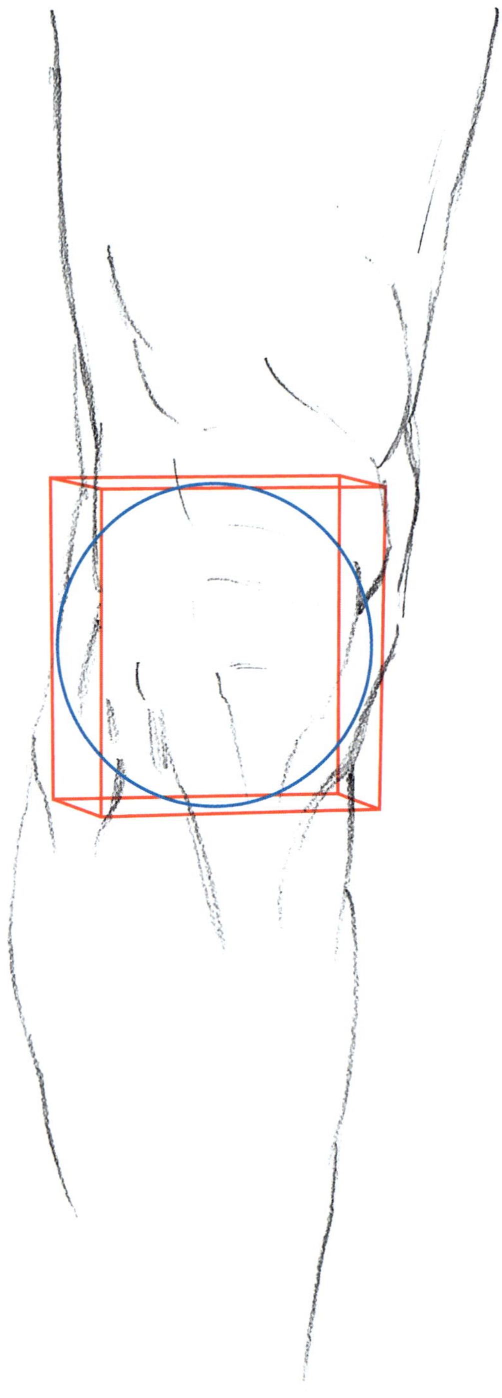

FOOT PROPORTIONS

The foot's widest point (where the toes meet the body of the foot) is equal to one-third the length of the foot, from the heel to the front of the toes. This measure is the same as from the ground plane to the ankle joint, where the foot meets the lower leg.

Because the height and width of the foot are the same, we can draw a square to describe it. And because that measurement is one-third the foot's length, we can determine the length of the whole foot by lining up three cubes in a row. Or given the length of the foot, we can divide it into three equal parts to find some significant landmarks. The back of the frontmost cube will mark where the toes join the rest of the foot. The back of the middle cube will mark where the shin meets the top of the foot.

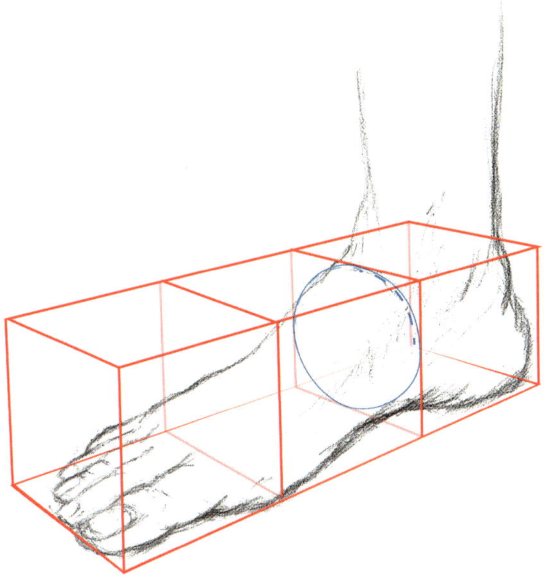

Foot Cube Divisions

Divide the foot into three cubes to find significant landmarks. Drawing a circle on the back of the middle cube gives us a quick, if approximate, way to easily trace the arc of the lower leg bones as they surround the foot at this juncture.

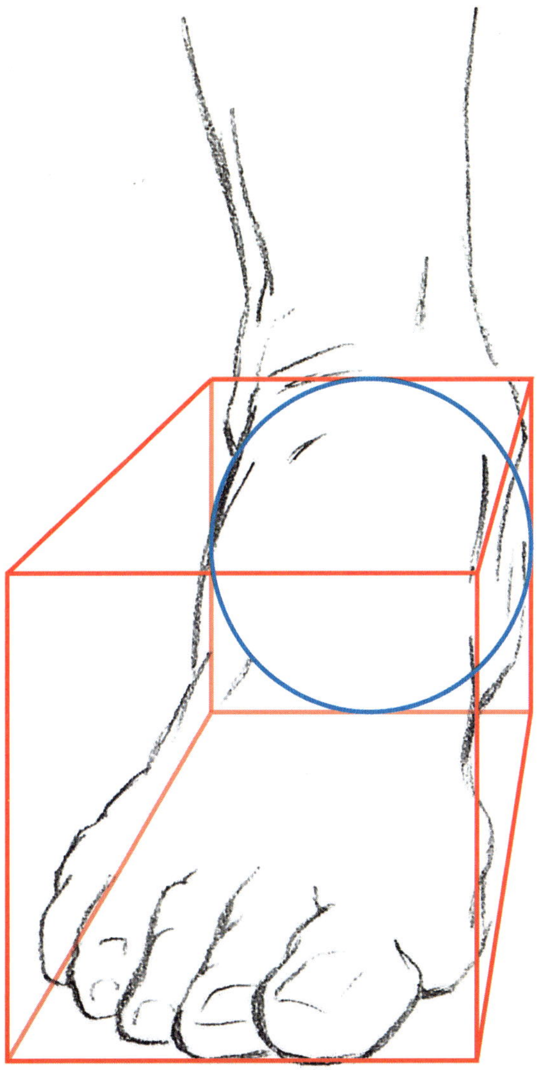

Foot Divisions in Perspective

Drawing the cubes in perspective can help you find the significant landmarks and draw the foot accurately.

THE BODY'S MAXIMUM VOLUME

In working out a composition, it's good to know from the outset how much area you want the figure to take on the page. If you know the height of the figure, remember that the figure will occupy the same amount of width with his or her arms outstretched. So be sure to leave enough room for that on the page.

You should also leave yourself a generous amount of page space if you want your figure to be twisting in space or if you want the figure to lift his or her arms overhead.

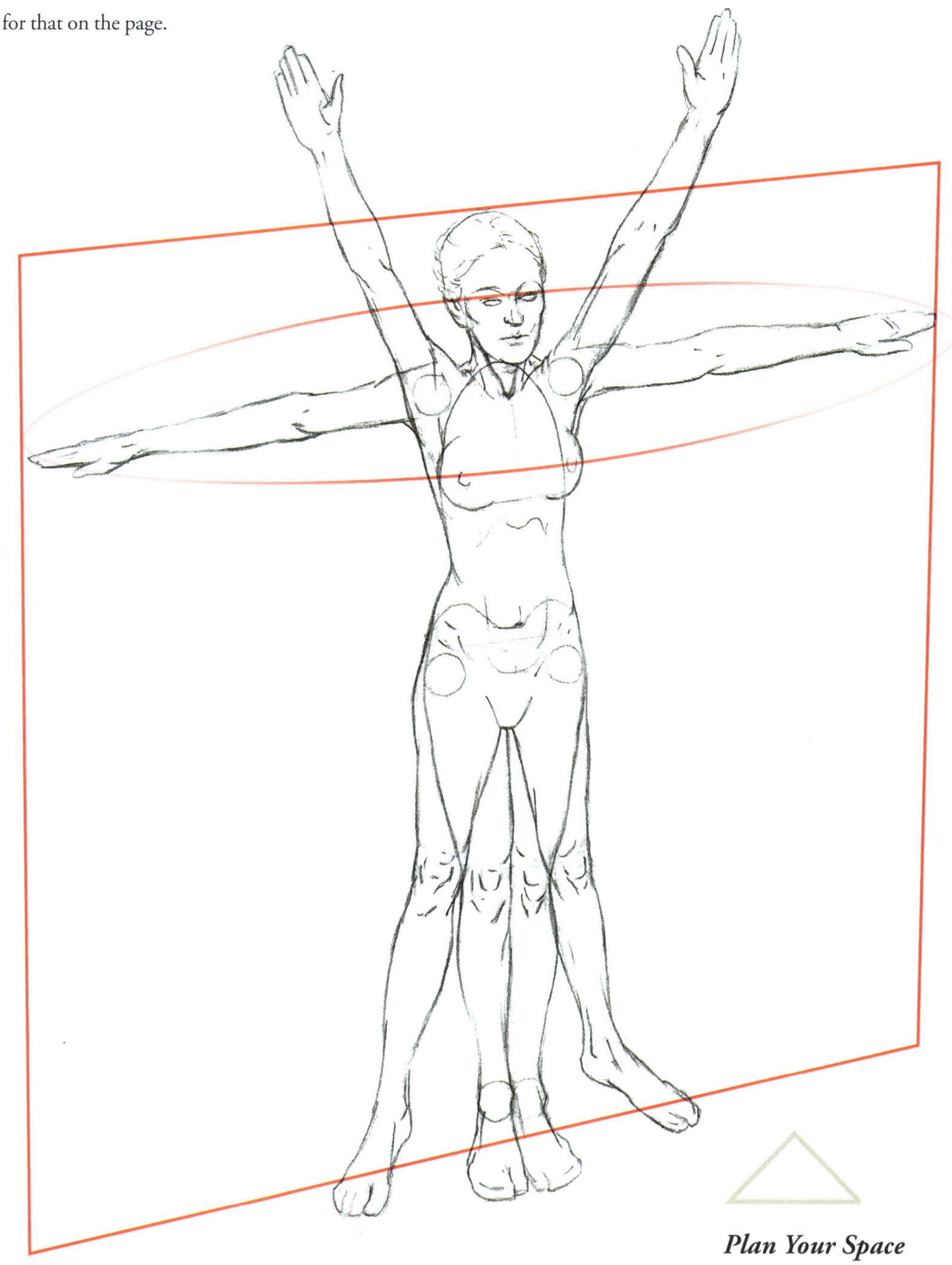

Plan Your Space

Keep the figure's maximum volume in mind as you place it on the page.

THE SEATED FIGURE

The easiest way to get a quick feel for the proportions of the seated figure is to remember the 2:1 ratio. There are two units of height above the seat line to one unit below the seat.

This makes sense because, as we saw earlier, the lower bracket and upper bracket of the figure are equal in height. When the figure is seated, the lower bracket is usually bent at something close to a 90° angle. Therefore, the lower bracket loses half its height while the upper bracket keeps its full length.

Unique Measurements
The exact measurements will depend on the height of the model, the chair and the way that the model is sitting. But using the 2:1 rule should set your drawing off to a good, solid start.

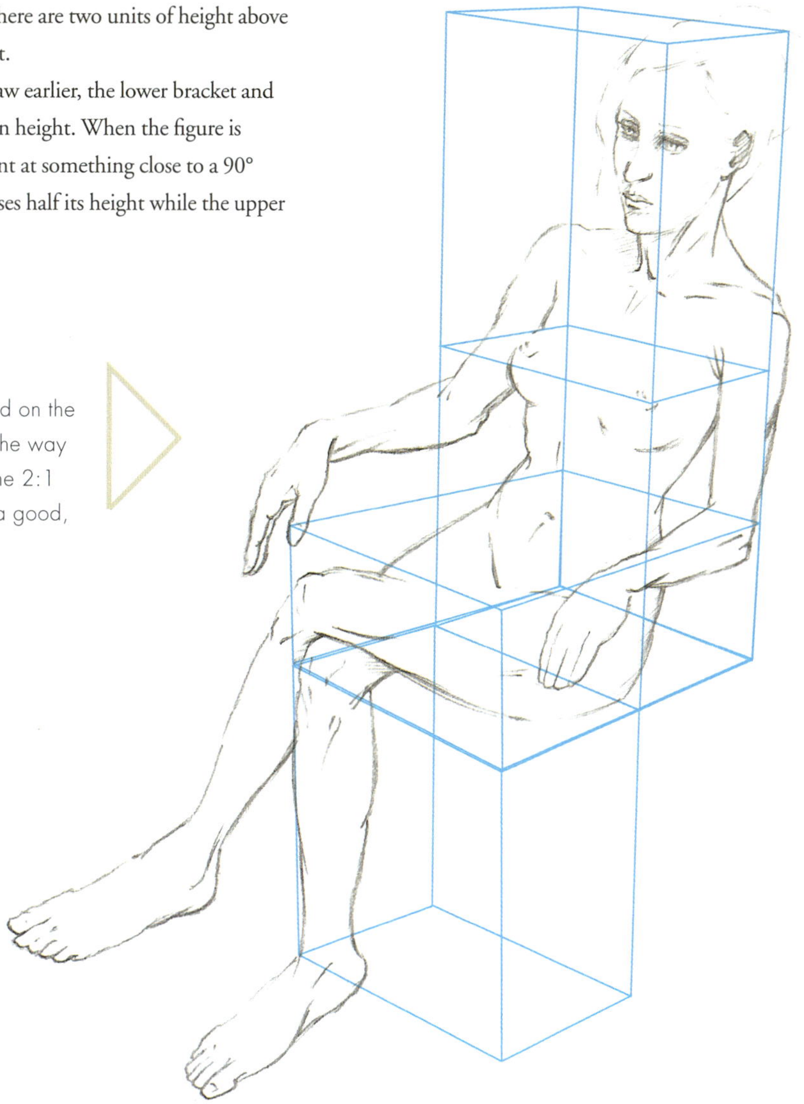

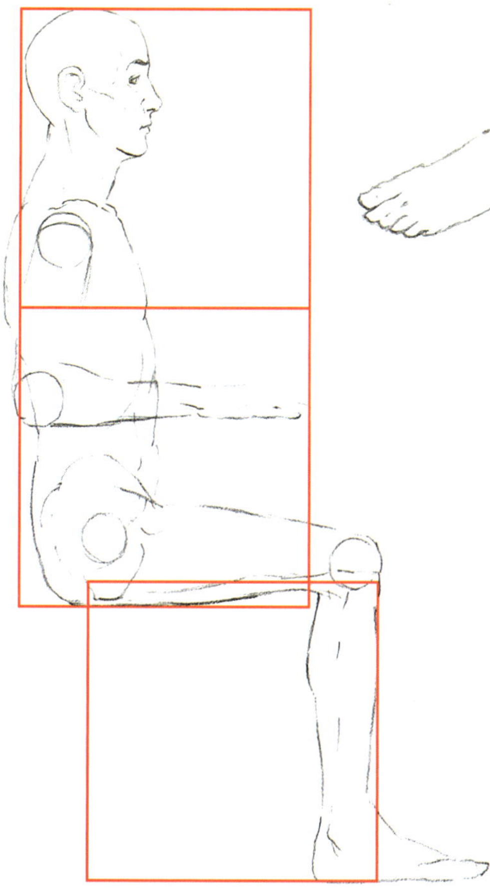

Use Squares to Find the Proportions
Here you can also see how to square off the area for the lower leg to find how far forward of the seat rest it will come.

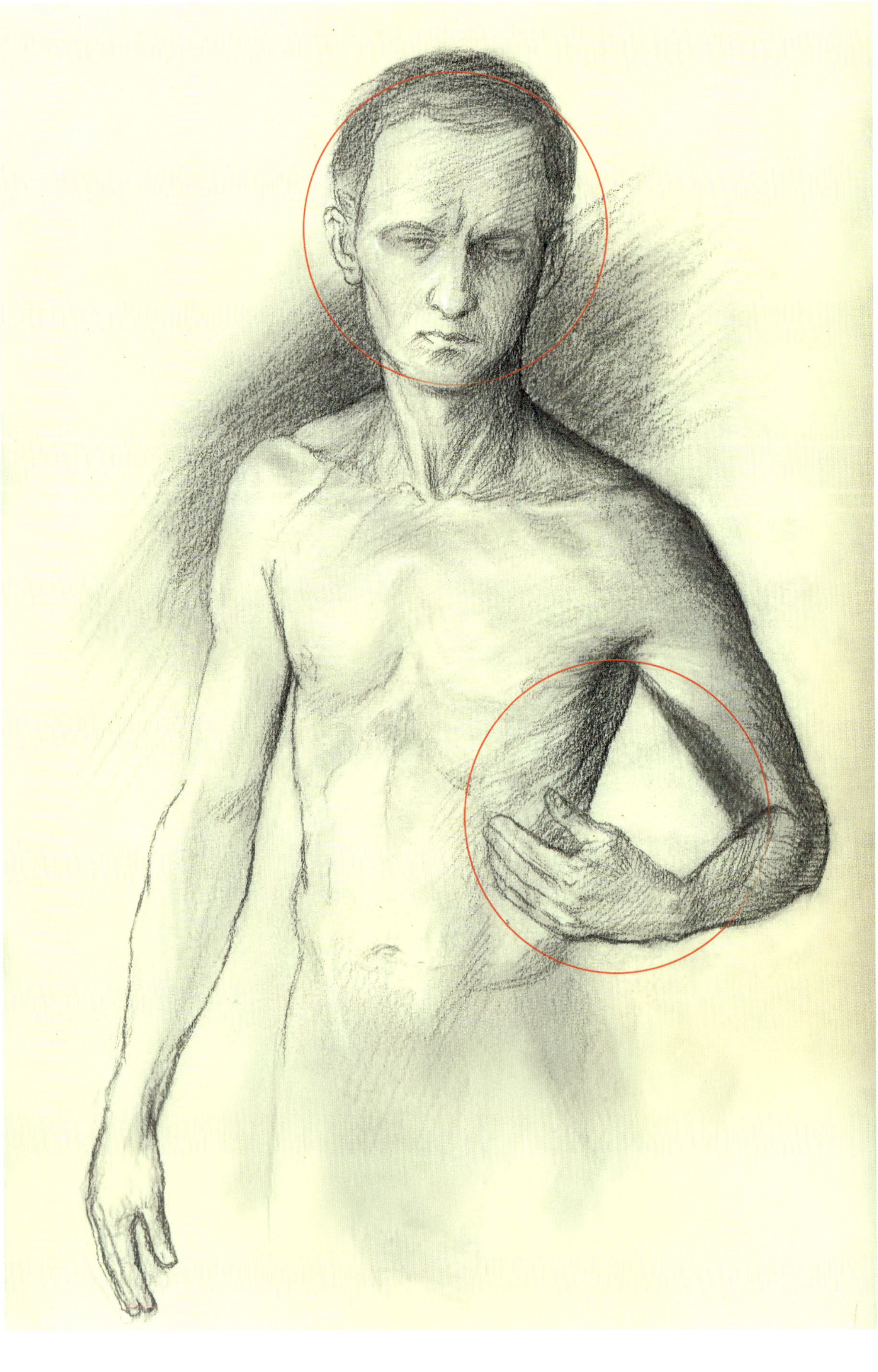

4

THE BODY'S COMPARATIVE PROPORTIONS

In Chapter 3 we looked at the internal proportions of the figure, each body part's own height, width and depth in relation to its other measurements. In this chapter we want to look at how some of these measurements compare with the height, width or depth of a different body part. Most especially, we want to look for simple proportions—any measurement that is the same size, twice the size or three times the size as another.

These simple comparisons are easier to recall than a table of abstract fractions, and they're easier to draw. We'll review some easy ways to keep them remembered. Always consider that your body doesn't vary that greatly from anyone else's, and neither does the figure in your drawing. So any comparative proportion you can find in your own body should also be valid for the figure on the page.

UPPER AND LOWER BODY BRACKETS

The upper body is equal in height to the lower body. And because the figure in your drawing can be as flexible as you want to create it, he or she would be able to bend perfectly in half.

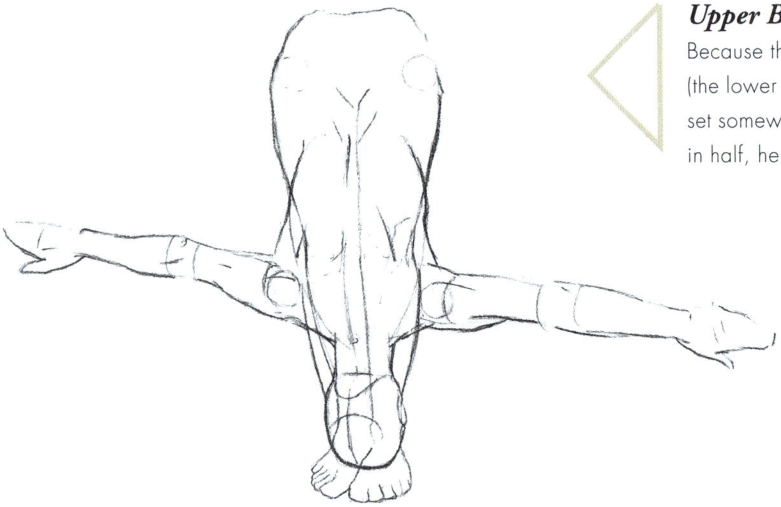

Upper Body Height

Because the hinge point of the hips, where the legs (the lower body) join to the trunk (the upper body), is set somewhat into the upper body, if the figure folds in half, her head will reach the top of her feet.

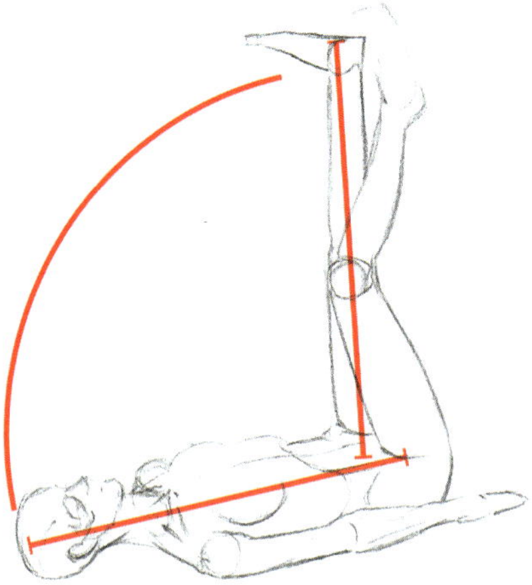

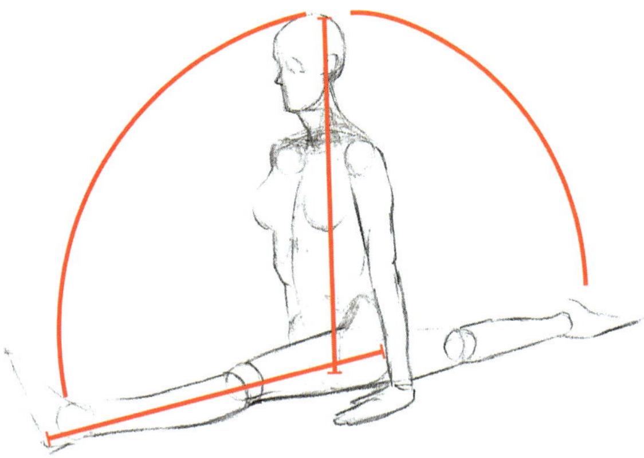

Upper Body Height in Varying Positions

The head should be able to reach the top of the feet whether the figure is on her back or even doing a full split.

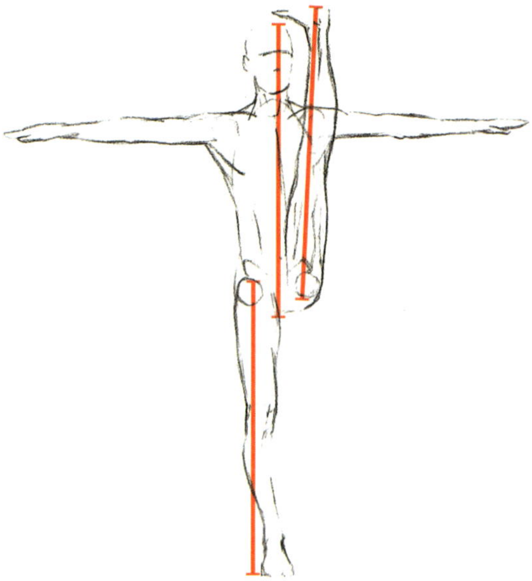

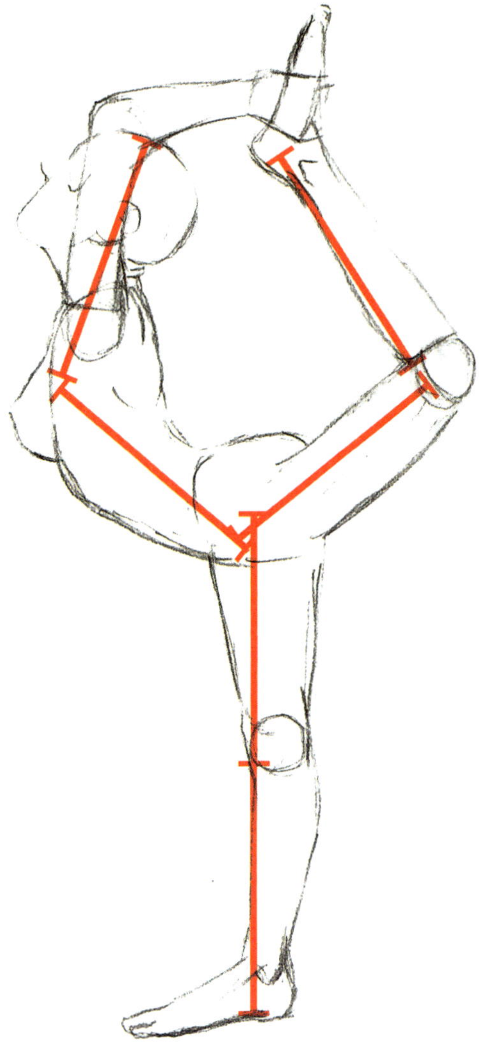

Direct Leg-Torso Comparison

Note how the legs and torso are of the same length. Though few people are this flexible, nothing stops your figure drawing from being so.

Bent Leg-Torso Comparison

Even when slightly bent, the upper brackets and lower brackets add up to the same length.

SHOULDER WIDTH

Because you know how to divide the upper body vertically into four, you can square off any of the vertical divisions to help find the proper width of the torso. If each of the quarter divisions makes a unit, then the balls of a male's shoulders should sit to the outside of the unit but should not be more than a full unit away from the vertical center line of the body.

The following comparison methods will help you position the shoulders more exactly, especially when you are not depicting the full torso in your work as when working on a portrait composition.

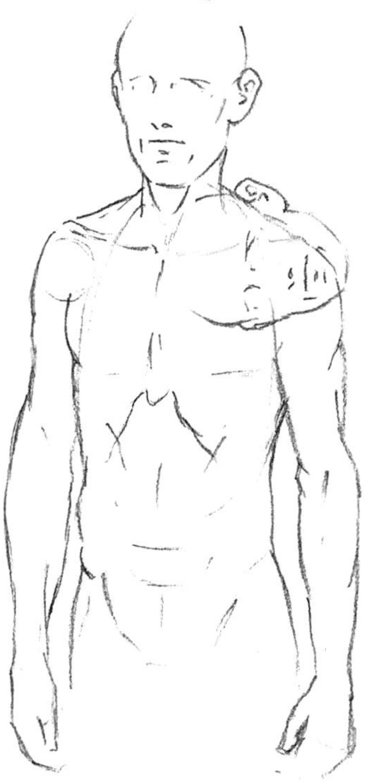

Shoulder-Head Comparison

An old song began "Put your head on my shoulder." You can use this to remember that the widest point of the shoulders for a strongly built figure (usually a male) will extend out the length of one head from the center of the body.

For a female or slighter figure, make the shoulders narrower than this limit.

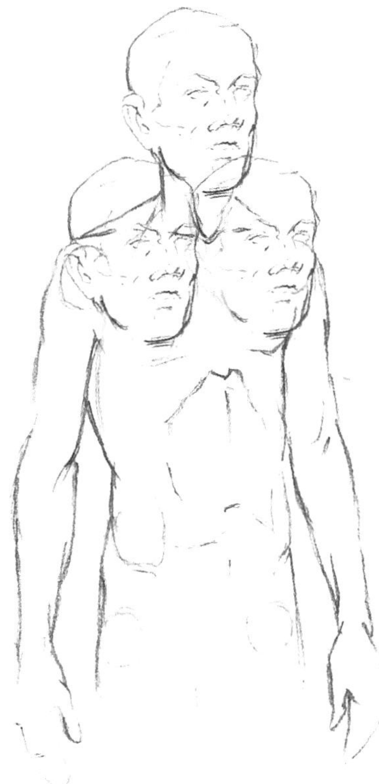

Clavicle-Head Comparison

The clavicle is equal in length to the width of the head. You can use a schema such as this to help you construct the shoulders.

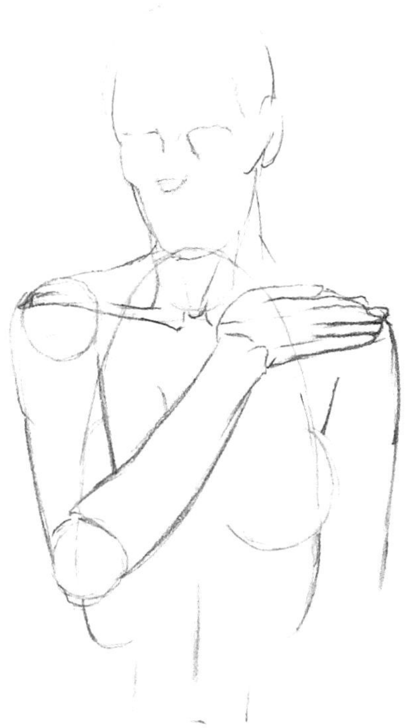

Shoulder-Hand Comparison

Your hand length is equal to the length of your clavicle plus the bony surface to the outside of it that belongs to the shoulder blade. So the hand should take up the distance from the pit of the neck to where the deltoid muscle begins.

UPPER BODY WIDTH

We already know how to divide the upper body vertically into four. Squaring off one of the units will give you a good idea of where the general mass of the torso falls. By drawing this mass as a solid, you can also indicate any twisting, bending or foreshortening happening in the drawing.

Use any of the following comparison methods to shore up the proper width of the torso.

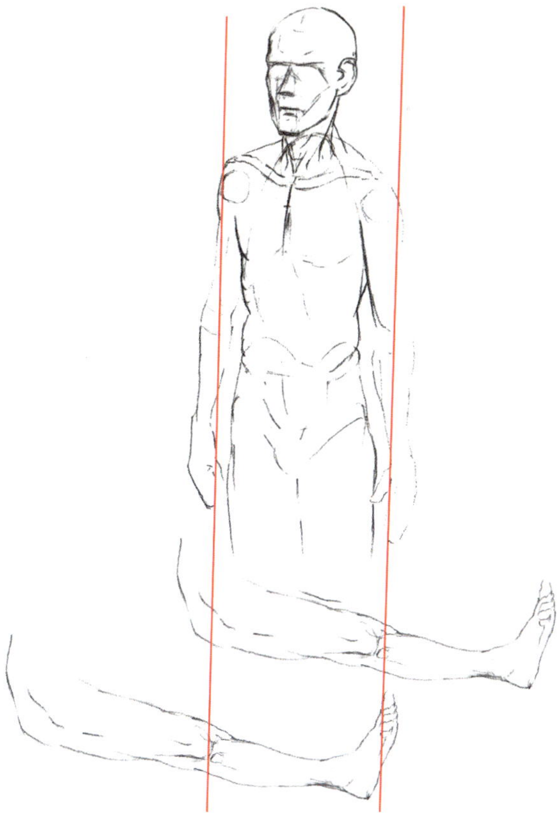

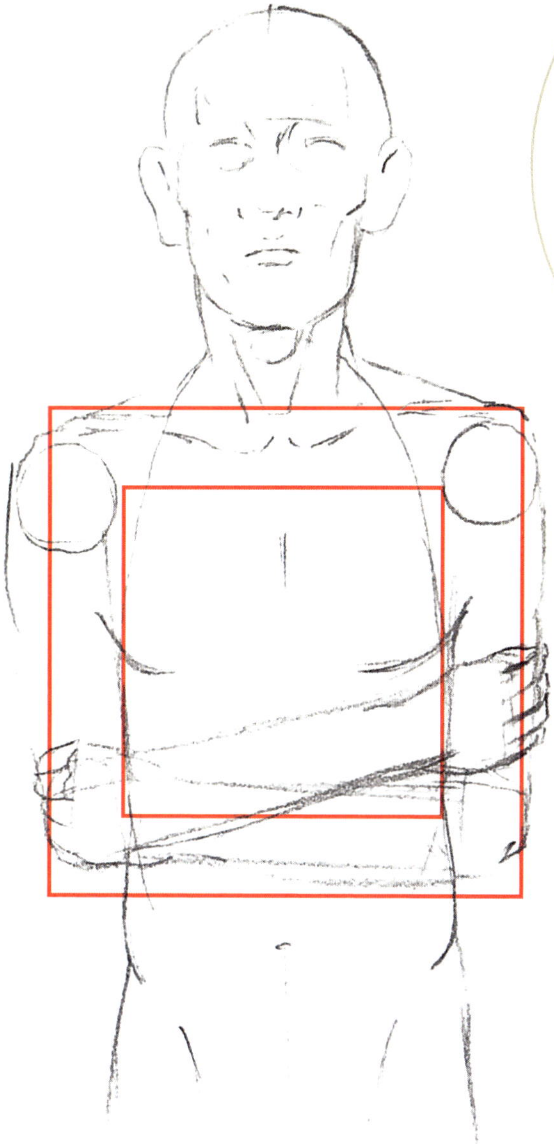

Body-Leg Comparison

Another way of sizing up the width of the body is to relate it to the length of either the upper or lower leg. Sit cross-legged on the floor, and you'll see that this is true. (Once again, we're talking about the widest part of a broad-shouldered person.)

Body-Arm Comparison

Because the length of the arm from the elbow to the knuckle is equal to the length of the arm from the elbow to the shoulder, we can draw a square around the arms of a figure who's grabbing his own arms by running a top line across the top of the clavicles.

We can also draw an inner square running from the top of the folded arms, up the insides of the upper arms, topped off by a line across the top of the armpits.

HEAD WIDTH, DEPTH AND HEIGHT

The head and face are so engaging in an artwork that it's easy to pay them too much attention at first, neglecting the proportion and composition of your drawing. Avoid this by trying to view the head, at least at first, as any other body part that makes up the figure. Having cemented its proper placement and size in the beginning, you will find you have much more time to devote to its details later.

The following comparison methods are good ways to relate the size of the head to other, relatively distant areas of the body.

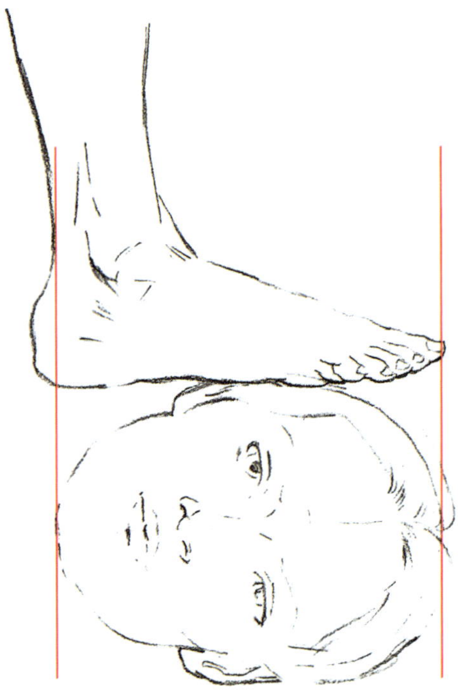

Head-Foot Comparison
Forget about the heels, and find the height of the head quickly (or vice versa to find the length of the foot).

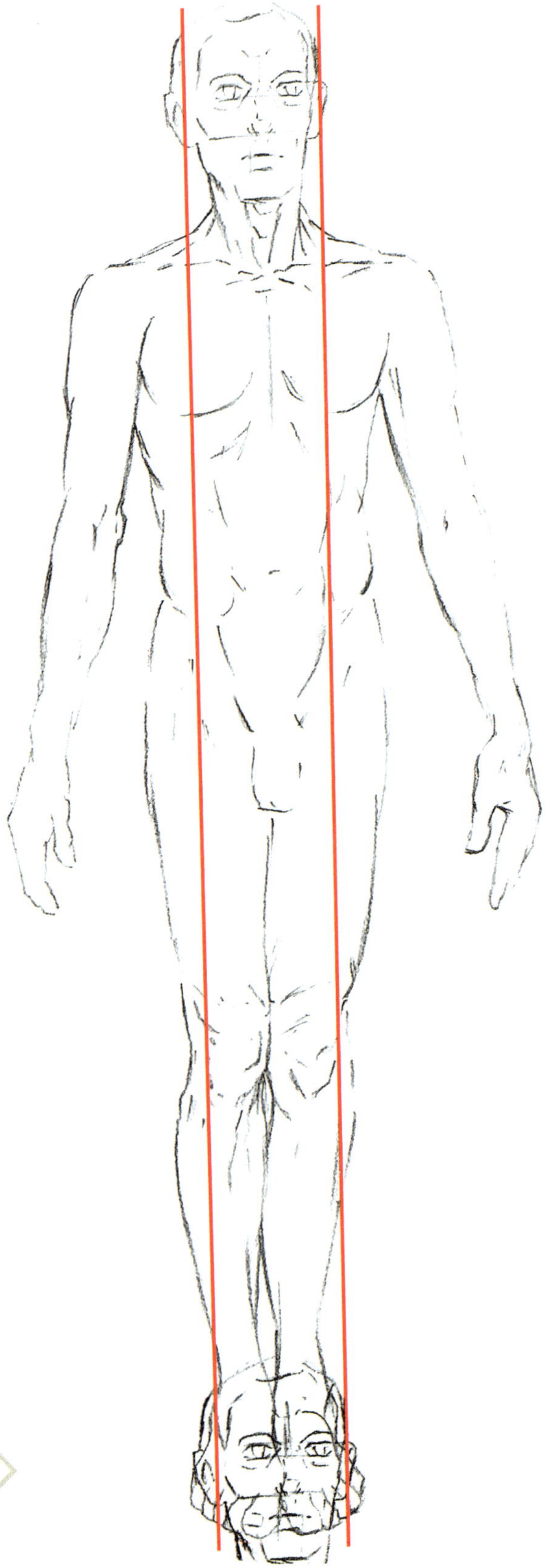

Head-Feet Comparison
Two feet placed side by side take up the same width as the head. You may want to make this comparison at the outset of your drawing. It's a quick way to establish some central proportions of your figure from head to toes.

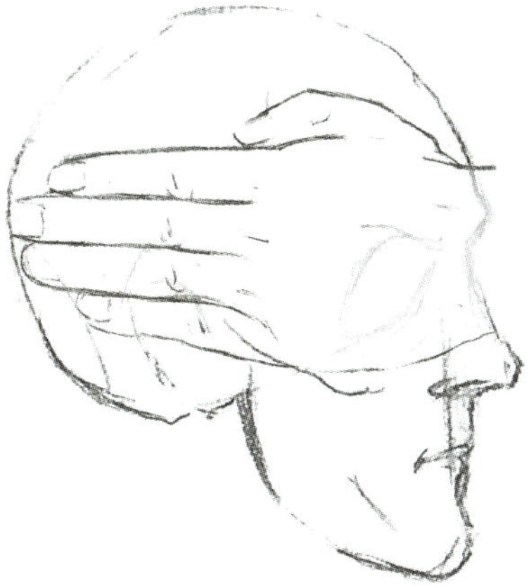

Head-Hand Comparison

Can't remember the proper depth of the head? Just take your head in your hands, and it should become apparent.

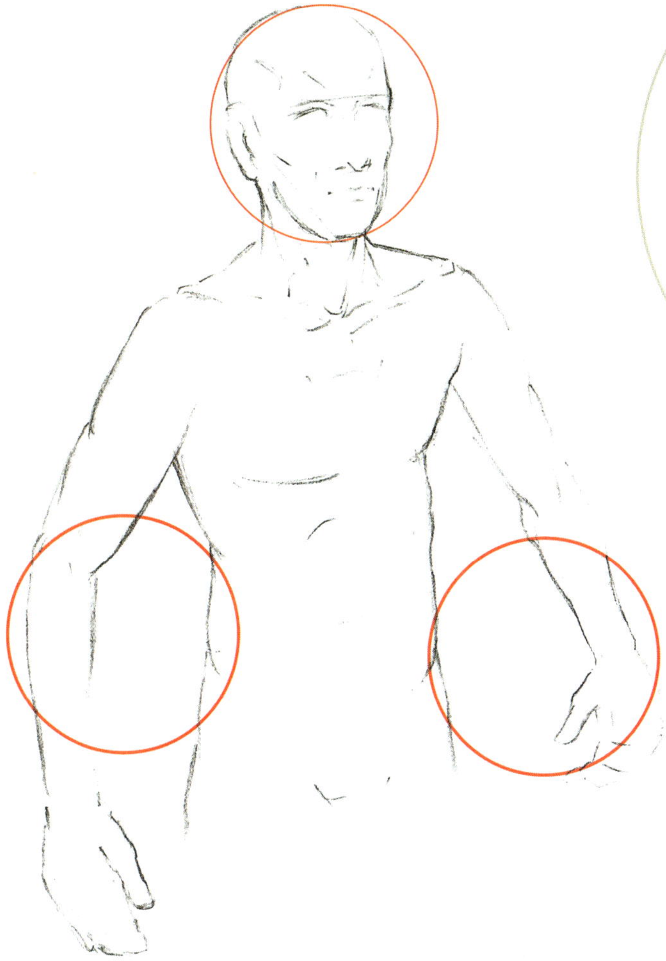

Head-Arm Comparison

If the height of a human head is about the same size as a regulation basketball, your figure should be able to cradle or palm a sphere that would hold his own head.

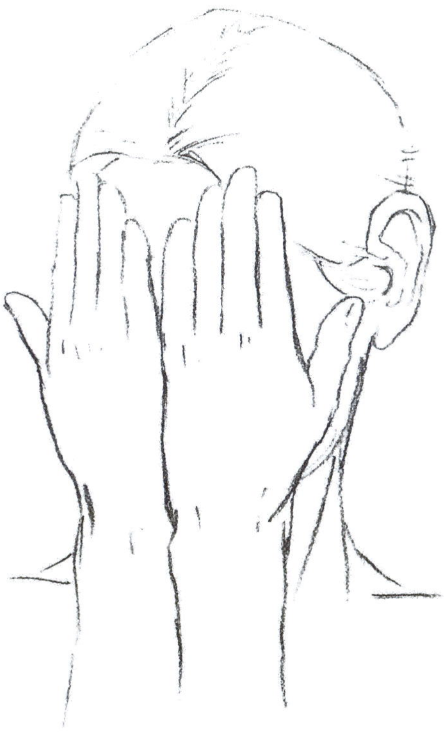

Head-Hand-Face Comparison

Playing peekaboo teaches us that the two hands together are the same width as the head, and they're also the same length as the face from hairline to chin.

NECK LENGTH AND HEIGHT

The neck is a complex bridge between the head and the torso. It is longer in the front than in the back because it sits on the rib cage, which slopes downward toward the front of the body. Nevertheless, if you first conceive of it as a cylinder (or, better yet, as a block) of equal height, width and depth, you will find it easier to draw.

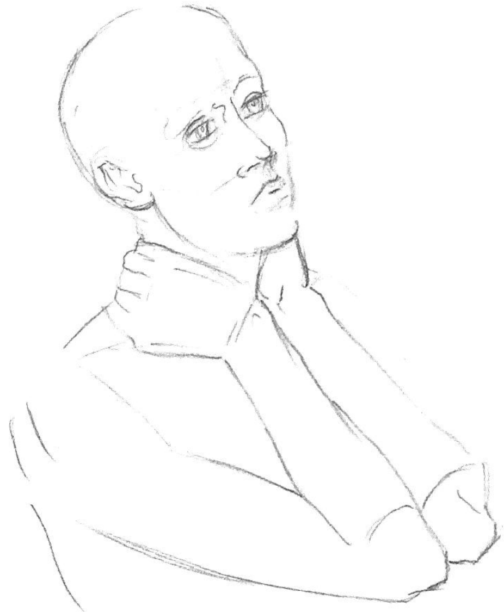

Neck-Hand Comparison

And if you want another way to find the height of the neck, just strangle yourself (gently, of course!), and you'll find that it's the same as the width of the hands.

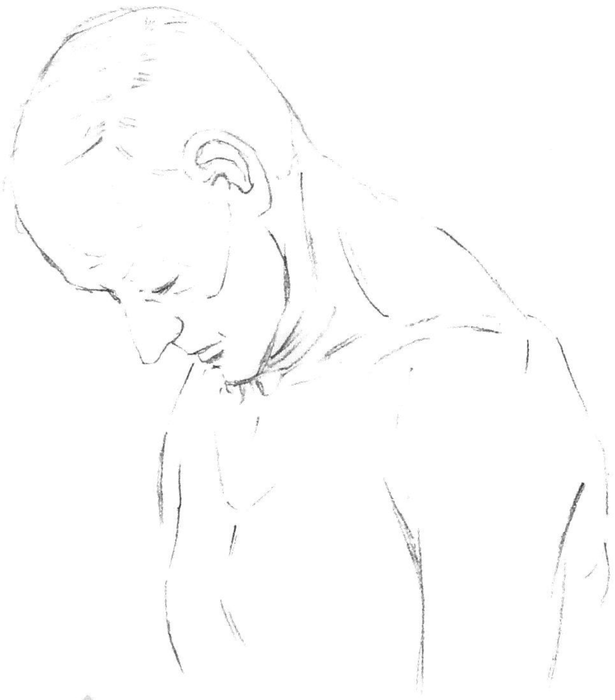

Neck-Chin Comparison

If you nod your head, your chin should reach the notch of your neck. The same should be true of the figure in your drawing.

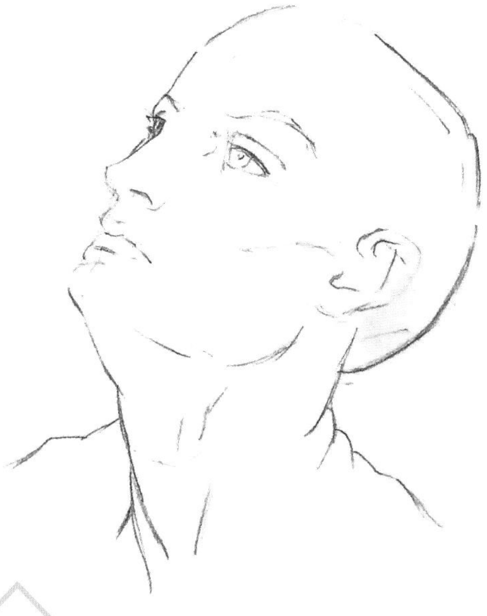

Neck-Back Comparison

We can't tilt our heads back so far that they hit our backs. But if we could, we would locate the proper length of the neck in back.

HIP WIDTH, DEPTH AND HEIGHT

The bony structure of the hips is only a little wider than it is tall. Its depth (front to back) is a bit narrower. The legs can change their positions wildly, but always indicate the block of the underlying pelvic girdle in your drawing. These comparisons can help keep you from having your proportions go too far astray.

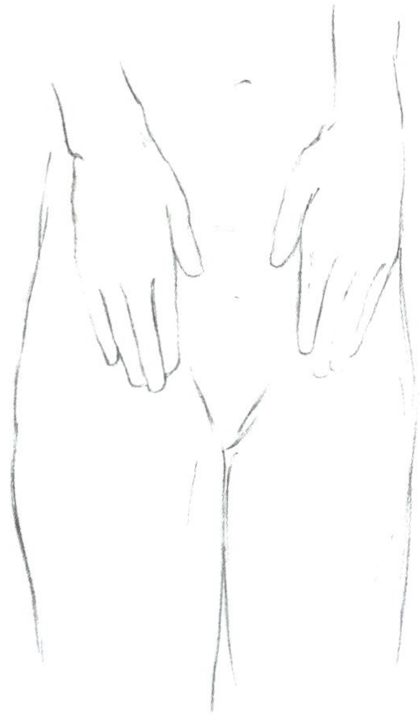

Hips-Hands Comparison

We are all used to sticking our hands in our pockets. If you pretend that the figure in your drawing is doing the same, it's easier to find the proper relationship between hips and hands.

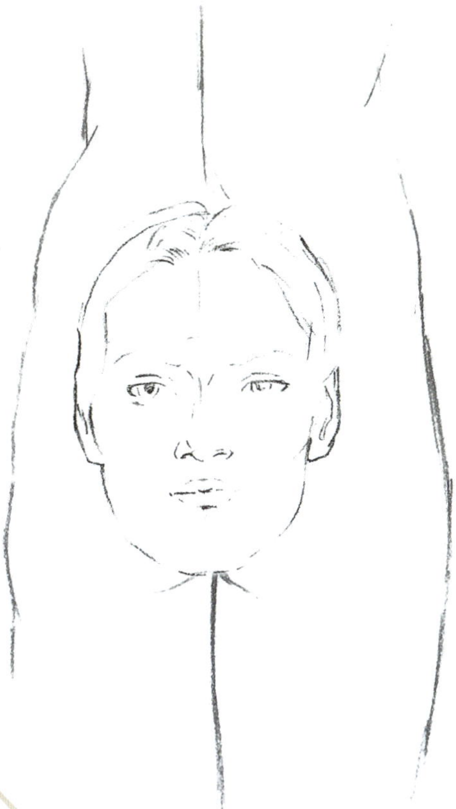

Head-Buttocks Comparison

Of course, it's not very polite to call someone a butthead, but you can use it to remember that the buttock area and the head are about the same height.

Hip-Hand Comparison

Once again, if you hold your own hand to your hip, you can get a pretty quick feeling of its depth front to back. Do the same with your figure drawing.

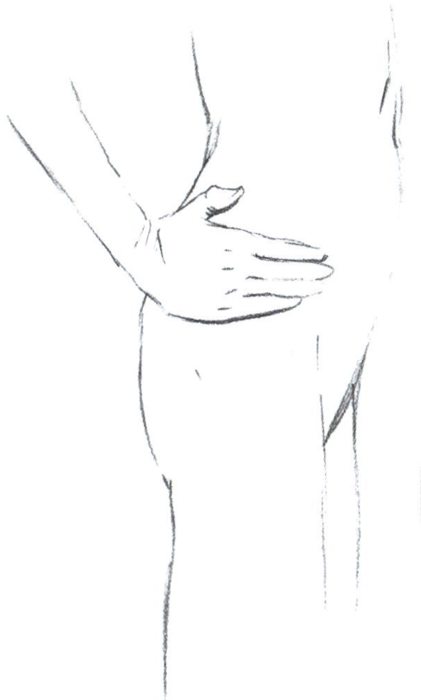

THIGH LENGTH

The thigh is the lengthiest single part of the body, and it is sometimes tempting to ignore its precise limits in your drawing, leaving the viewer to guess where it should properly end. Try instead to move the thighs in your imagination so that you can compare their dimensions with other body parts. The following comparisons should help.

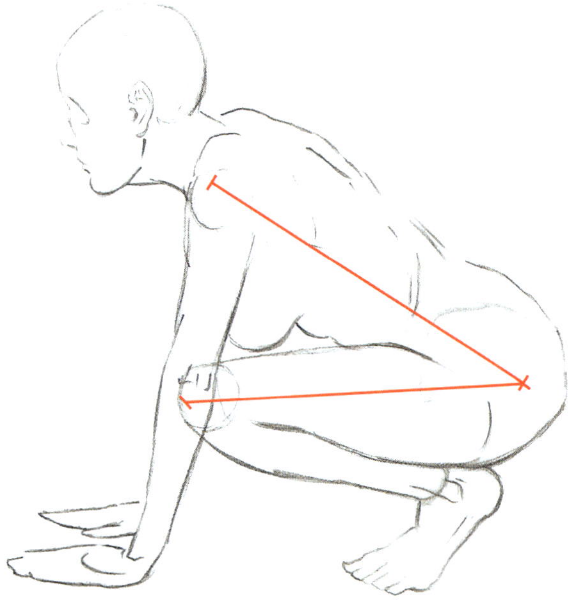

Thigh-Chest Comparison, Crouching
When a person's thighs are flexed to the limit, the knees will hit the chest right below the collarbone.

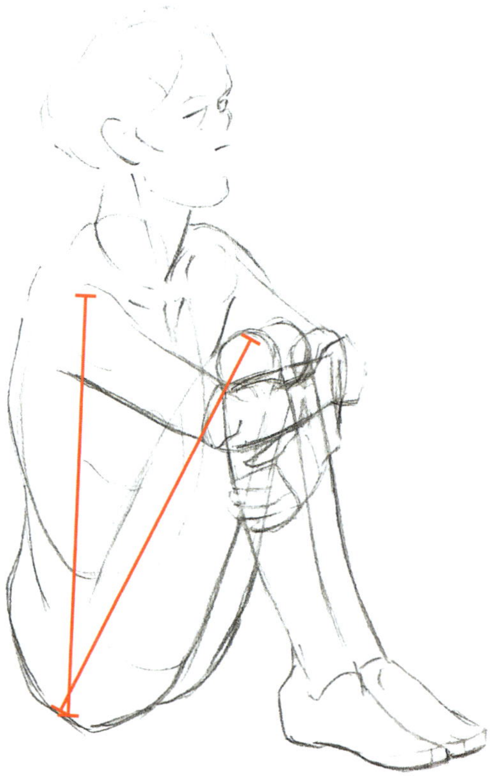

Thigh-Chest Comparison, Sitting
The same comparison works for a seated figure.

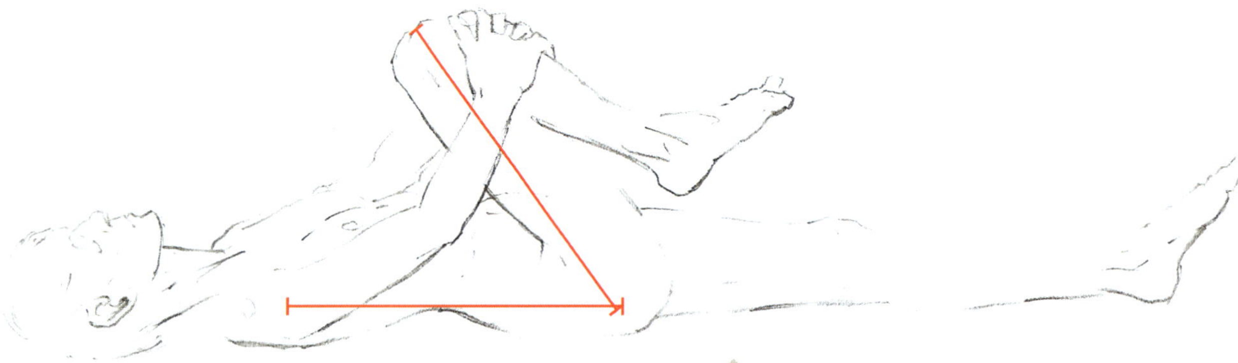

Thigh-Chest Comparison, Reclining
Likewise, the tops of the knees should reach just below the collarbone when the legs are drawn up into a tight ball.

KNEE WIDTH AND DEPTH

Where the knee begins and ends is somewhat arbitrarily determined. Here, we include not only the kneecap but the bony regions of the bottom of the upper leg and the top of the lower leg. Given this definition, you can draw the knee as a cube—a box of equal width, height and depth. (Properly portraying the slopes of such a cube will lend dynamism and credibility to your drawing.)

The following comparisons show how easy it is to compare the knee with other body parts.

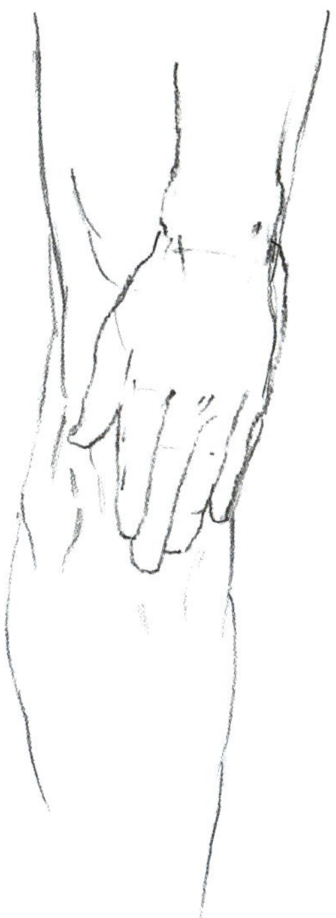

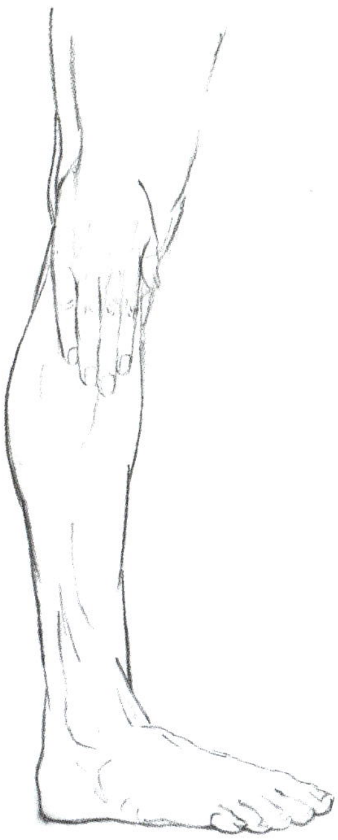

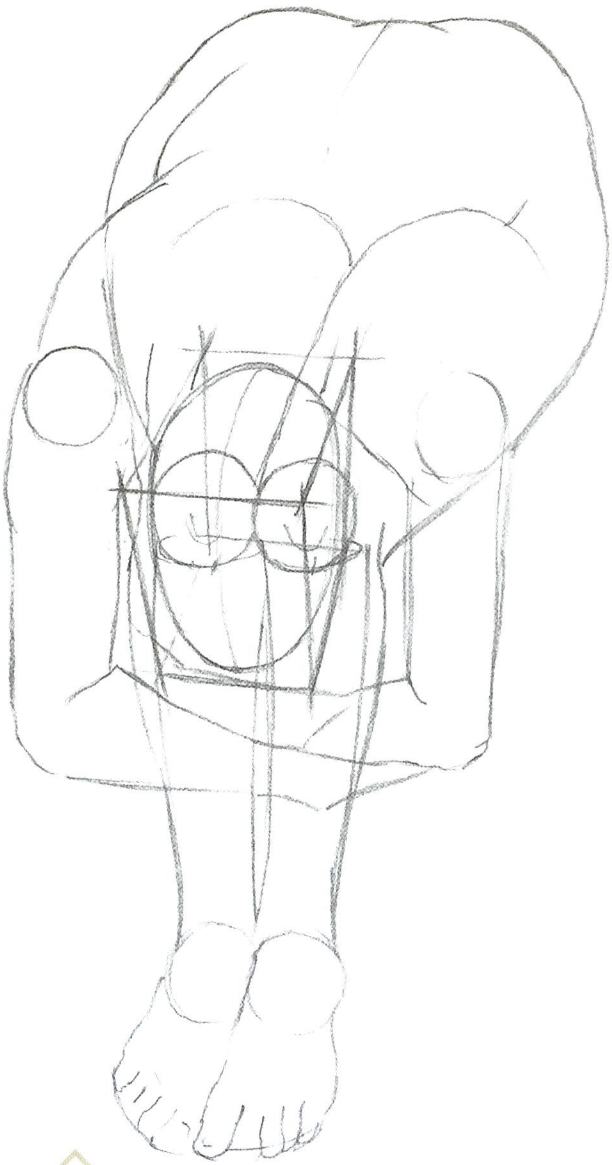

Knee-Palm Comparison, Front

Which is wider, your palm or your knee? It's a trick question! They're both the same width. Check it and see.

Knee-Palm Comparison, Side

While you're at it, move your hand to the side of your knee joint, and you'll find that its width is the same as the knee's depth, too.

Knees-Head-Feet Comparison

Assuming a "crash position," you (and the figure in your drawing) will find that the width of your head is equal to that of your knees put together.

It's also, by the way, equal to the width of your feet put together.

LOWER LEG LENGTH

Sitting, running, kneeling, kicking—to draw a figure in any of these exciting positions, you must know the proper comparative distance between the top of the shinbone and the bottom of the foot. Don't forget that the lower leg is one-half the lower bracket of the body.

The following comparisons will show additional ways to determine the lower leg's proper dimension by rotating it in space and by comparing it with other body parts.

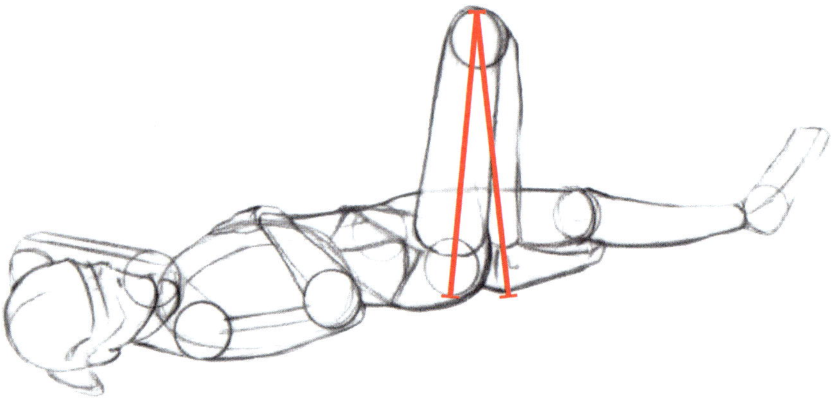

Lower Leg-Upper Leg Comparison, Reclining

If a figure lying on his back bends his knee, it is easy to see the equivalence between the lower and upper leg lengths. The heel and the top of the thigh bone will both sit on the ground plane.

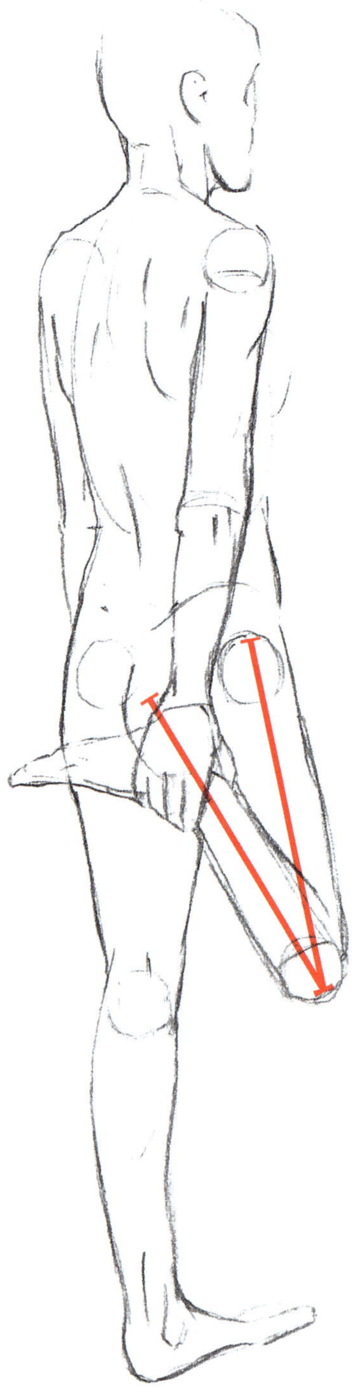

Lower Leg-Upper Leg Comparison, Standing

Ever feel as if you could kick yourself in the butt, sometimes? Make sure that the figure in your drawing can do so as well.

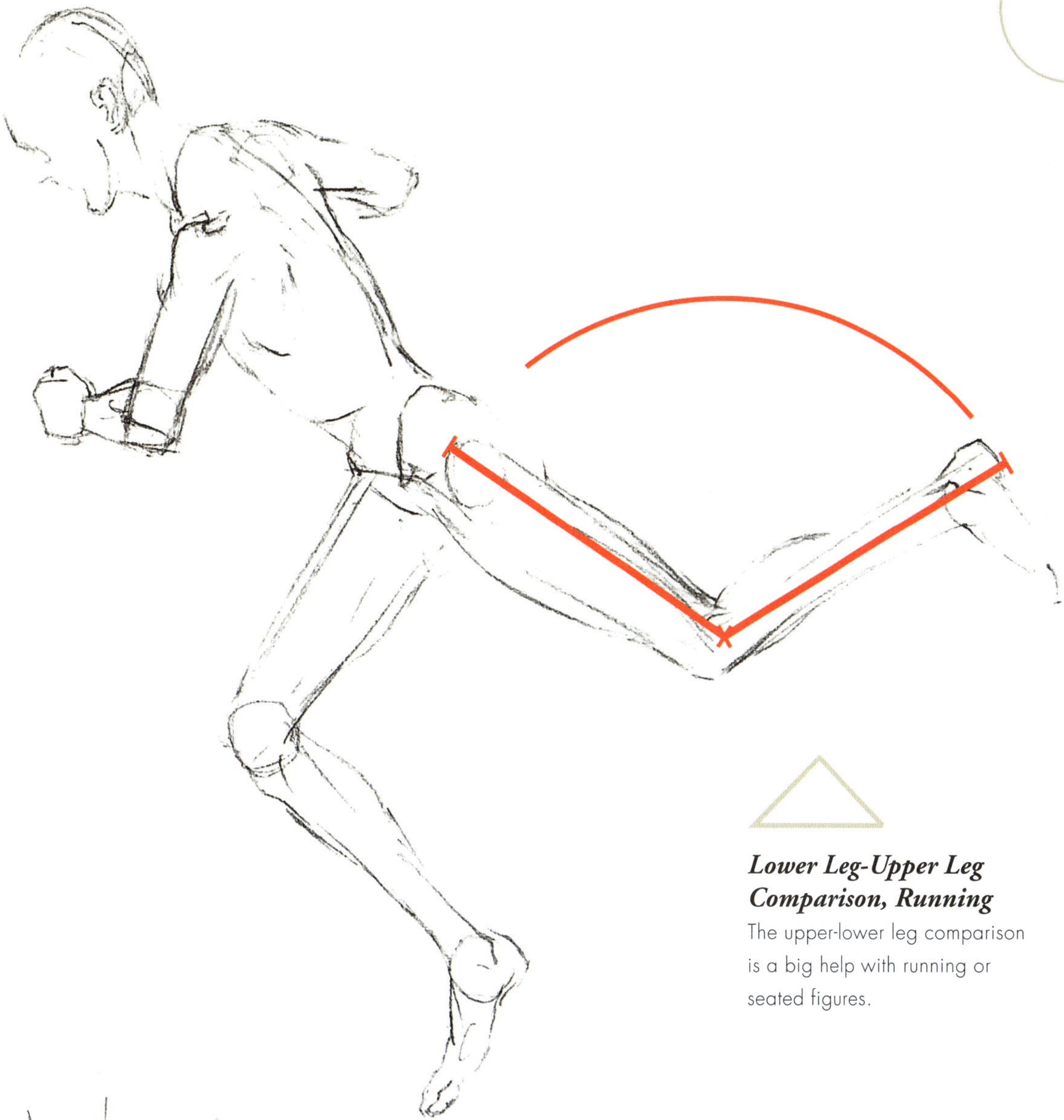

Lower Leg-Upper Leg Comparison, Running

The upper-lower leg comparison is a big help with running or seated figures.

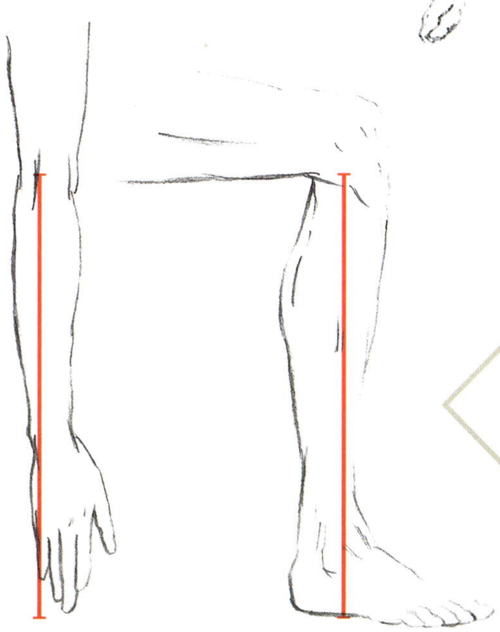

Lower Leg-Lower Arm Comparison

The lower leg (from the top of the lower leg bones to the sole of the foot) is the same length as the lower arm (from the elbow to the fingertips). Try it yourself and see.

FOOT LENGTH, WIDTH AND HEIGHT

In Chapter 3 we divided the foot into three cubes, which will help you draw it in proportion for your figure. The foot's width, length and height are also easily compared to other parts of the body as shown in the following examples.

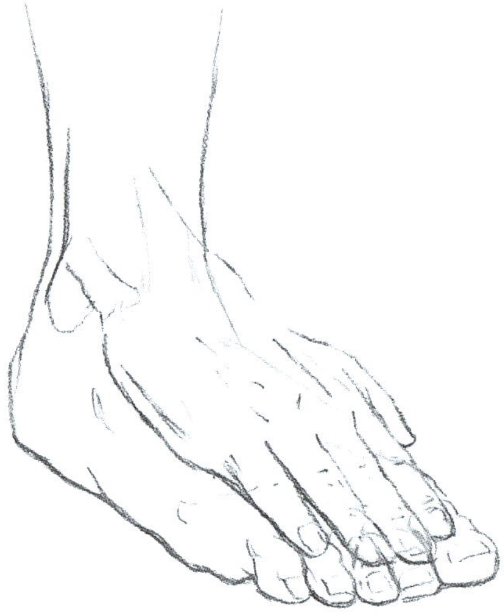

Foot-Hand Comparison

Lay your hand on top of your foot. You will find that it's the same width and the same length from the front of the ankle to the toes.

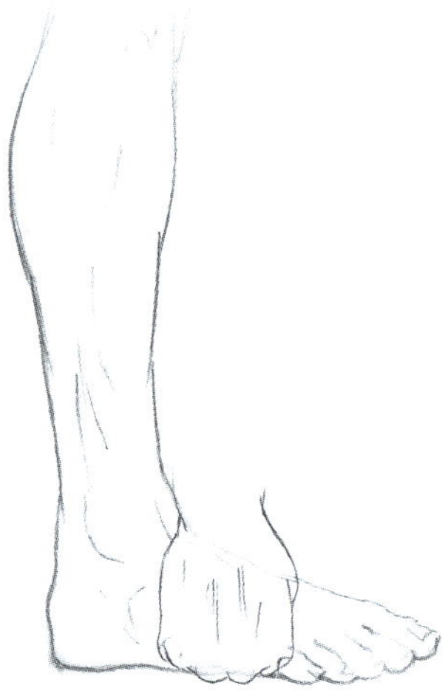

Foot-Palm Comparison

The height of the foot is the same as the length of the palm of the hand.

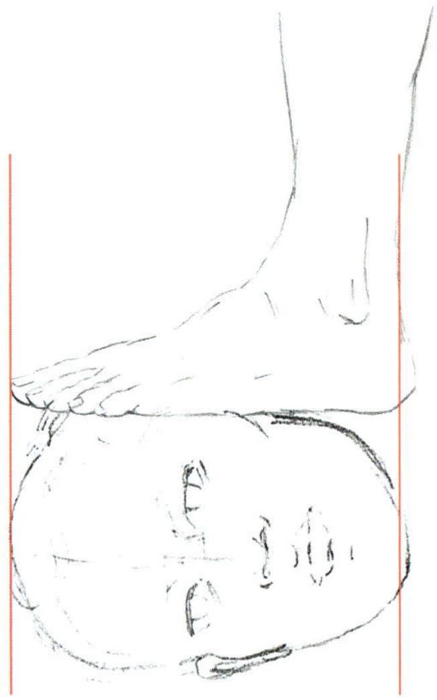

Foot-Head Comparison

The length of the foot without the heel is the same as the height of the head.

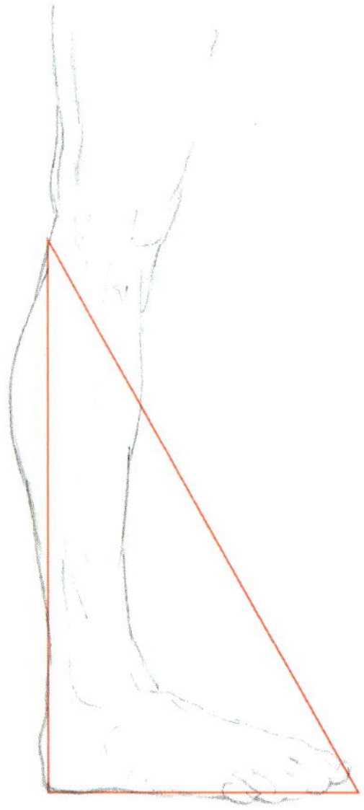

Foot-Triangle Comparison

You can use a 30-60-90° triangle to find the end of the toes given the back part of the knee bones, the middle of the knee joint and the floor plane. Remember to draw this triangle in the same perspective as your figure drawing. (Don't worry. It sounds harder to do than it is.)

FULL ARM LENGTH

The arms are the most mobile parts of the body. While both arms are rarely kept perfectly straight, knowing the length of the full arm will make finding its component parts easier.

Use the comparisons below to help you determine the length of the full arm.

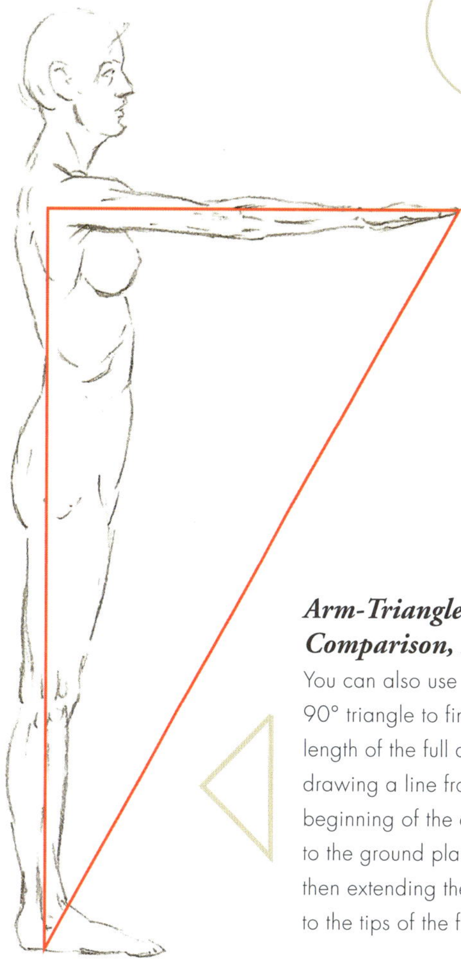

Arm-Triangle Comparison, Front

You can also use a 30-60-90° triangle to find the length of the full arm by drawing a line from the beginning of the arm bone to the ground plane, and then extending the triangle to the tips of the fingers.

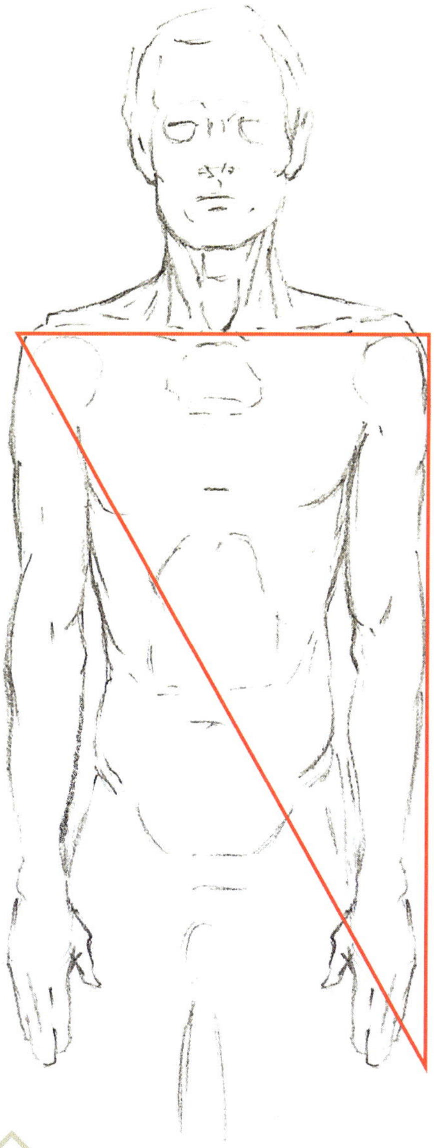

Arm-Triangle Comparison, Relaxed

You can use the same triangle, measured from shoulder to shoulder, to find the length of a relaxed arm.

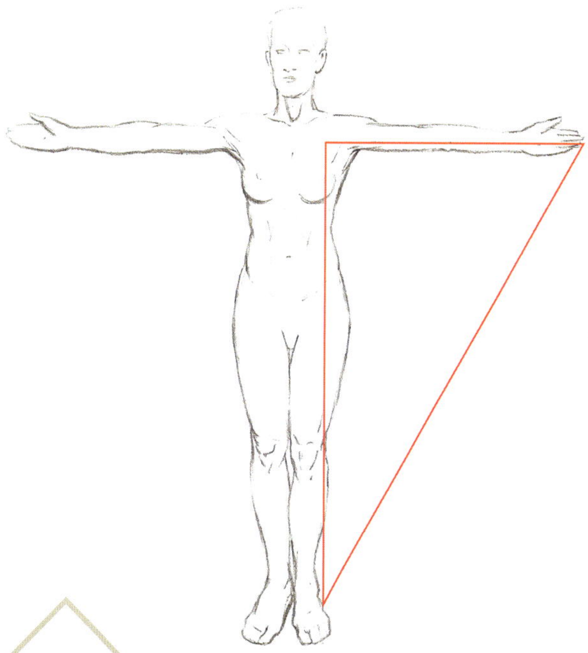

Arm-Triangle Comparison, Side

The triangle trick also works when the arm is held out to the side.

LOWER ARM LENGTH AND WIDTH

Whether you are drawing a figure with an open fisted or half-fisted hand, you can determine the length of the lower arm by measuring from the elbow to the knuckles (the end of the fisted hand). Then draw the full hand from there if needed.

In either case, the following comparisons will help you get the proper proportions.

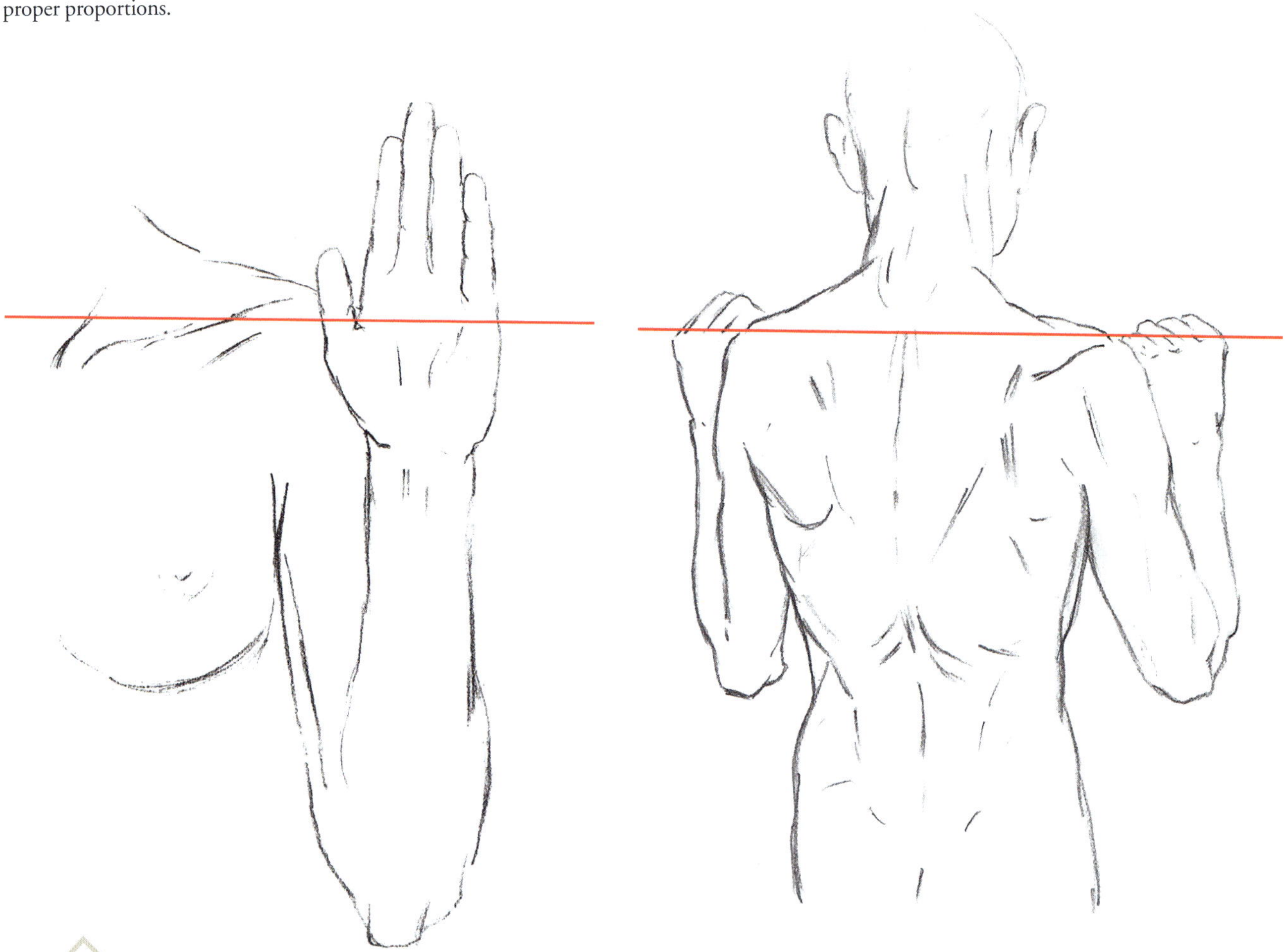

Lower Arm-Collarbone Comparison

Raise your arms to your shoulders as if you're going to do military presses. You'll find that your knuckle line (or that of your drawn figure) lines up with the bottoms of the collarbones.

It doesn't matter whether the hand is closed or open—promise!

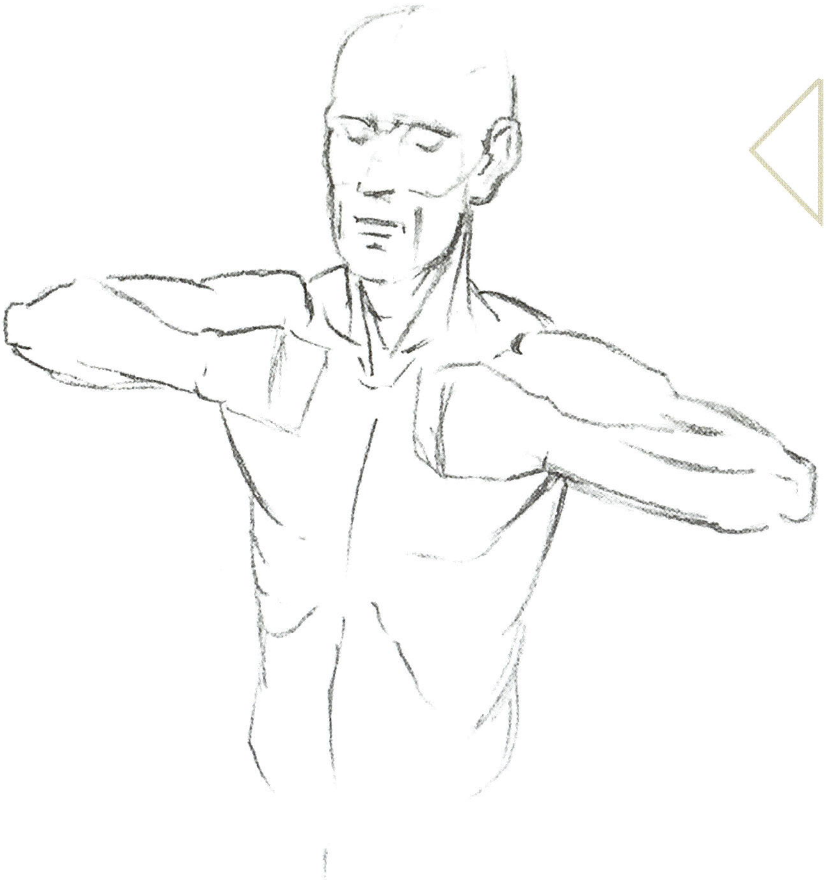

Lower Arm-Chest Comparison

Put on a pair of suspenders or just pretend that you have or that your drawn figure has. It will show you exactly where the fisted lower arm reaches on the chest when the elbows are elevated to the sides.

Forearm-Palm Comparison

The fleshy part of the forearm is the same width as the bony part of the palm, which means that you should draw the wrist thinner than the rest of the lower arm.

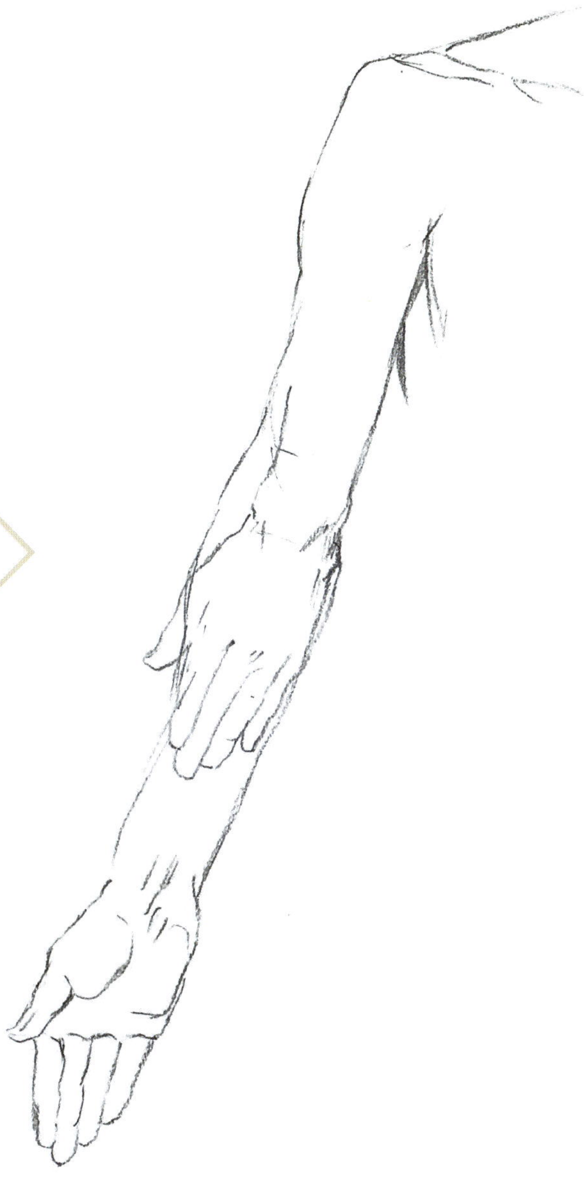

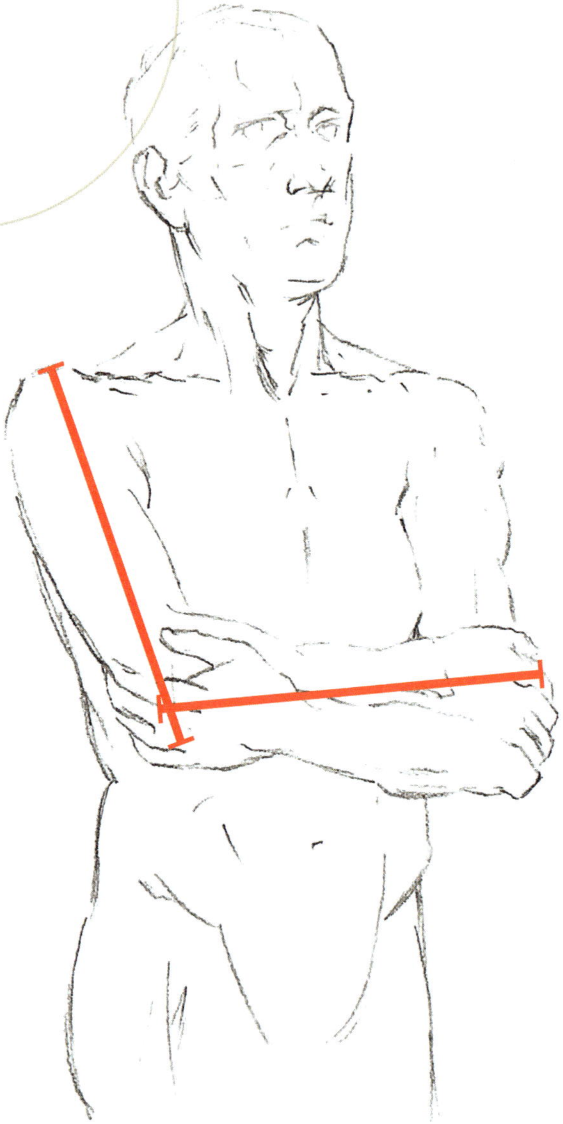

Lower Arm-Upper Arm Comparison

The lower arm, from the elbow to the first knuckle line, is the same length as the upper arm, from shoulder to elbow.

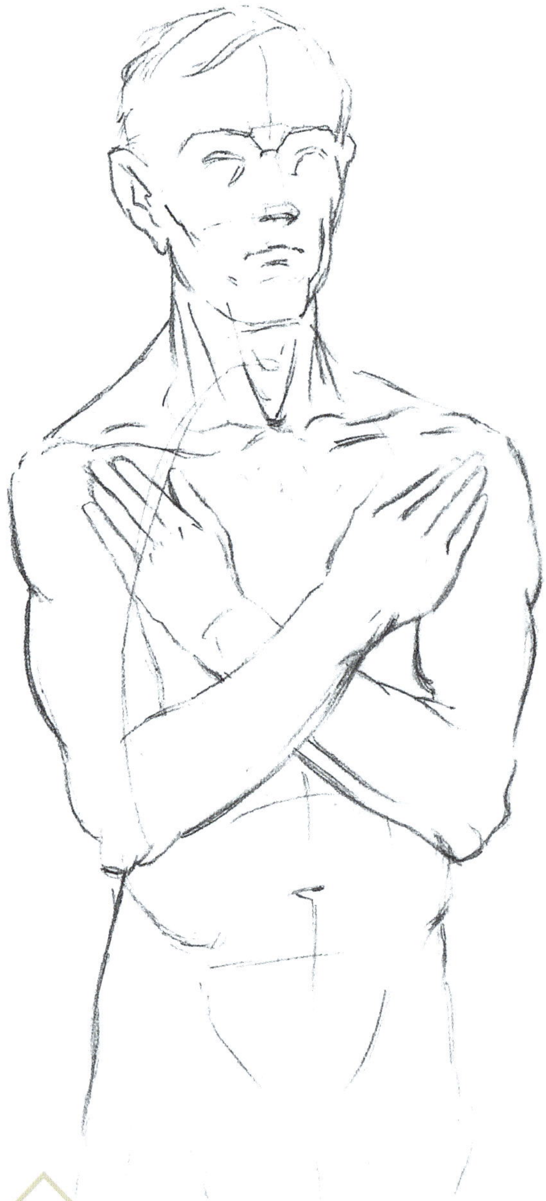

Lower Arm-Shoulder Point Comparison

When the fingers are outstretched, they're just able to point to the shoulder points.

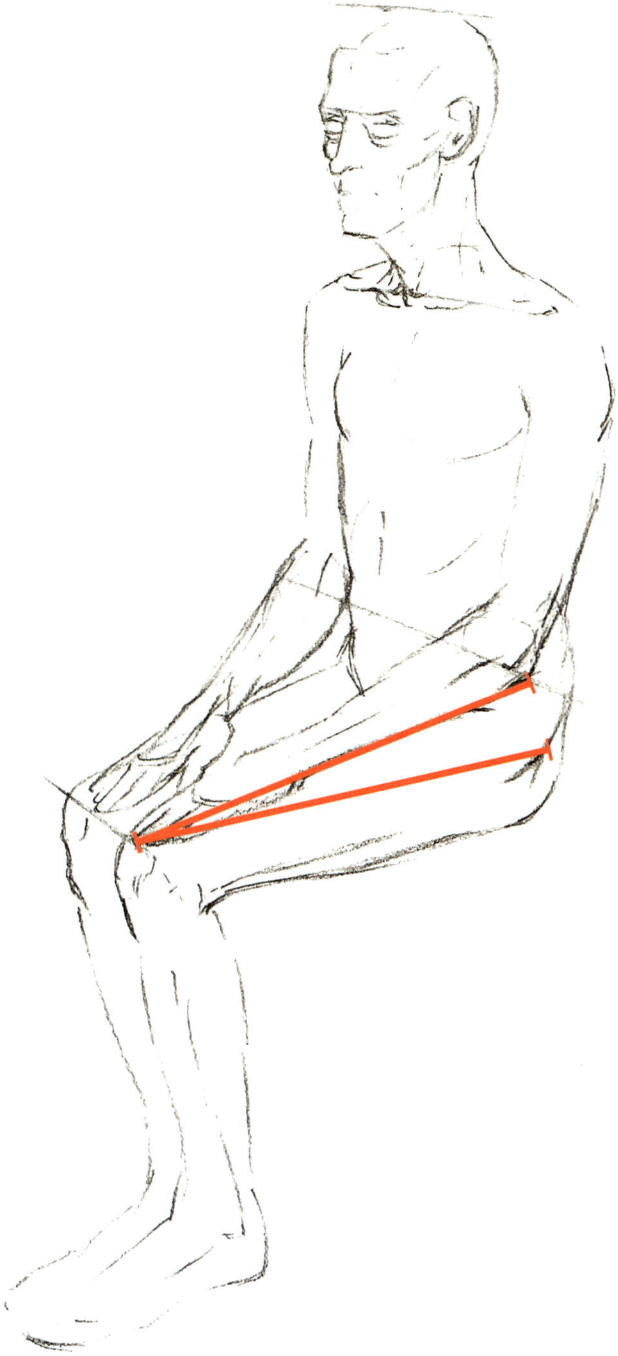

Lower Arm-Upper Leg Comparison

The lower arm is also the same length as the upper leg bone, from the top of the ball of the hip to the far end of the thigh. You can sense this easily in yourself when seated.

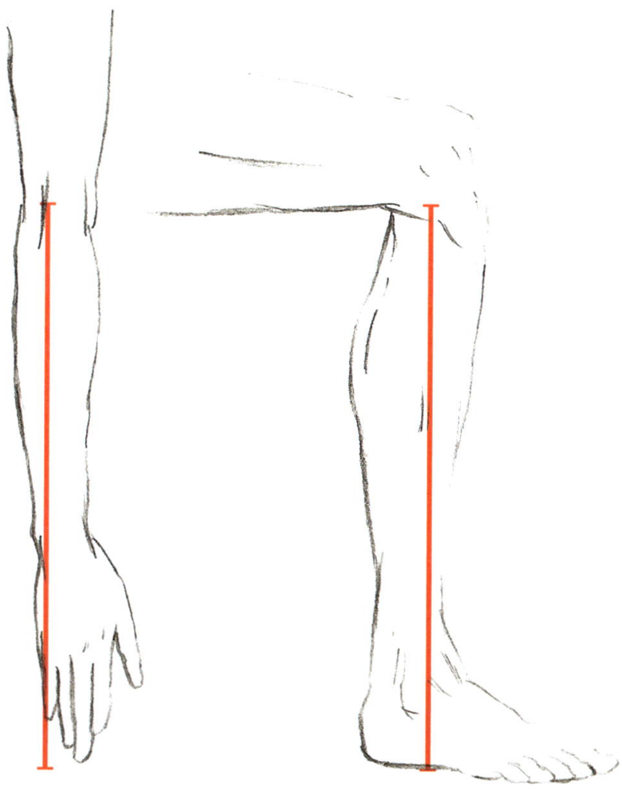

Lower Arm-Lower Leg Comparison

The lower arm, from the elbow to the fingertips, is the same length as the lower leg, from the top of the tibia (lower leg bone) to the sole of the foot.

UPPER ARM LENGTH

When resting completely at ease, the elbow reaches to the waist, the area between the rib cage and the top of the pelvis. You can use that measurement to determine the proper length of the upper arm in a variety of positions: frontwards, upwards, outwards and so on.

The following comparisons will also help.

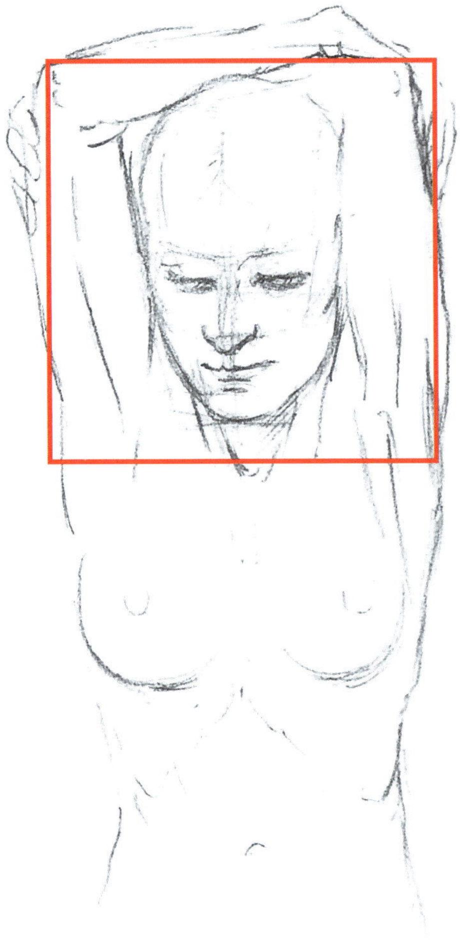

Upper-Lower Arm Comparison, Raised

The top of the square will be at the top of her head if she raises her arms and grabs her elbows. Try it yourself, and you'll feel your arm bones resting on the top of your head.

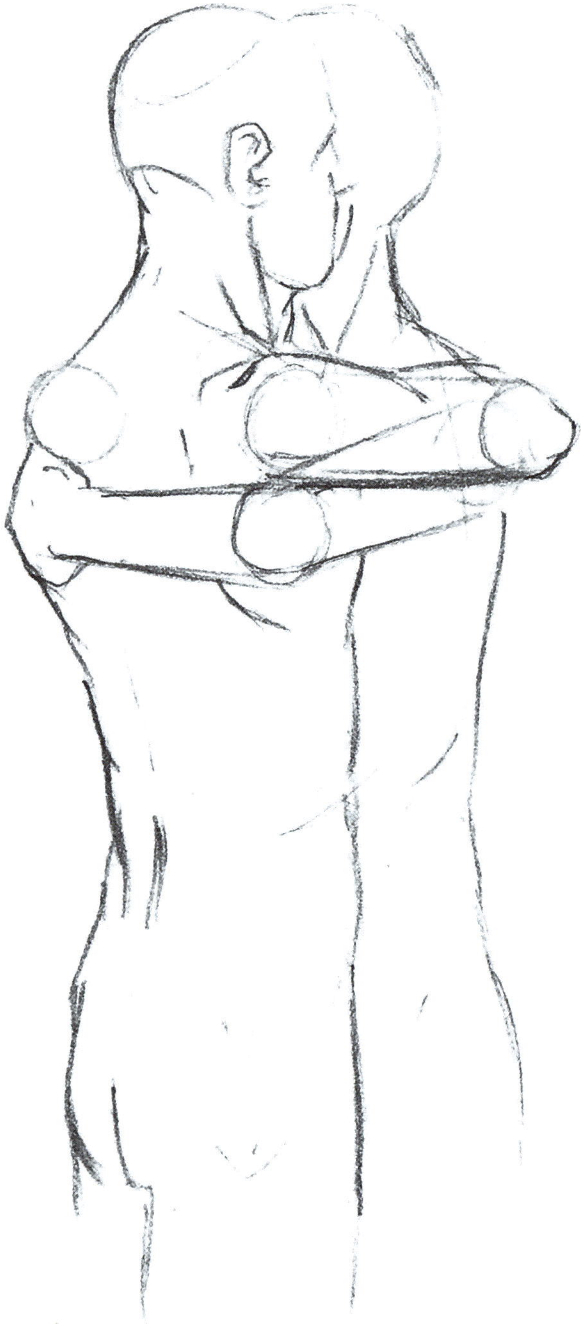

Upper Arm-Body Comparison

Could it be that we were designed to give each other hugs? In any case, you will find that there is just enough length in the upper arm to accommodate another body thickness.

HANDS

You use your hands to create your drawings, but don't forget that they are good references to compare to the sizes of other body parts as well as the size of their component parts, the fingers, thumb and palm.

The following comparisons offer some useful suggestions, but you can discover more by making your own careful observations.

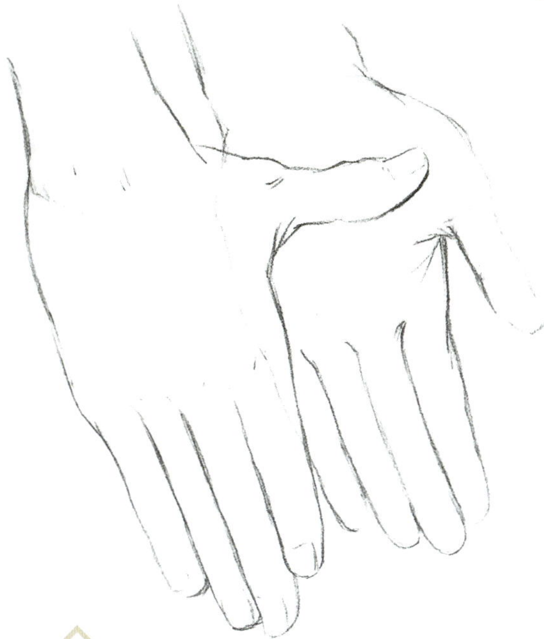

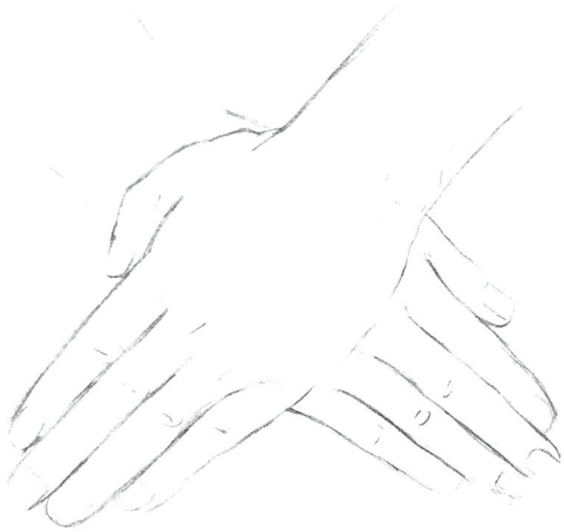

Thumb-Palm Comparison

The thumb (measured from the end of the big, bony knuckle to its tip) is the same width as the palm of the hand.

Palm Length and Width Comparison

Note how the palm of the hand is as wide as it is long (measured from the wrist to the first knuckle line). Try it on yourself and see, back to back, palm to palm or palm to back.

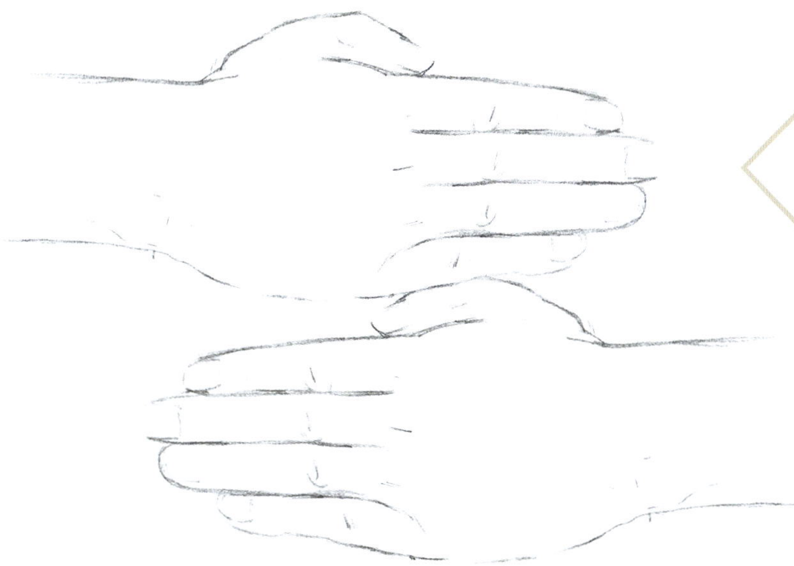

Thumb-Little Finger Comparison

The thumb is also the same length as the little finger, which also means that the little finger is as long as the palm is wide.

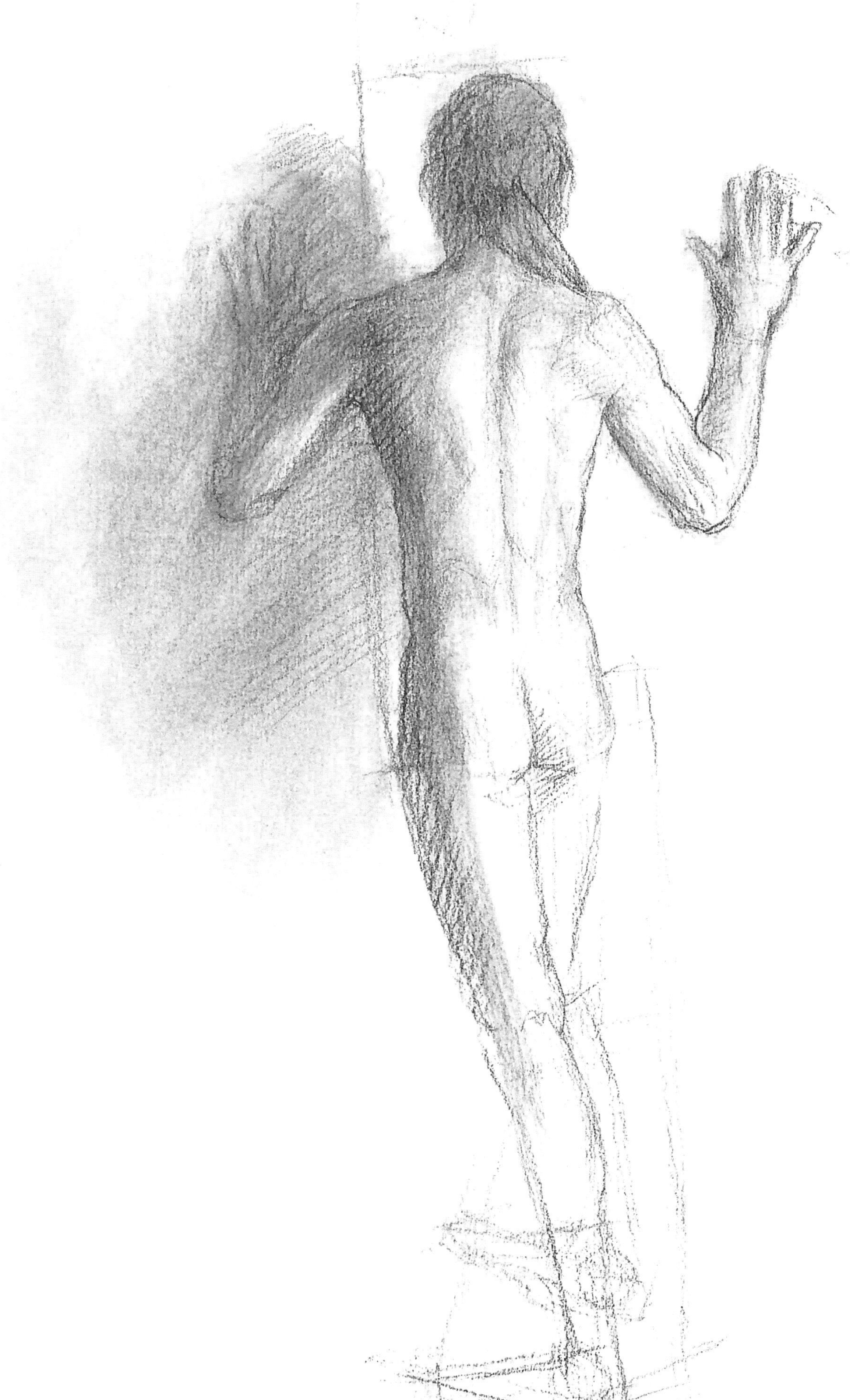

5

FIGURE DEMONSTRATIONS

In this section we will take the internal and comparative measurements we've discovered and apply them to our figure drawings.

If you keep looking, you will discover even more useful measurements of your own.

Demonstration

Standing Male

At first glance, a standing pose such as the one pictured here may seem the easiest to draw, as there's little foreshortening to deal with. However, with the figure presented in one relatively stretched out length, there aren't a lot of interesting negative spaces to help divide the figure vertically or to help us find its proper width.

Use your knowledge of how to divide the upper and lower brackets to find the major proportions, and remember that the folded arms form a square to help you with that area.

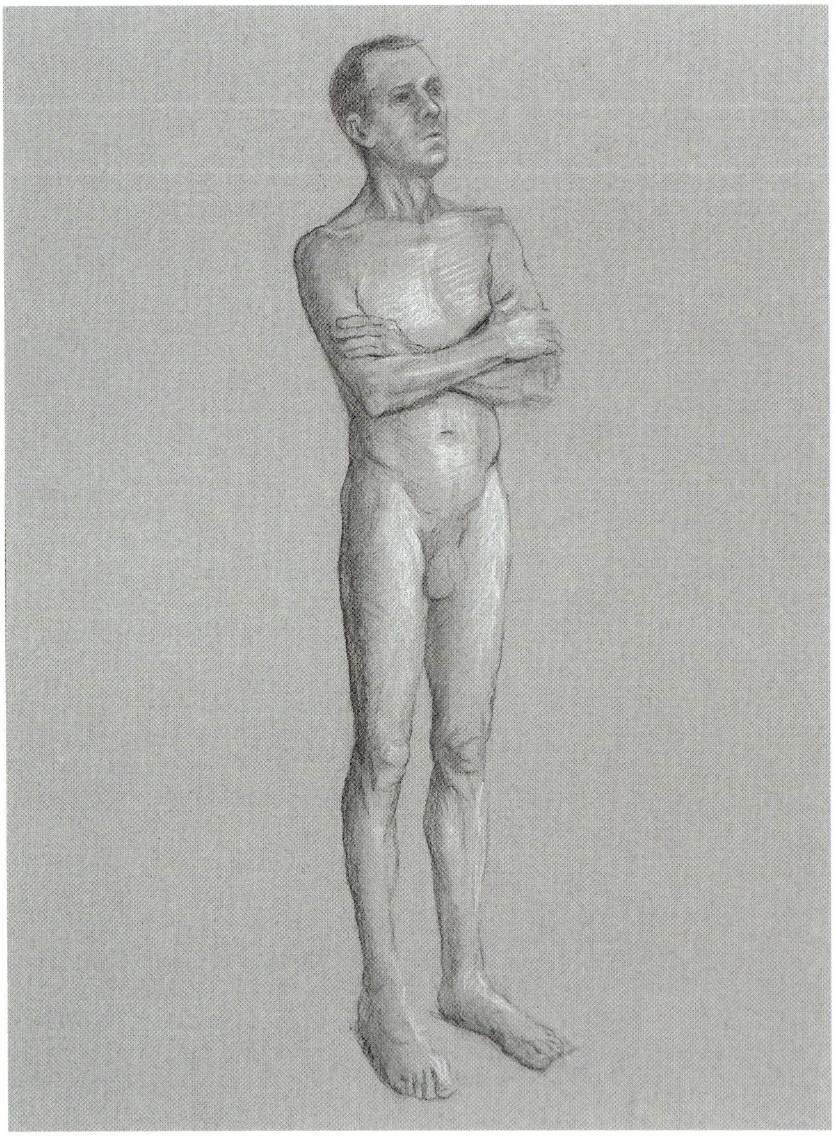

Proportional Challenges

At first glance, a standing pose may seem easy, but it presents proportional challenges, too.

MATERIALS

Surface

gray Canson Mi-Teintes 98-lb. (160gsm)

Charcoal Pencils

HB, 2B, 4B and white

Other Supplies

chamois cloth

kneaded eraser

paper towel

Place the Figure on the Page

Using a light gesture with an HB charcoal pencil, indicate the placement of the figure on the page.

Draw a top bracket in a line suggesting the general movement of the upper body. Draw in lower brackets that represent the centerlines of the legs.

The upper and lower brackets should be the same length and overlap each other by one-eighth of the length of either bracket.

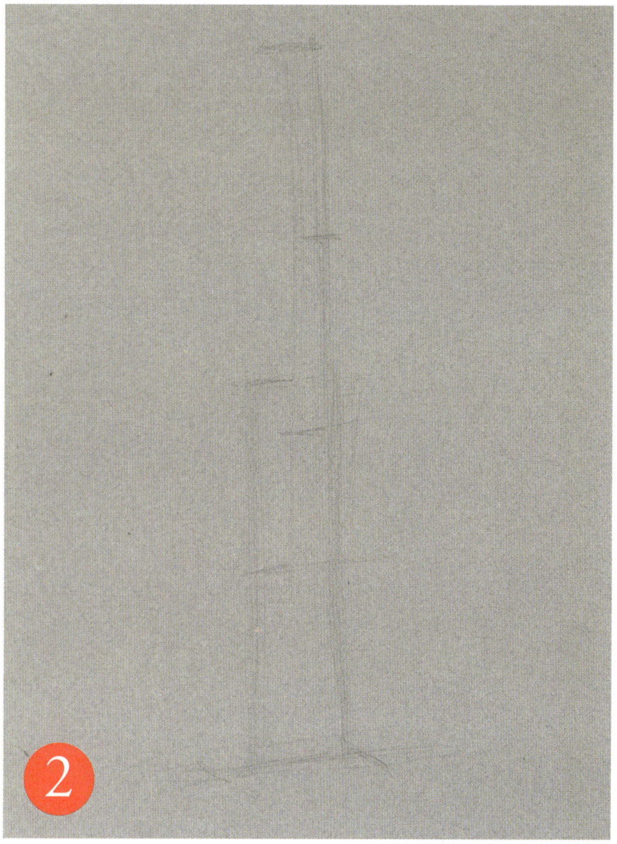

Divide the Brackets

Continuing with an HB charcoal pencil, divide the upper and lower brackets in half. The halfway marks of the lower brackets will position the center of the knee joints.

Could your figure kick himself in the head by raising his leg straight up?

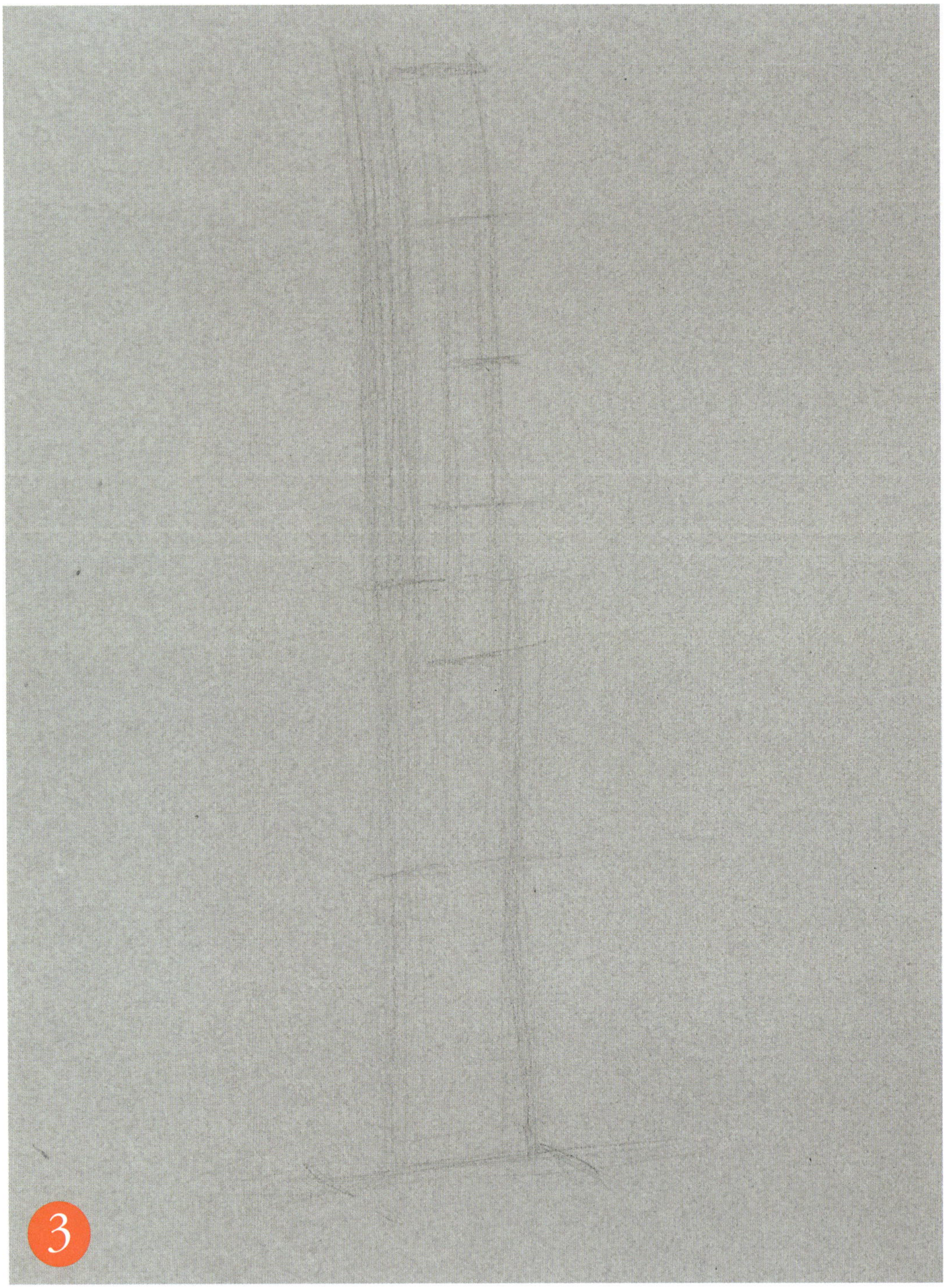

Subdivide the Upper Bracket

Continuing with an HB charcoal pencil, divide your upper bracket again. The topmost quarter of the upper bracket will give you the height of the head. The lowermost one will give you the size of the pelvis.

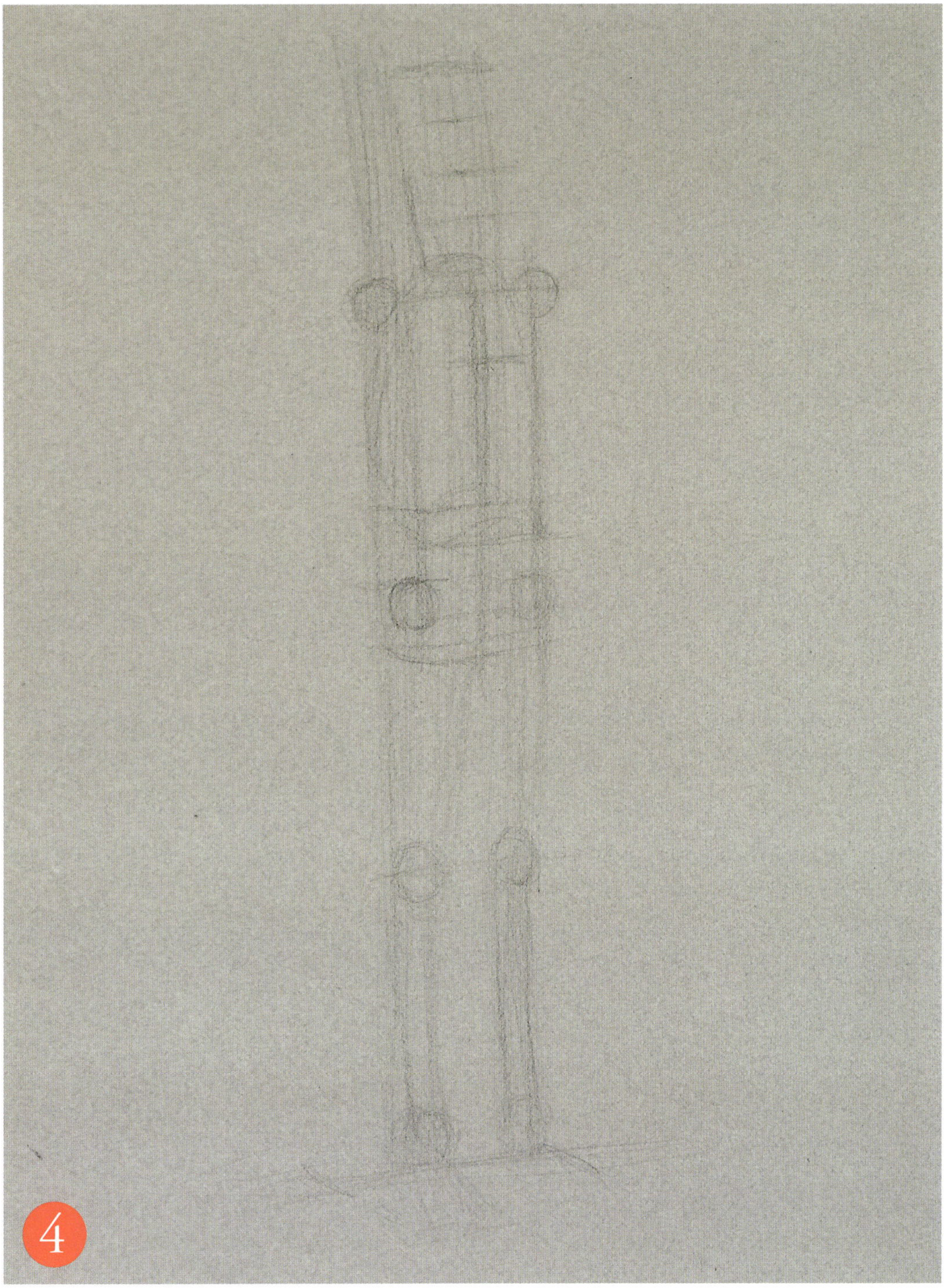

Start the Torso, Hip Joints and Shoulders

Continuing with an HB charcoal pencil, square off the lower bracket and draw lines straight up to give yourself guidelines for the sides of the torso. Set the balls of the hip joints midway on the torso lines and the balls of the shoulders to the outside of the lines. The balls of the shoulders will also sit on a line midway between the second-highest quarter of the top bracket.

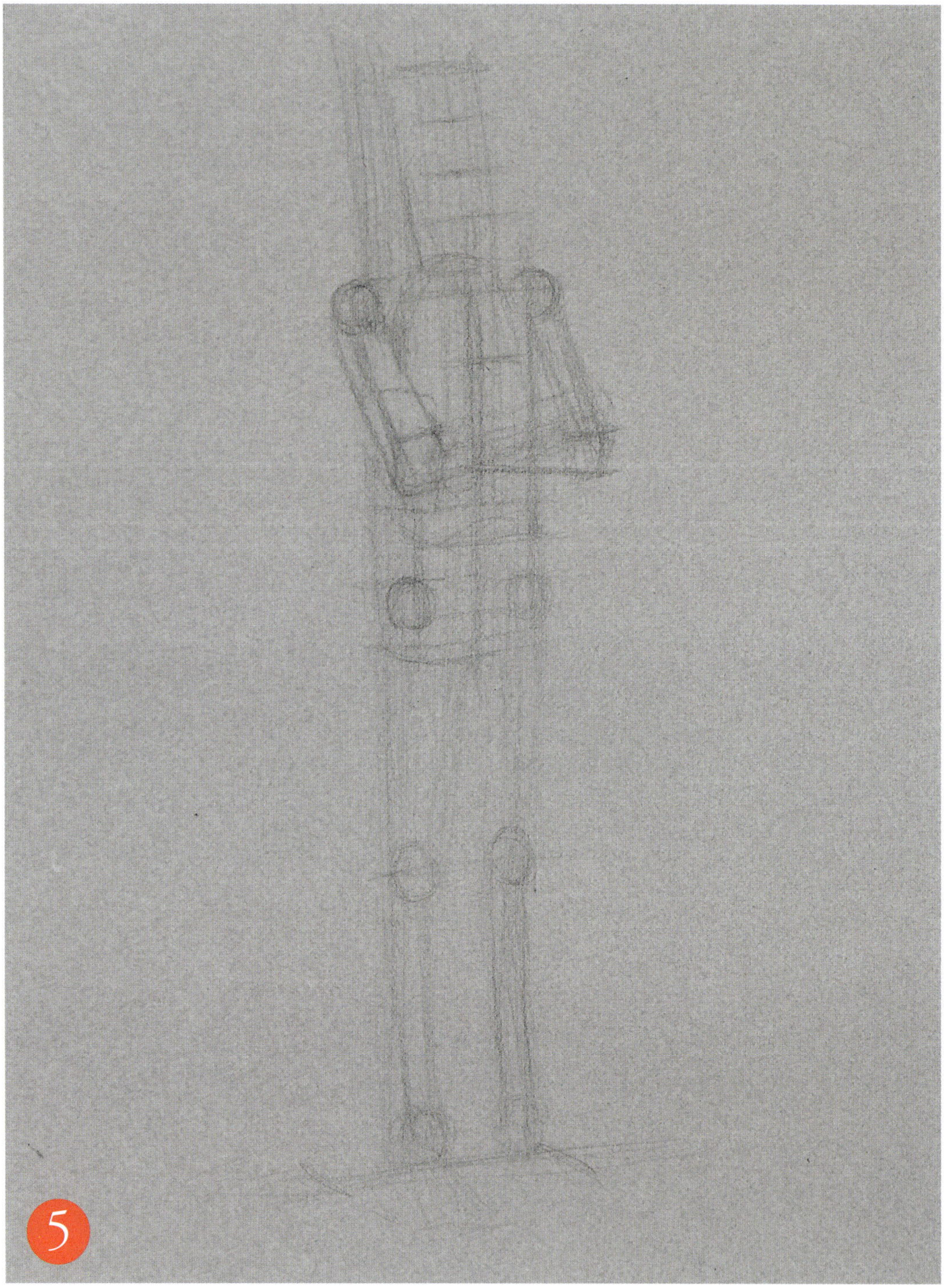

Indicate the Remaining Major Joints

As you dimensionalize the figure, use an HB charcoal pencil to add baseball-sized spheres for the knees, ankles and elbows, keeping them the same size. Remember that the folded arms will form a square that could also sit on top of the head.

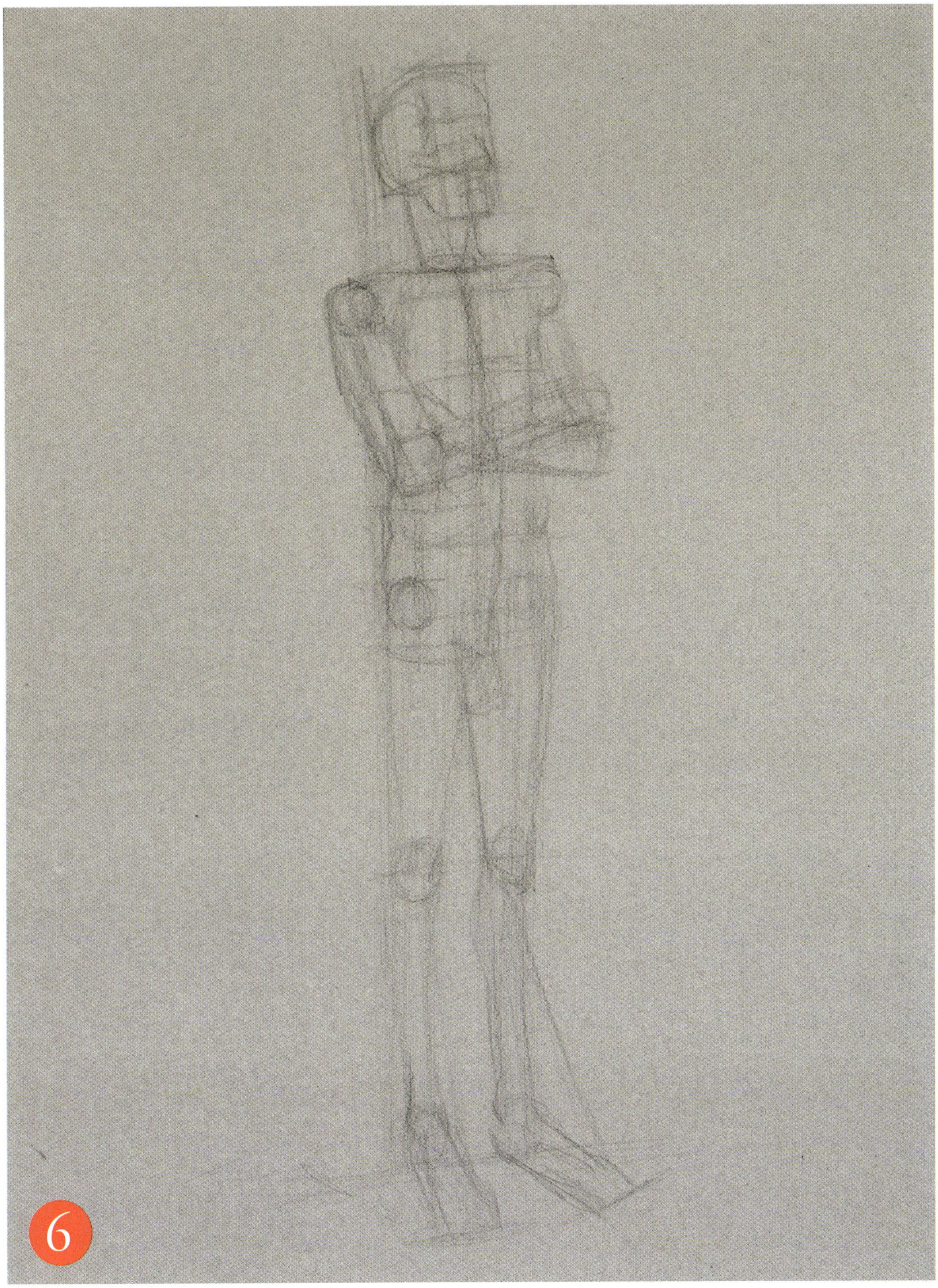

Add the Feet and Contour Lines

Continuing with an HB charcoal pencil, find the length of the feet by drawing 30° angles (in perspective) from the knee joint to the floor plane. You can start adding contour lines that you see in the model.

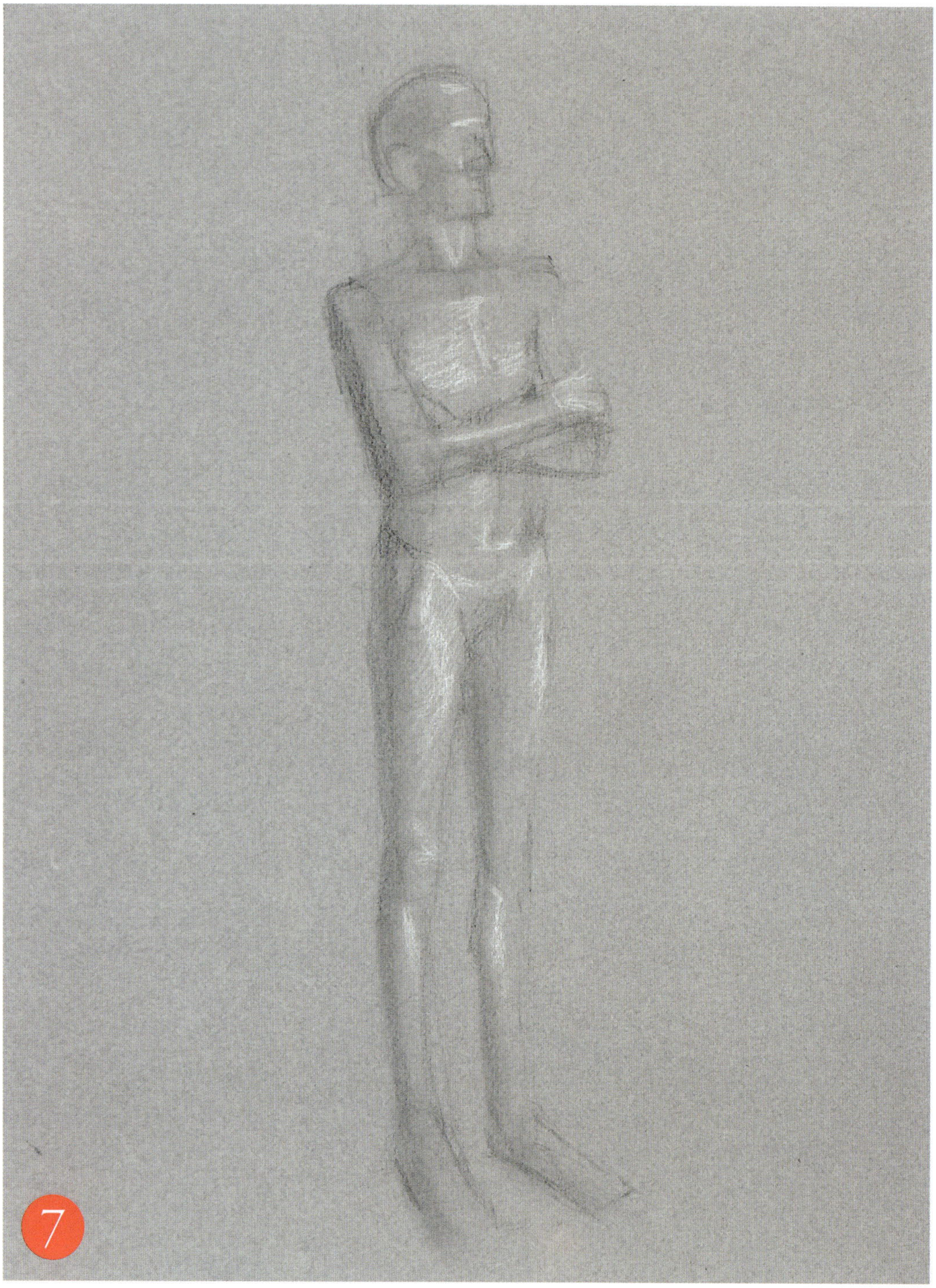

Clean Up the Guidelines and Add Darks and Lights

With your blocking already established, it is easy to rub it all out using a chamois cloth or paper towel and still keep a good sense of the figure's proportions. Use a kneaded eraser to clear all the lighted areas of the figure of any charcoal and to transition the tones from the gray background to the dark.

With a 4B charcoal pencil, add your darkest tones. Add the most brightly highlighted areas with a white charcoal pencil. All the other tones will be somewhere between these two extremes.

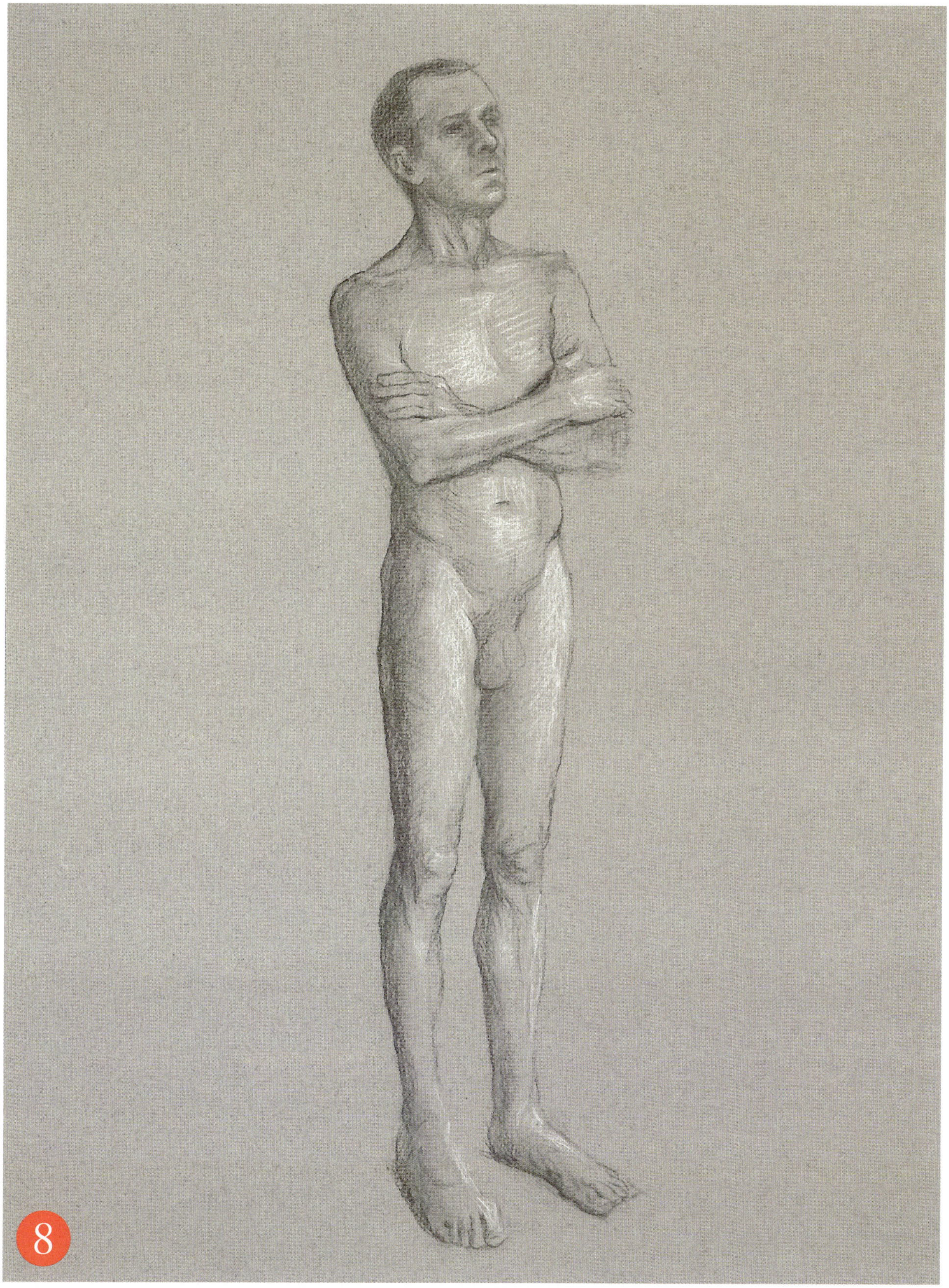

Complete the Contours and Details

Continue to work from the model, adding contours and details with all the pencils until you feel your work is done.

Demonstration

Standing Female

This pose offers a strong stance with lots of interesting negative spaces. Use the spaces to find the position of the staff, which has no natural law of proportion attached to it. Keep in mind that the model's bent left arm is in a vertical plane on a 45° angle to the viewer.

Because her legs are spread, her center point (top to bottom) will be closer to the ground than if her legs were together. Compensate for that when you find the vertical subdivisions of the upper and lower body.

MATERIALS

Surface
light blue Canson Mi-Teintes 98-lb. (160gsm)

Charcoal Pencils
HB, 2B and 4B

Other Supplies
chamois cloth
kneaded eraser
paper towel

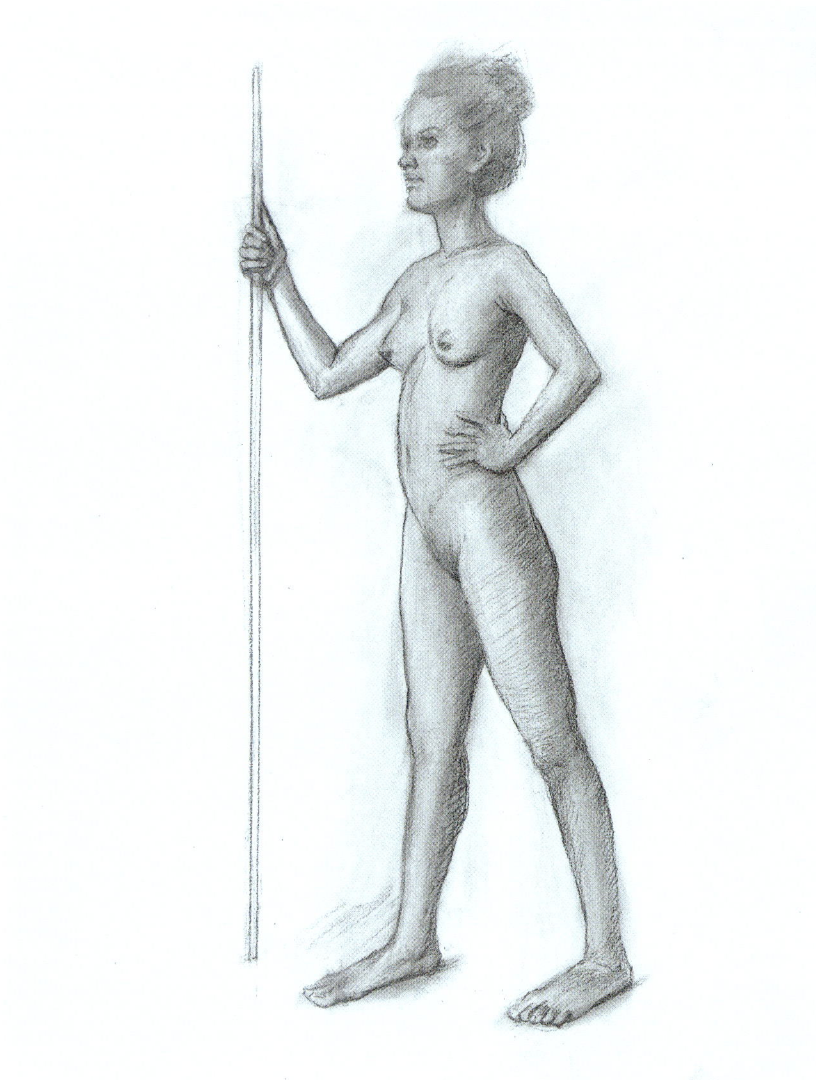

Dynamic Stance
This dynamic stance presents strong abstract shapes to work with.

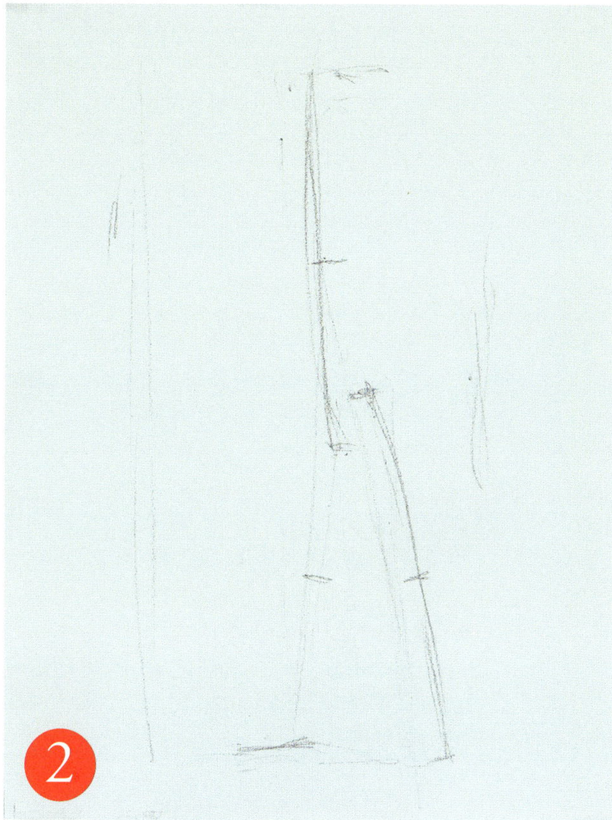

Place the Figure on the Page

Start with an HB charcoal pencil by setting the limits of the figure, indicating where you want it to appear on the page.

Draw a top bracket in a line suggesting the general movement of the upper body. Draw in lower brackets that represent the centerlines of the legs.

Divide the Brackets

Continuing with an HB charcoal pencil, divide the upper and lower brackets in half. The halfway marks of the lower brackets will position the center of the knee joints.

Could your figure kick herself in the butt by flexing her knee?

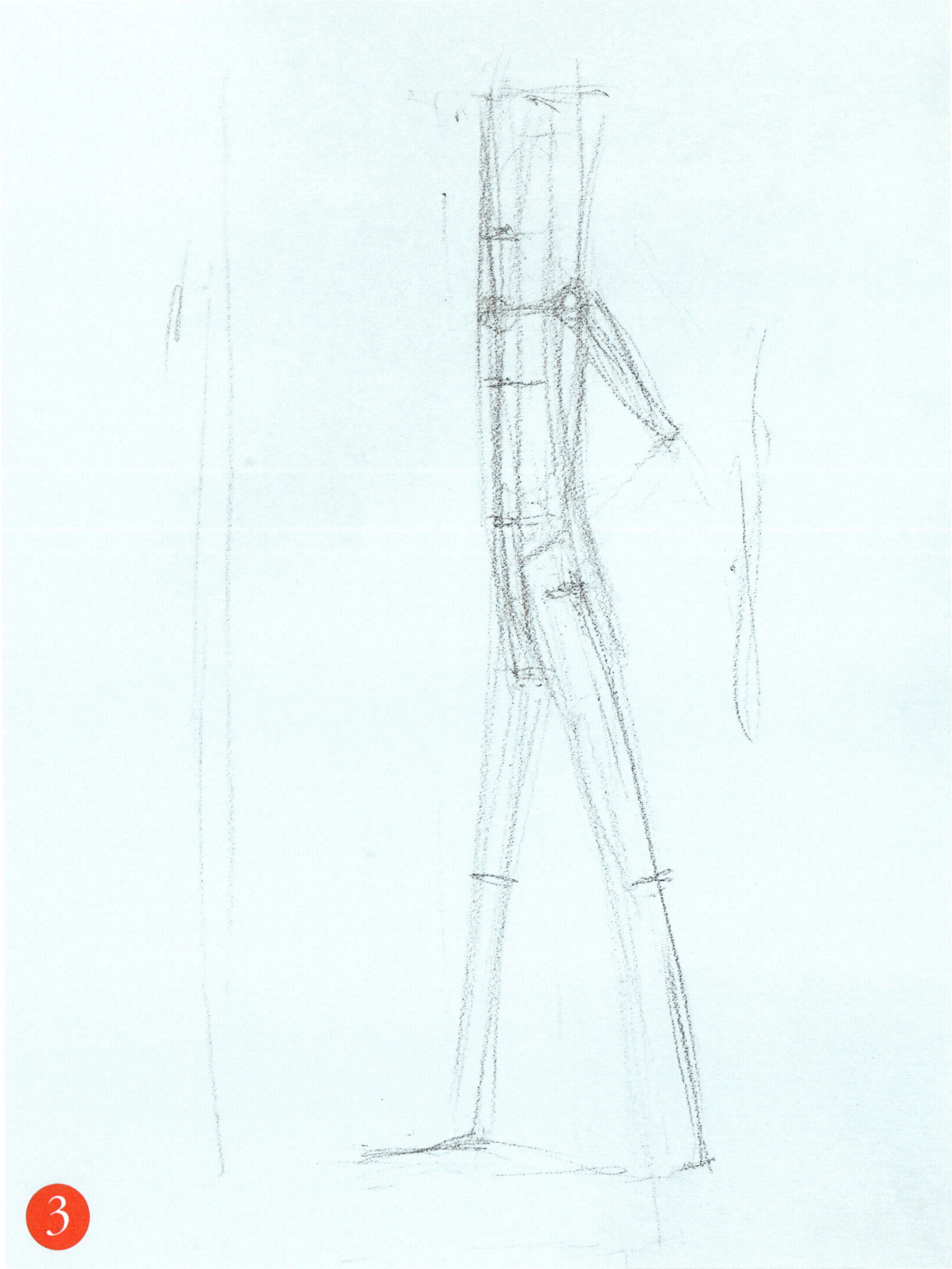

Subdivide the Upper Bracket

Continuing with an HB charcoal pencil, begin to lightly draw solids for the figure, starting to establish its three-dimensional space. Divide the upper bracket into quarters so that you know the heights of the head and the pelvis.

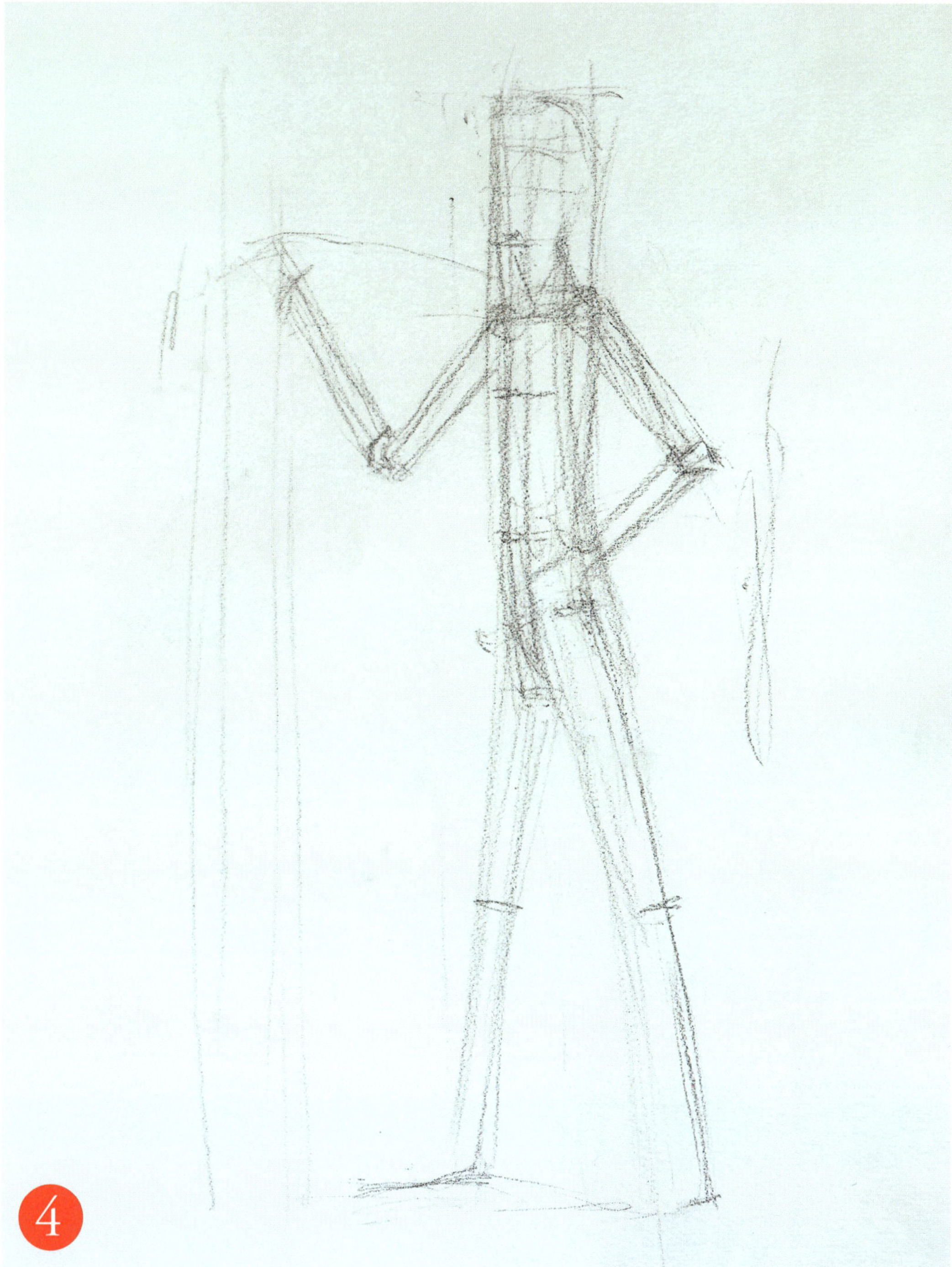

Position the Arms

As you set the position of the arms with an HB charcoal pencil, ask yourself if this figure could draw her elbows to her waist. Would her knuckles reach the top of her shoulder joint if her elbows were completely flexed?

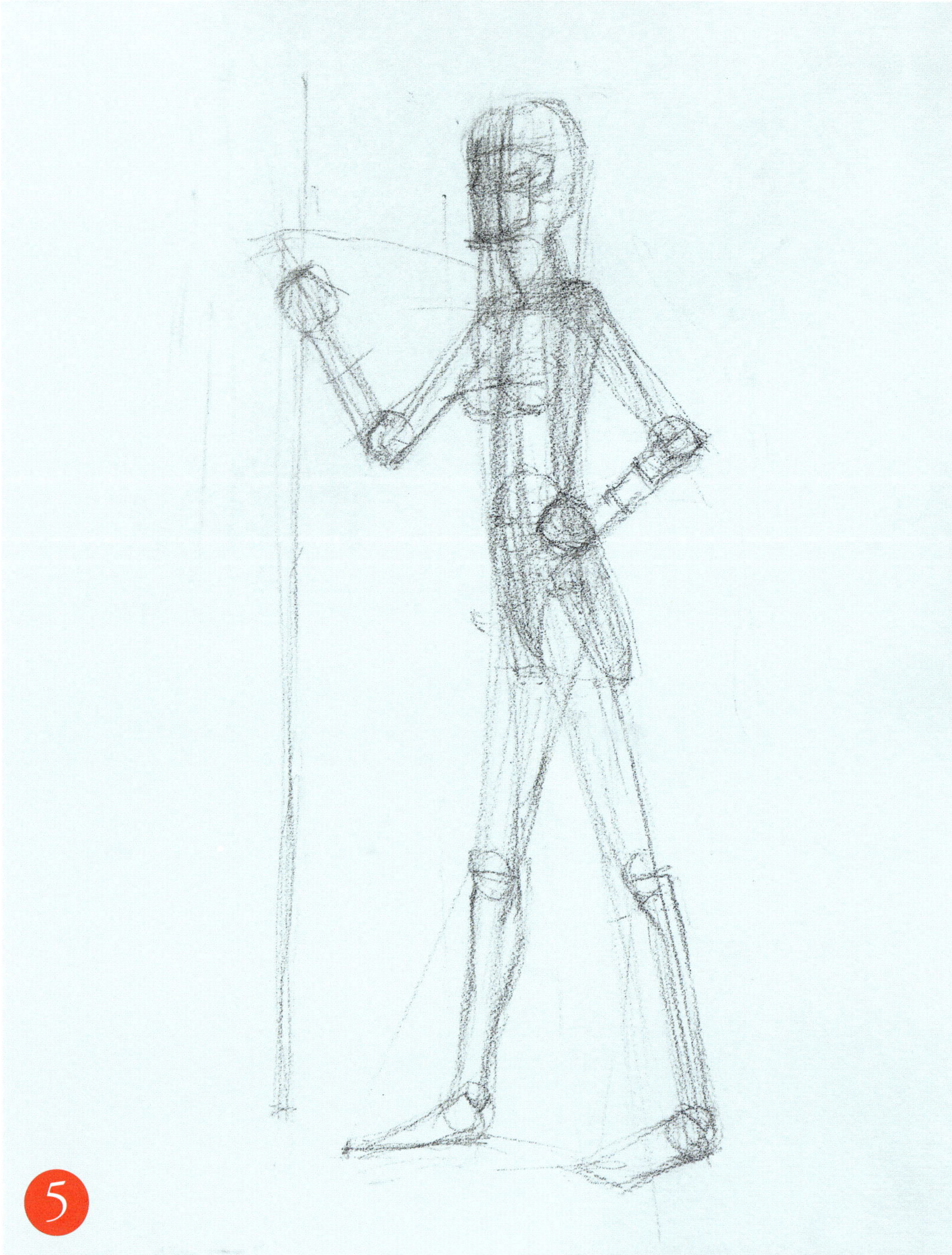

Solidify the Figure

As you start to solidify the figure, keep checking the widths and depths of the various body parts. Are the widths of the knees, feet, palms and elbows equal?

Use an HB charcoal pencil to lightly draw right triangles (in perspective) to find the length of the feet, or make sure that each foot's length (without the heel) is equal to the height of the head.

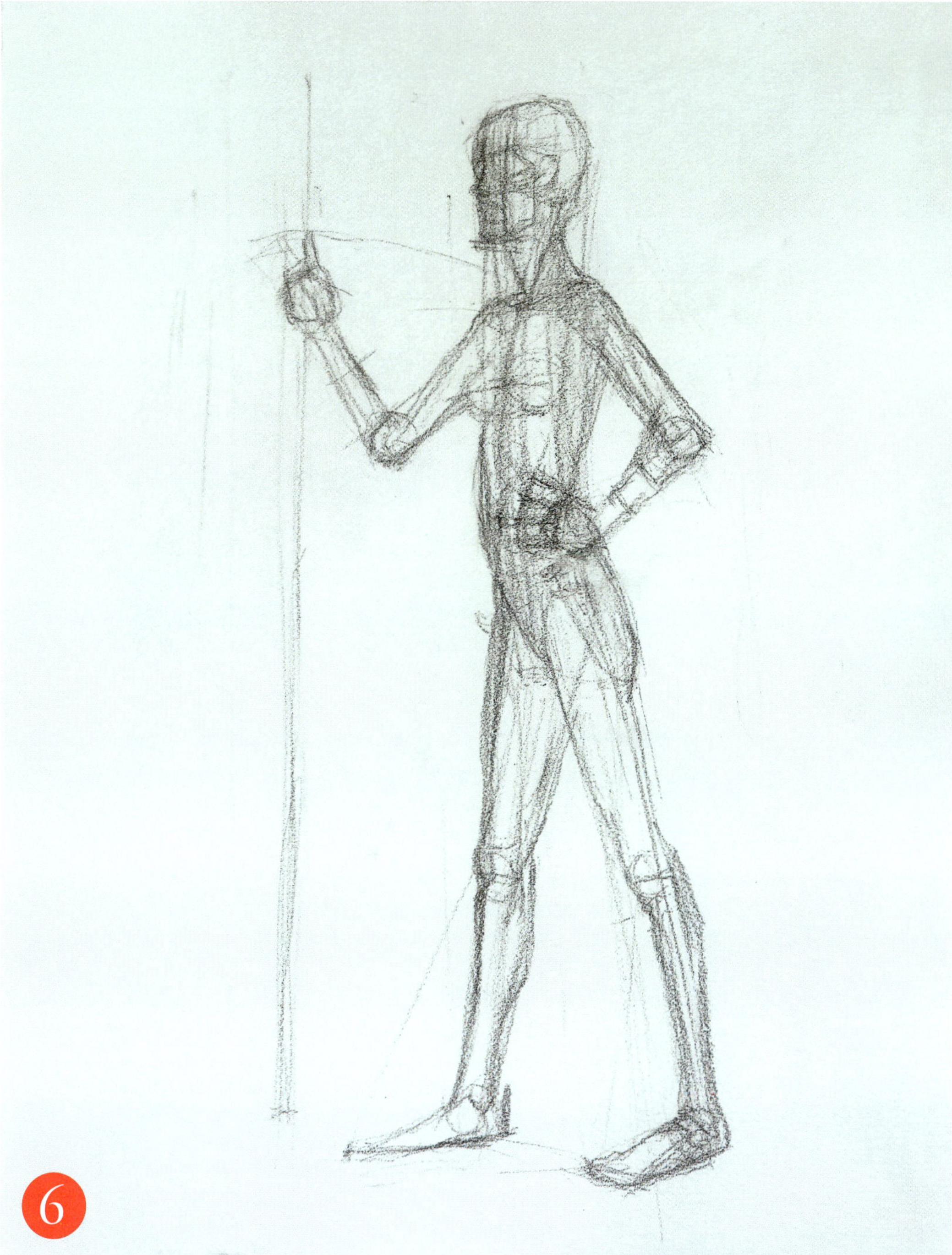

Add Some Contour Lines

As you start adding some of the contour lines that you see in the figure, keep reminding yourself that your figure can move. Keep checking, for example, that this figure could cradle her arms, bend her head to the insteps of her feet and so on. You can begin to use a softer grade pencil (2B), but keep the volumes light and airy.

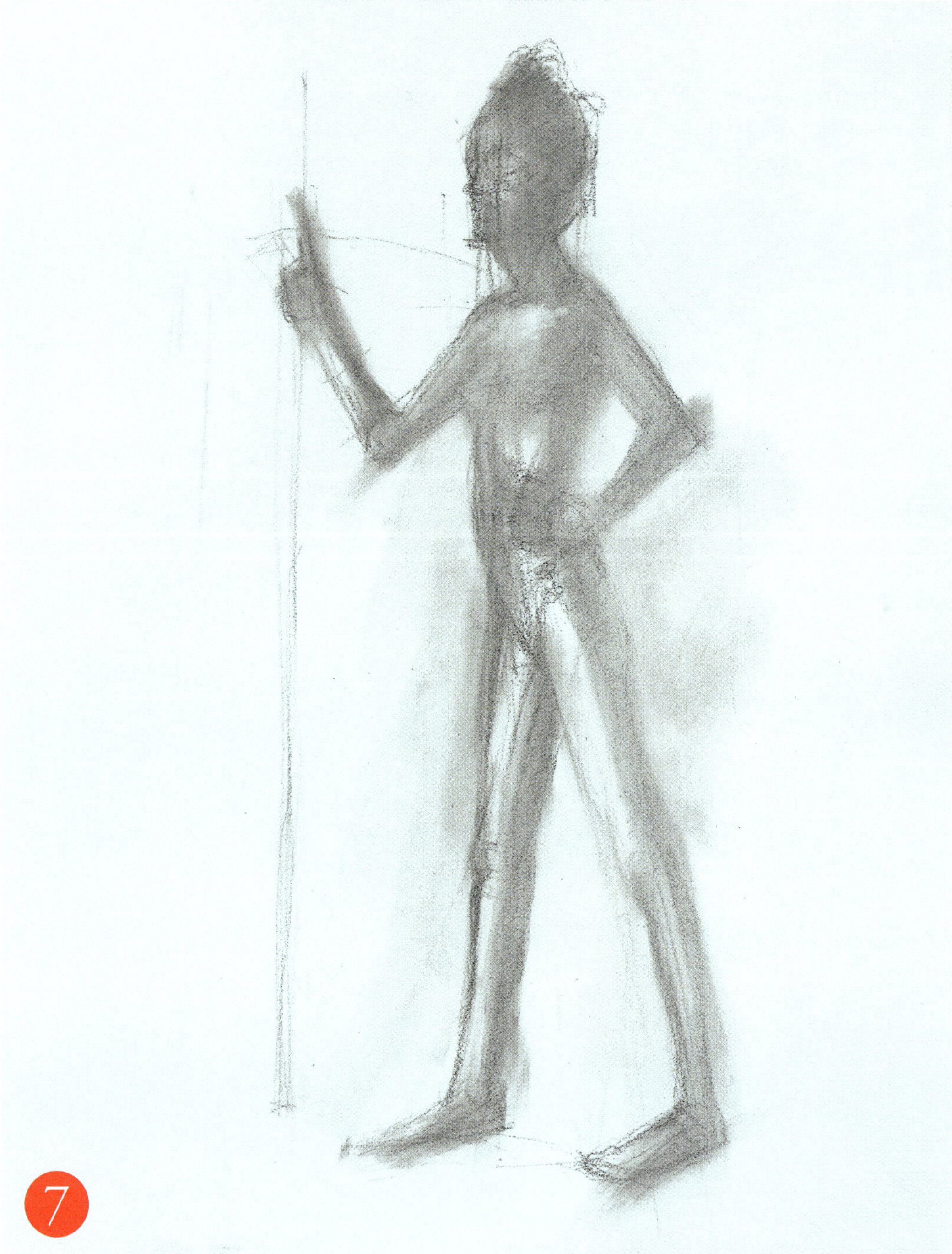

Erase the Guidelines and Begin to Shade the Figure

Once you are happy with the proportions and positioning of the figure and its various limbs, feel free to rub out your drawing with a chamois cloth or a paper towel, shading the figure's left side and back planes while keeping her top and front planes light.

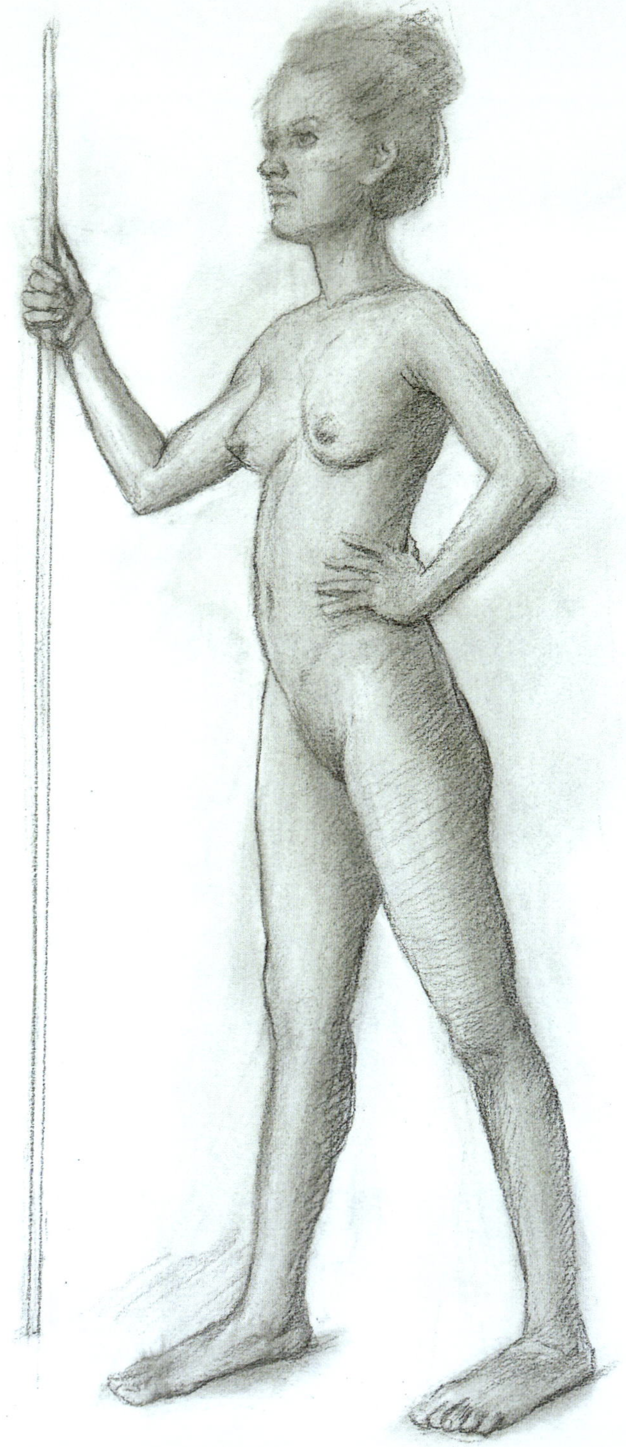

8

Finish Adding the Details

Finish the figure drawing as you normally would, adding details and particular characteristics from your model. Use a soft pencil (4B or even darker) sparingly to accent the darkest parts of the contour lines, cast shadows and hair.

Demonstration

Seated Male

The simple guideline of 2:1, upper body to lower body, from the end of Chapter 3 will help to quickly establish the proportions for this pose. The thigh and the lower leg are of the same length, so you can draw a square to roughly find the relationship of the upper leg to lower leg, when the leg is bent at a right angle.

The trick is to watch out for the subtle perspective at play—the model is seated at a three-quarter angle to the viewer, and most of the figure is situated below eye level.

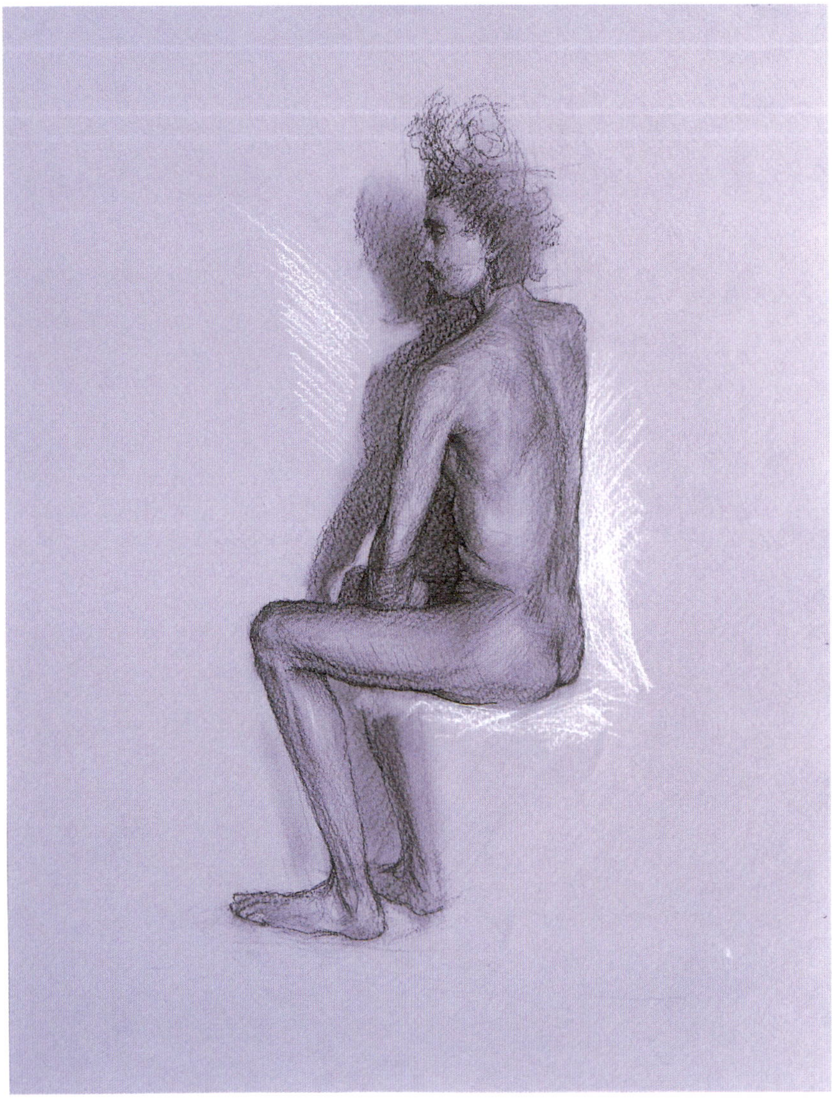

Divide to Find the Dimensions

Draw the large squares (in perspective) first, into which you can situate the body. Then subdivide to find the various dimensions of the body parts.

MATERIALS

Surface

purple Canson Mi-Teintes 98-lb. (160gsm)

Charcoal Pencils

HB, 2B, 4B and white

Other Supplies

chamois cloth

kneaded eraser

paper towel

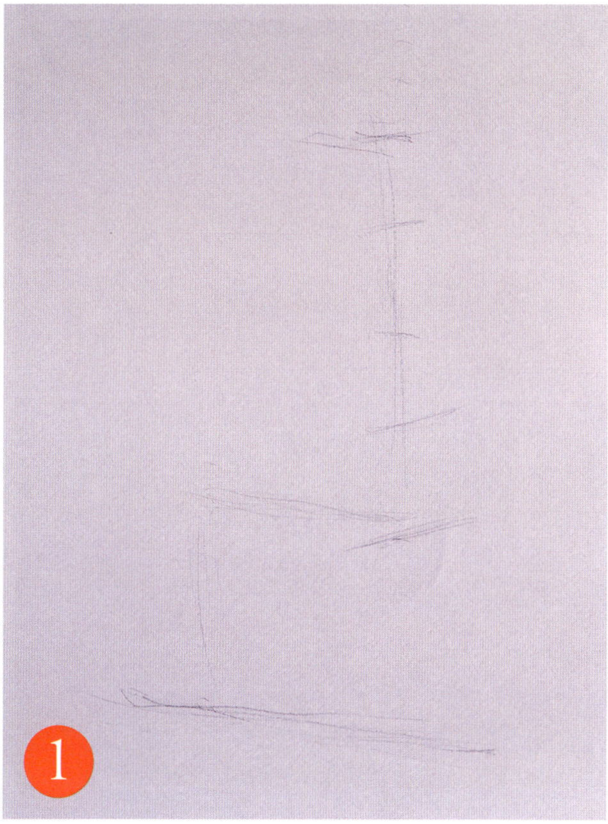

Place the Figure and Brackets

For a seated figure, remember the guideline: two units for the body above the plane of the seat to one unit for the body below the plane of the seat.

The upper bracket sits above the seat. Divide it into fourths as usual. It's not too early to draw these as diagonals, which will establish a perspective for the drawing.

At the knee the lower bracket bends into a square. Use an HB charcoal pencil to indicate these areas.

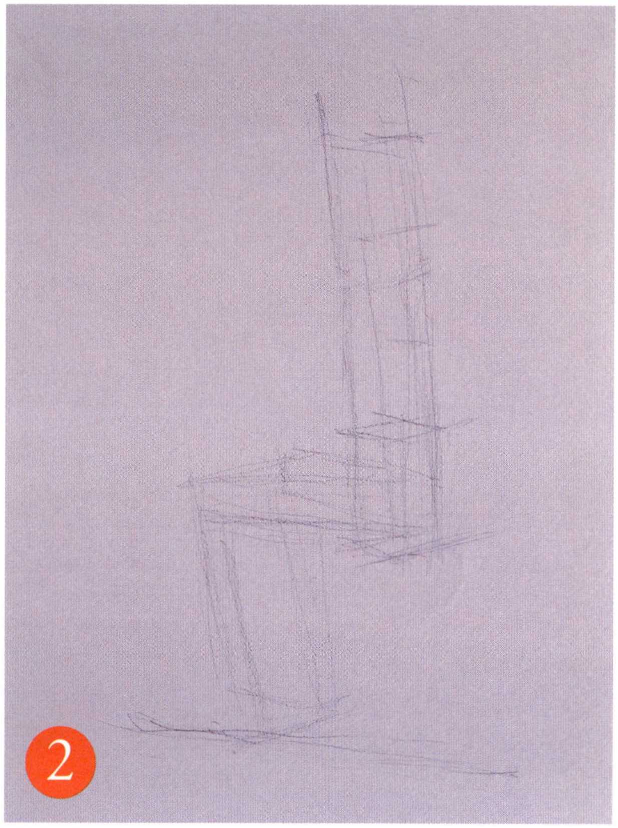

Find the Shoulders, Hips and Head

Continuing with an HB charcoal pencil, indicate the line of the shoulders.

Begin to draw the solid forms. Square off the lowest fourth of the upper bracket (in perspective) to find the width of the hips.

The head is only seven-eighths deep as it is tall.

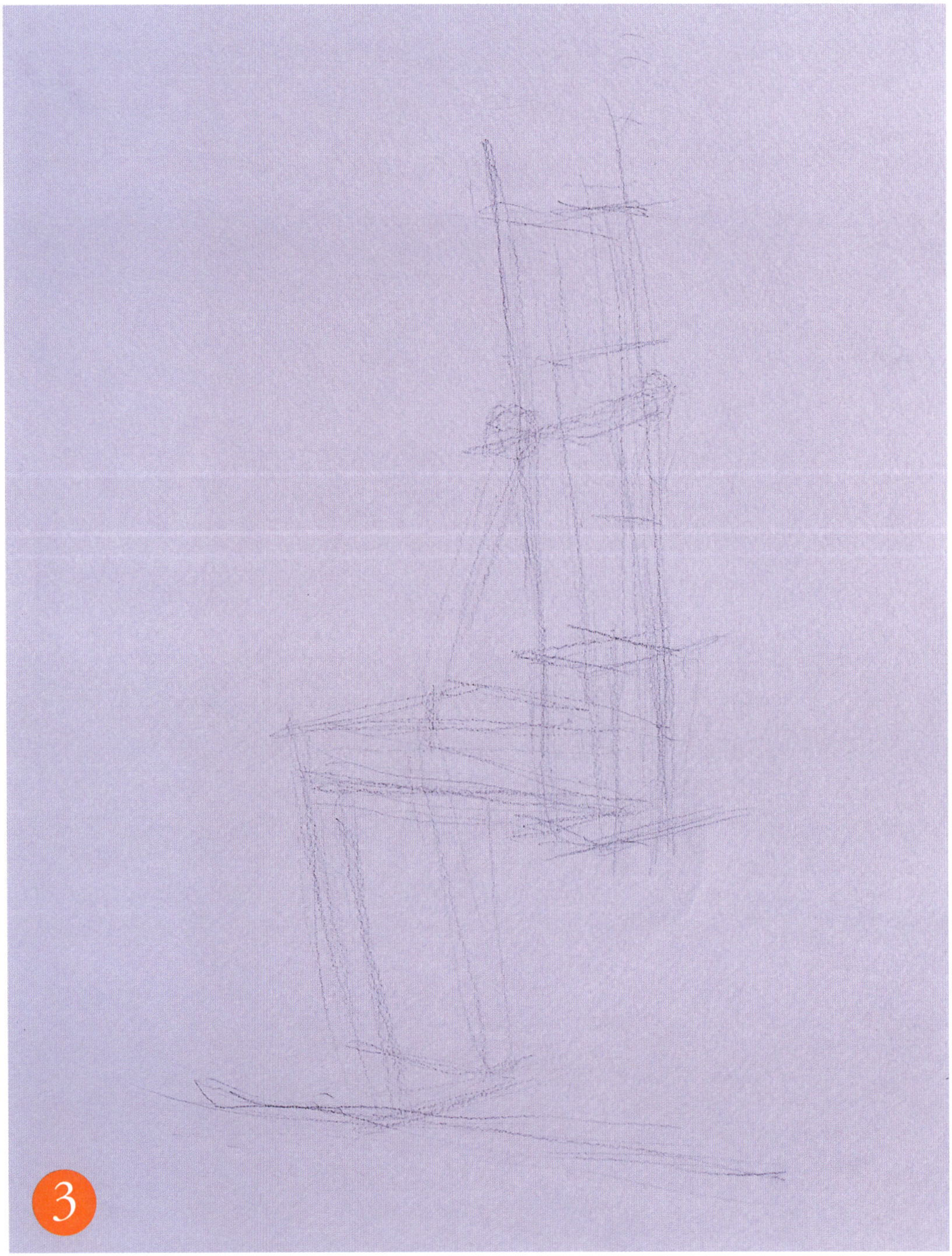

Start the Feet and Arms

The length of each foot (without the heel) is the same as the height of the head.

Continuing with an HB charcoal pencil, sketch in the direction of the upper arms even if you can't see the one on the far side of the body.

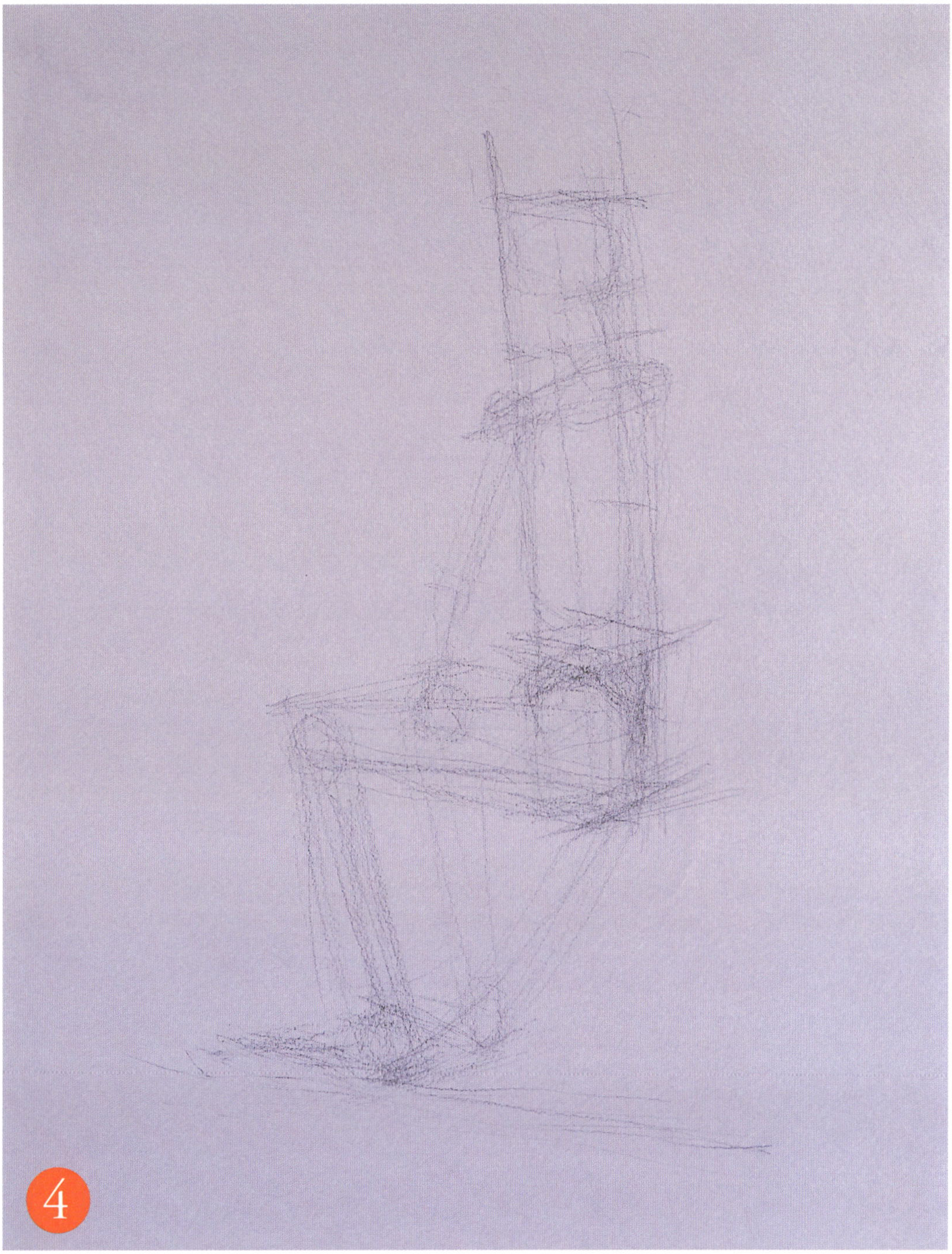

Check Measurements and Sizing

Double-check that the figure can kick himself in the butt with his heels to be sure that the thighs and shins are the proper length.

The knees, the balls of the shoulders and the height of the feet should all be the same size.

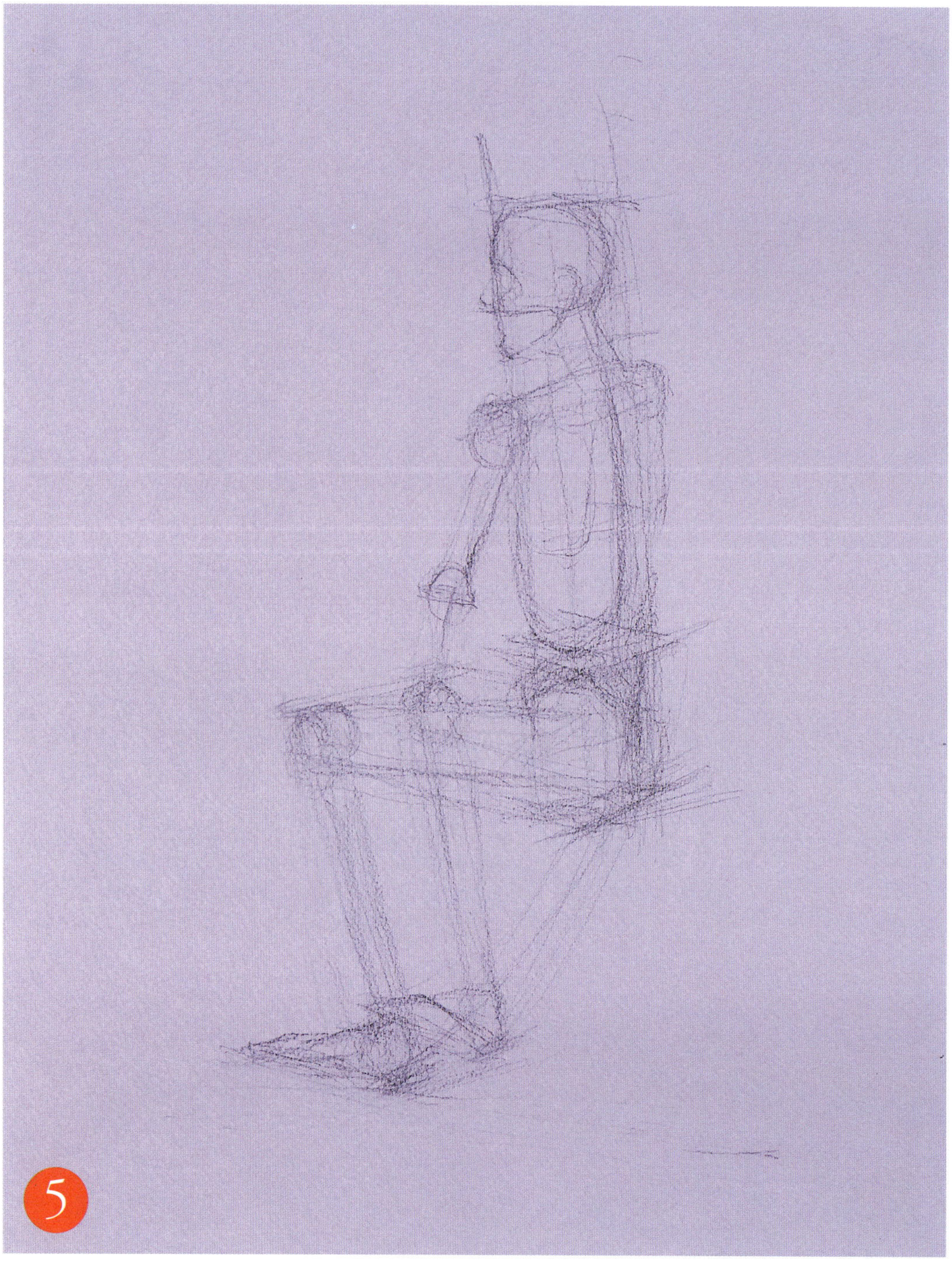

Add Bony Shapes and the Elbow Joint

Continuing with an HB charcoal pencil, sketch in the proper bony shapes for the head, hips and shoulder blade.

Indicate the proper width of the elbow joint. (You can use the same size sphere that you used for the other limb joints.)

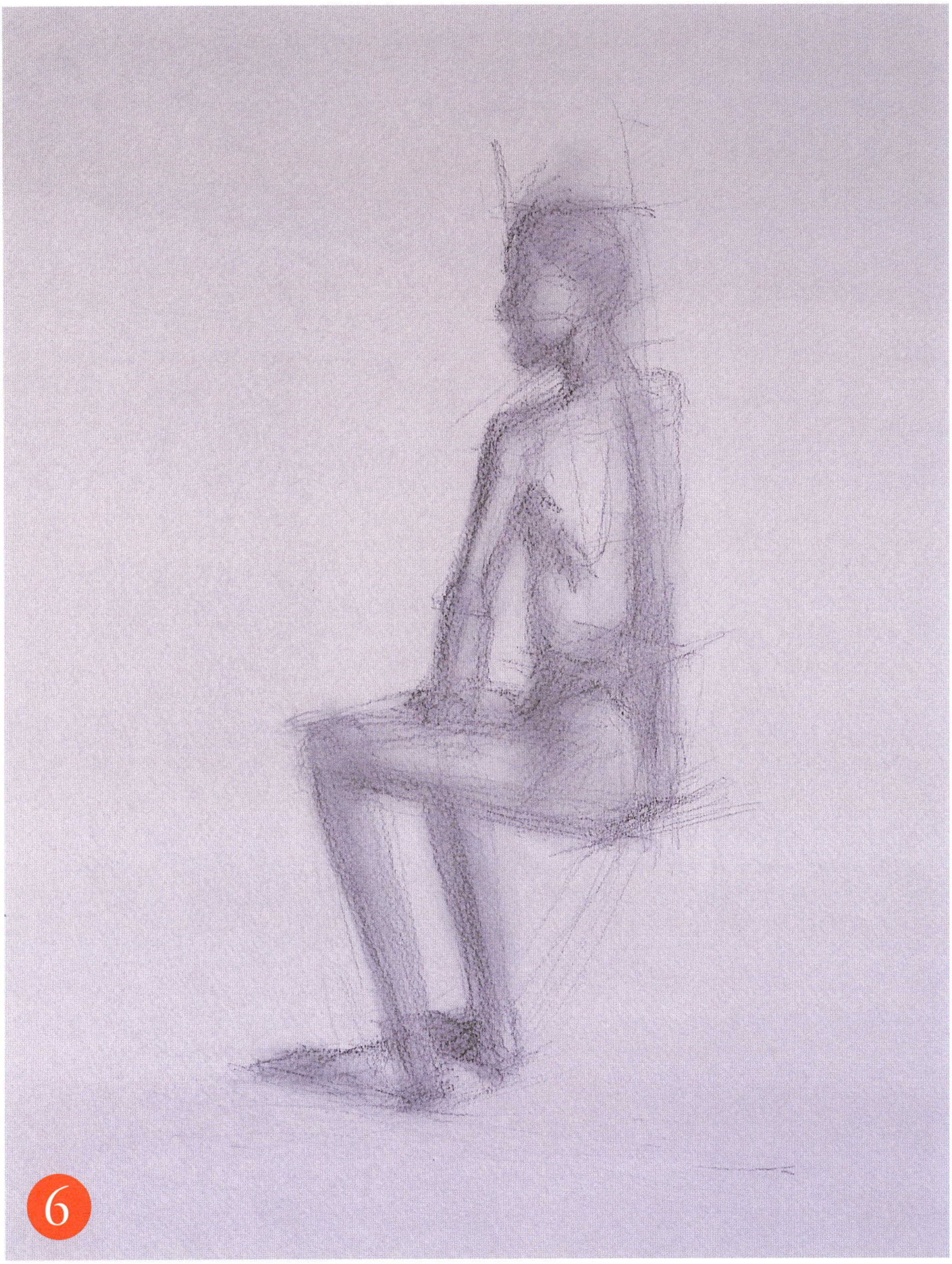

6

Begin to Block In Shading

At this point you can choose to block in your basic shading. Shadow covers the planes turned away from the light source. Light hits those planes turned toward it. Use a medium-grade pencil to evenly shade the shadow areas. Rub those areas out with an even tone using a chamois cloth or paper towel, then blend the shadow area to the light area with a kneaded eraser. Keep the light areas large. Run your eraser over them to "draw" the light falling upon the figure.

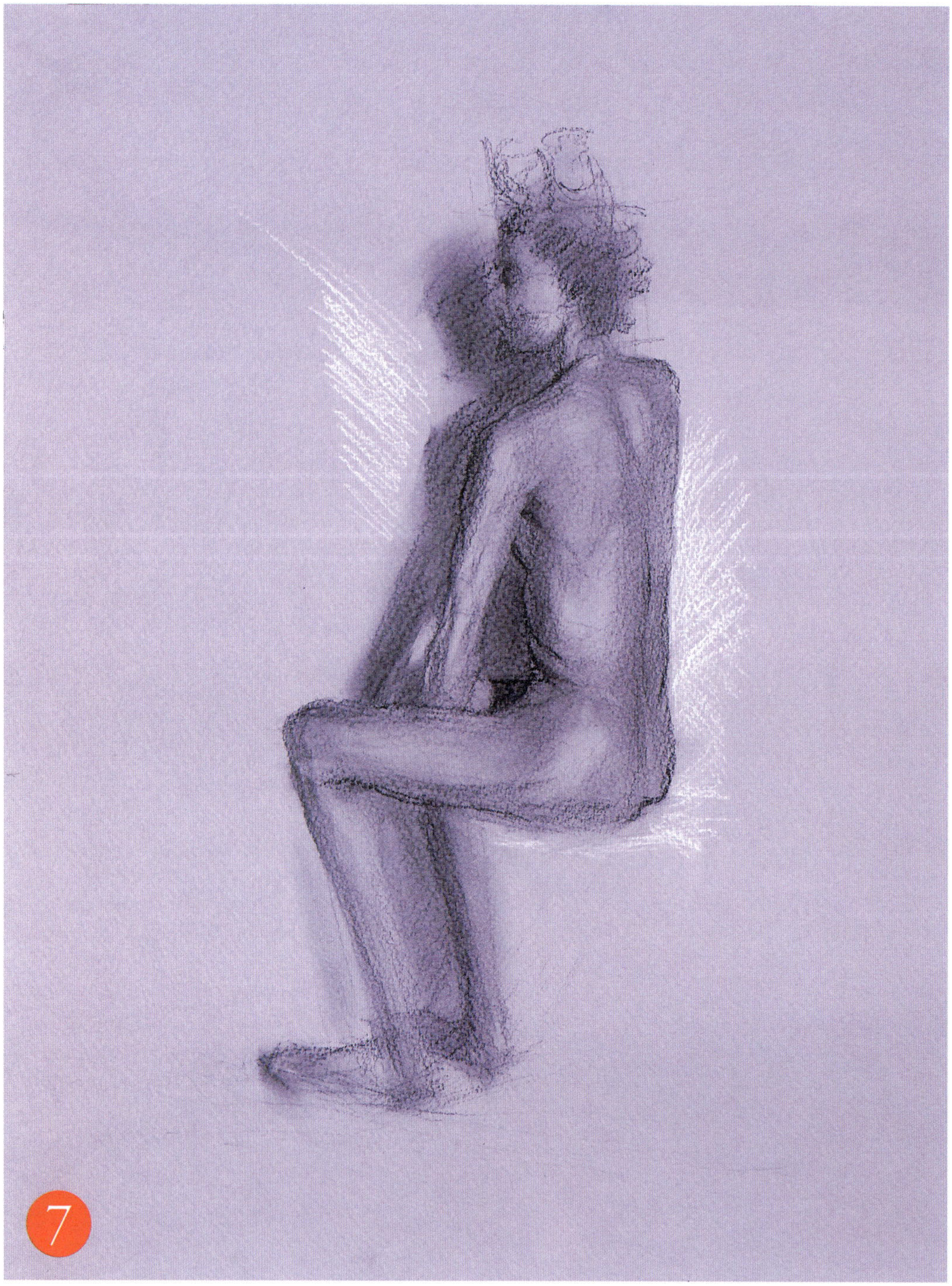

Add More Shading and Highlights

Continue to model the figure. Use a 4B charcoal pencil to add cast shadows to reinforce the darkest contour lines and to color in the hair.

Use a white charcoal pencil to indicate the most strongly illuminated portions of the background and the plane that the figure is seated on. Use the white pencil sparingly to add the lightest highlights within the lighted areas of the figure.

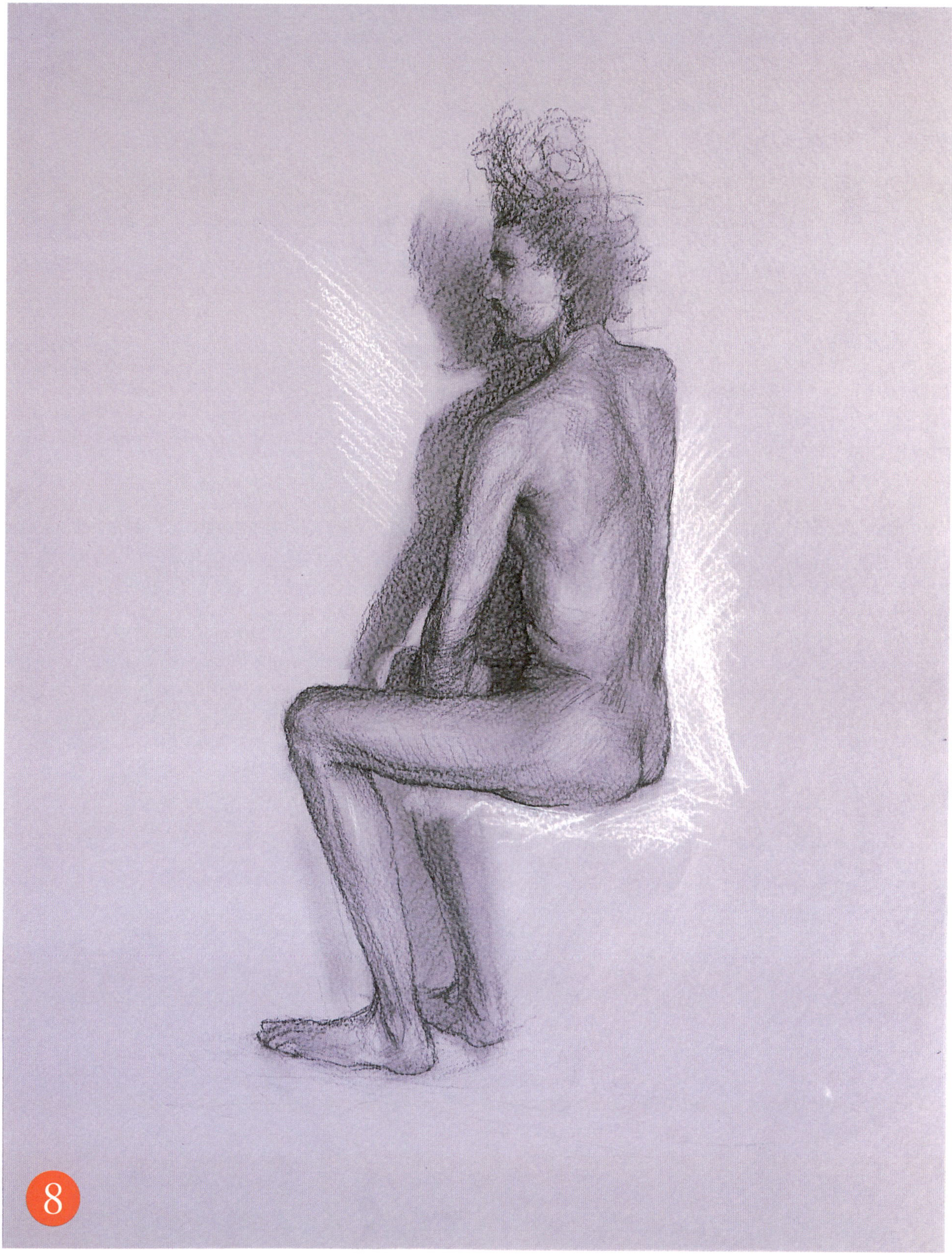

Complete the Contours and Modeling

Use your direct observation of the model to cement the proportions and tighten up the contours and modeling of your figure. Be cautious not to overwork or overly model the figure by keeping the tones within the range of lights and darks you already set.

Demonstration

Seated Female

Conté pencil is another excellent medium to try for your drawings. The greasier binder means that you can get very sharp lines and very dark darks that will hold. But be careful—Conté is very difficult to erase, so start lightly.

With the model's right thigh in mid-flexion, you can easily trace the arc that it would make when fully rotated in the hip socket. Note how that compares to the position of the model's left thigh, which rests at a typical angle for the seated figure.

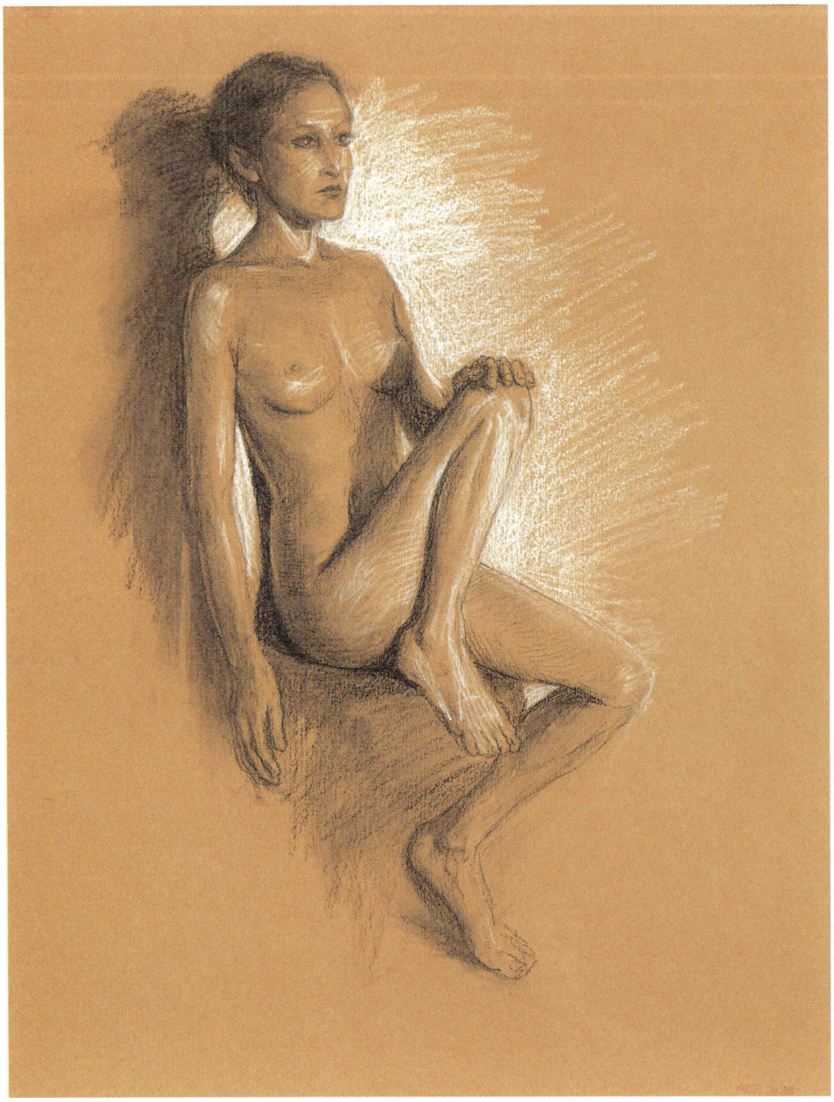

MATERIALS

Surface

orange Canson Mi-Teintes 98-lb. (160gsm)

Conté Pencils

HB, 2B, 4B and white

Other Supplies

chamois cloth

kneaded eraser

paper towels

Animated Drawing

Animate the figure drawing in your mind to find where the limbs would end up if the model curled up into a ball. Both heels would touch the buttocks and the arms would comfortably wrap around the shins. Then relax the figure back to its actual position and compare the relative dimensions.

1

Place the Figure and the Brackets

When using Conté, be sure to keep your guidelines very light. Use an HB Conté pencil to sketch in the brackets. Set up the two above, one below ratio. Note how the seated figure can still kick herself in the butt.

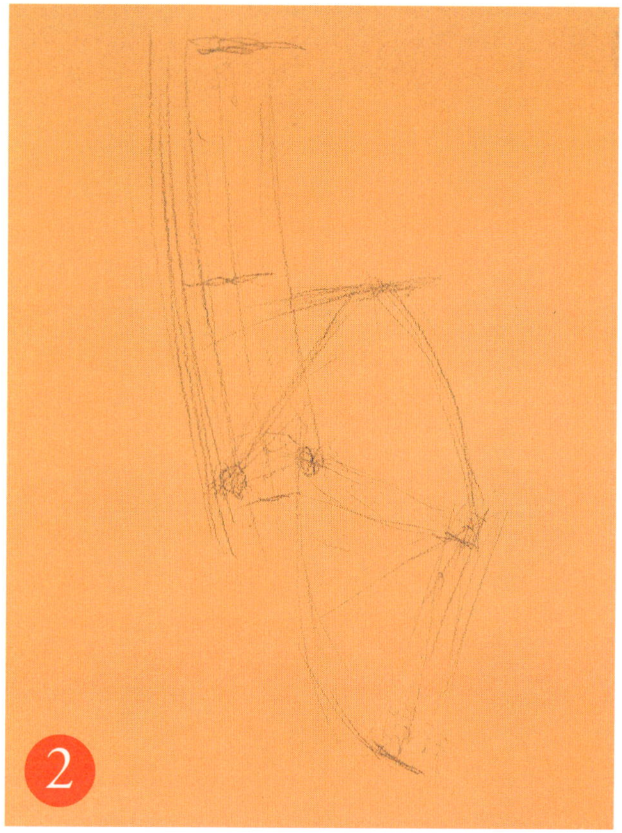

2

Adjust the Thigh Placement

By establishing the perspective early on, we can then swing one of the thighs upwards. You can assume it will be the same length as the thigh you already drew.

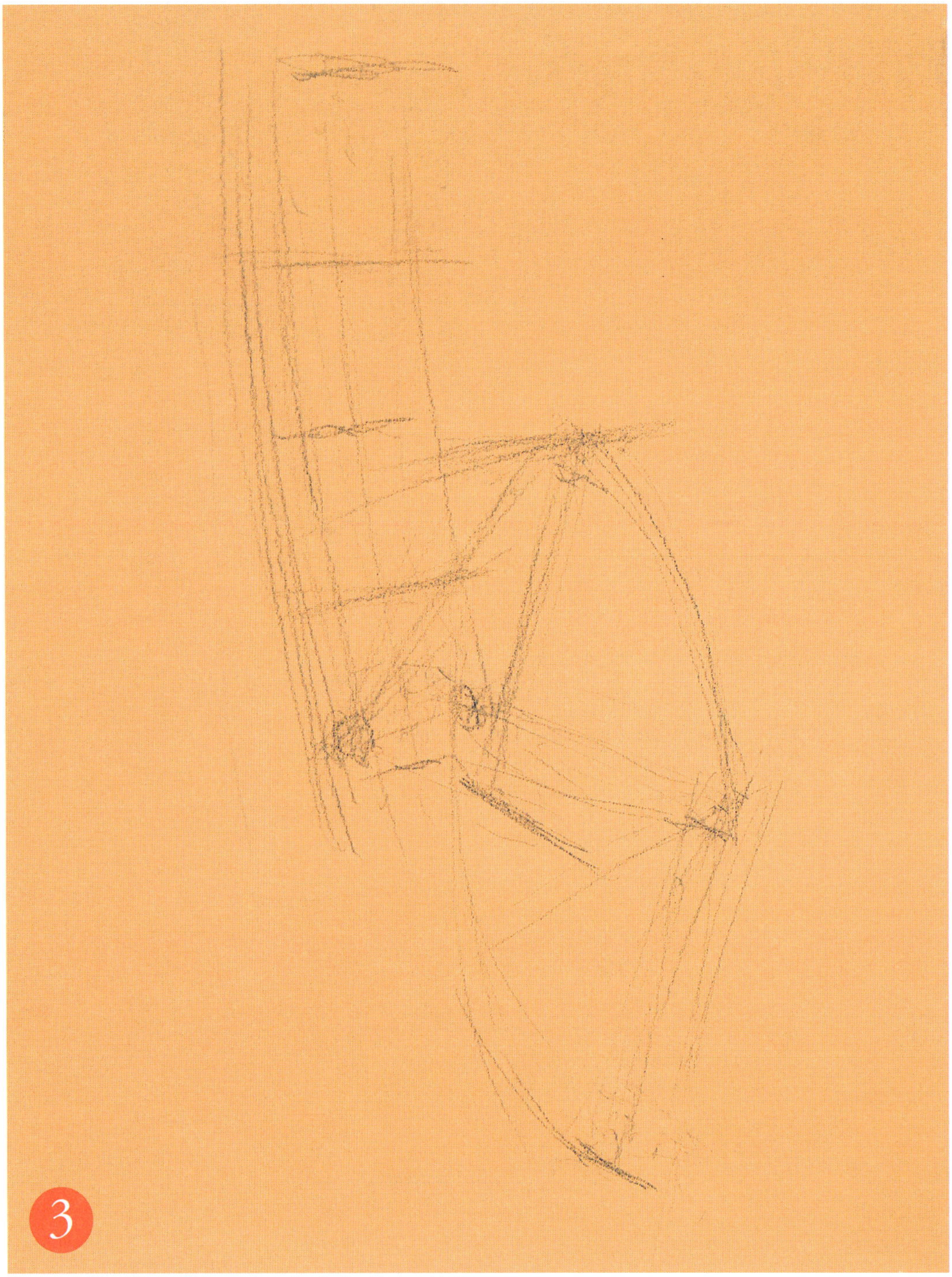

Develop the Upper Bracket and Feet

Continuing with an HB Conté pencil, divide the upper bracket into quarters and add thickness, front to back, following your perspective scheme.

The feet (without the heels) should be the same size as one of the upper bracket quadrants.

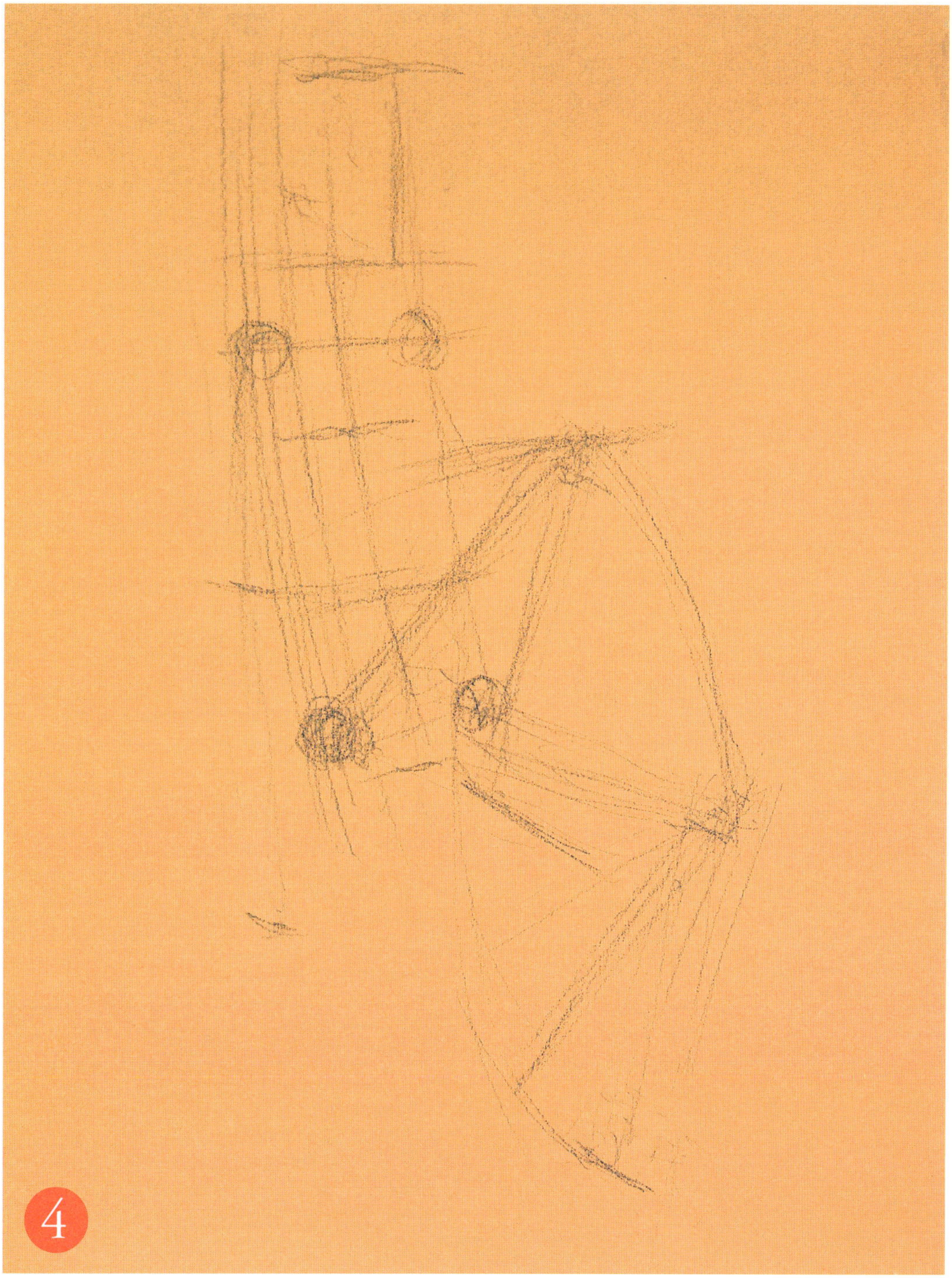

Develop the Shoulders and Hips

Continuing with an HB Conté pencil, establish the shoulder line by subdividing the second topmost quadrant into two, top to bottom. Draw equal spheres for the balls of the shoulders and hips.

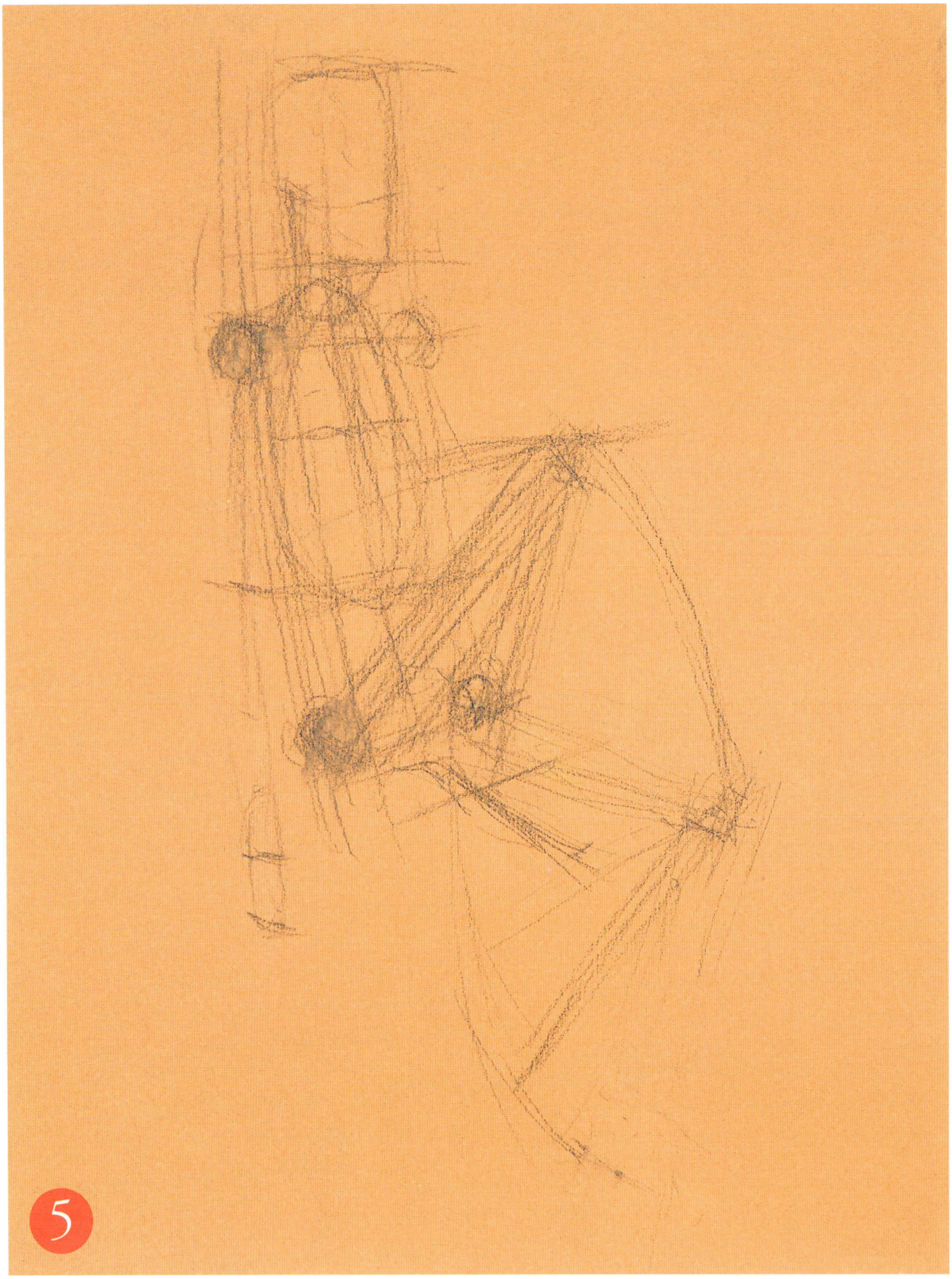

Continue Developing the Forms

Continuing with an HB Conté pencil, draw in primitive forms for the skull, rib cage and hips.

You can establish the length of the hanging arm easily, knowing that the distance from the top of the arm to the elbow is equal to the distance from the elbow to the first knuckle line of the hand.

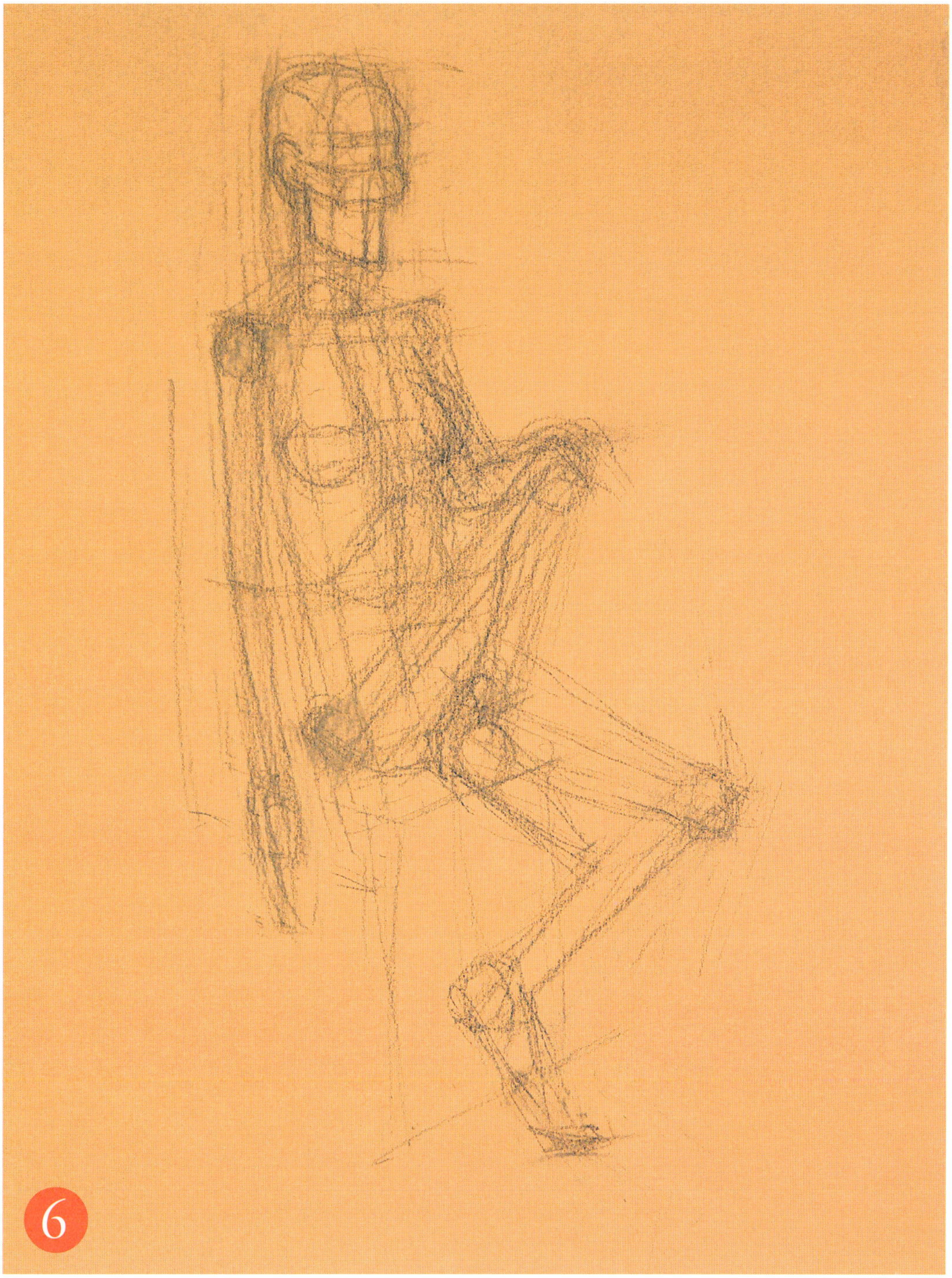

Develop the Limbs

Continuing with an HB Conté pencil, establish the rest of the thicknesses of the limbs. Most will be equal to a palm's width, which is also equal to the height of the neck.

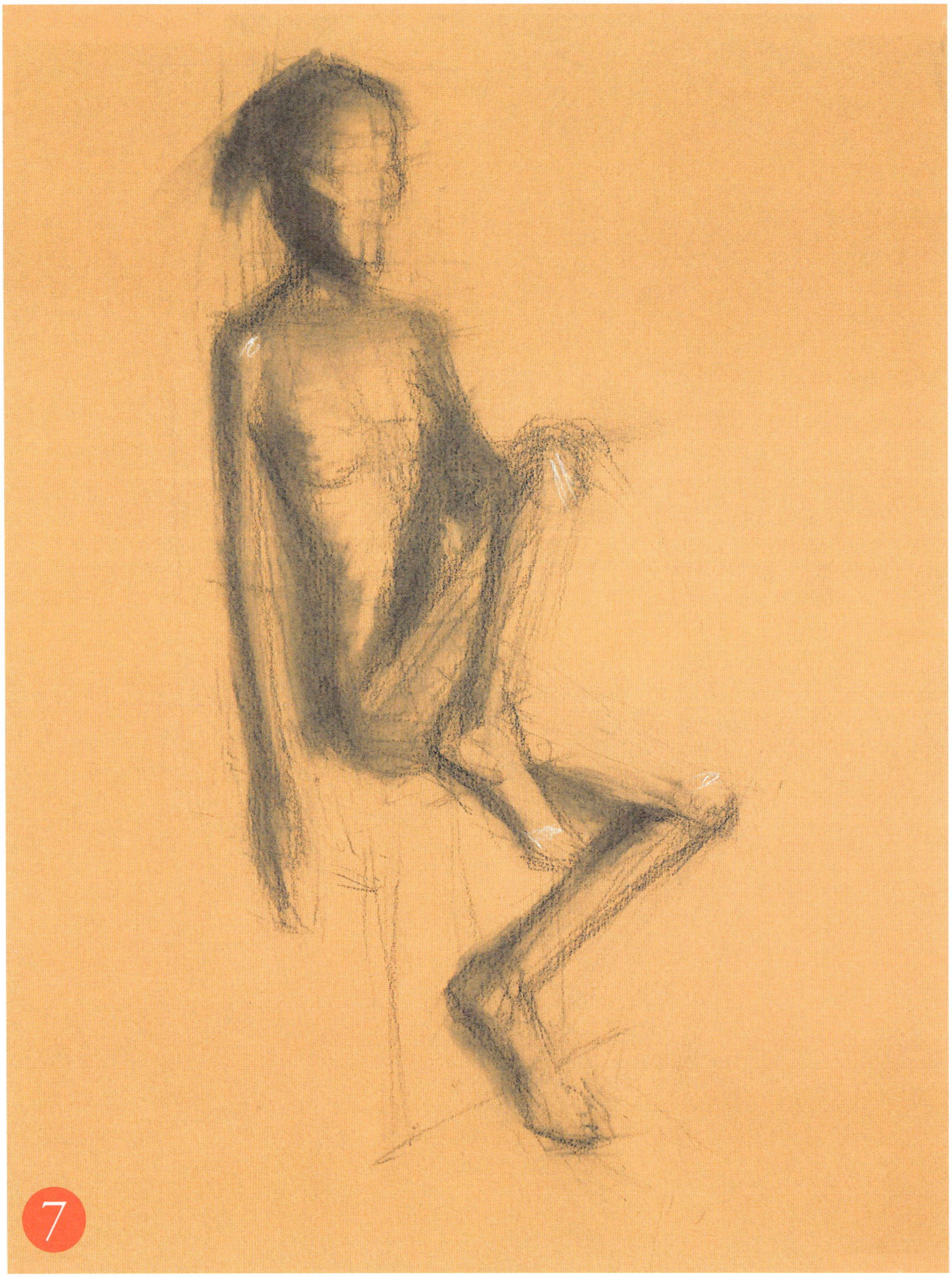

Erase the Guidelines and Begin Shading

At this point you have established enough information for the figure that you can rub out the guidelines, and add shading to the surfaces in shadow. The HB Conté that you used up to this point should be dark enough to give a good shadow tone when rubbed with a paper towel, chamois cloth or rag. But be careful—Conté is hard to erase. Add darker touches, where needed, with a 2B or 4B Conté pencil. Keep your lighted areas clear of dark pigment with a kneaded eraser, and add some highlights to the form with a white Conté pencil.

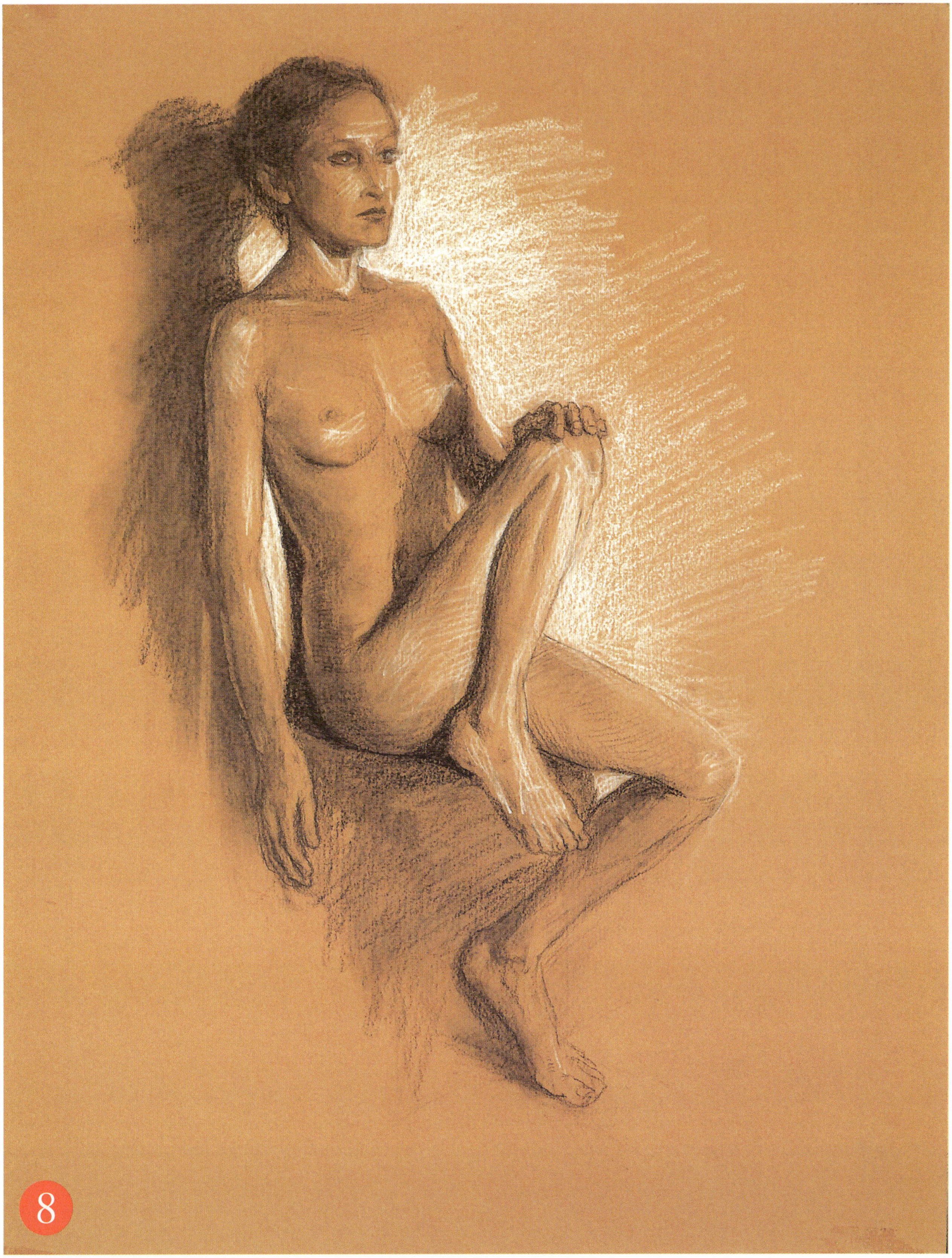

8

Refine the Contours

By refining the contours of the figure and smoothing the transitions in your modeling, you can quickly arrive at a satisfactory drawing.

Demonstration

Reclining Male

Don't be intimidated by reclining poses. Because most of the limbs are not foreshortened, they generally present the same amount of difficulty as standing poses. They're just turned on their sides.

As with standing poses, use the divisions of the upper and lower body to find the positions of the major joints. You will need to draw your upper bracket on a curve to represent the flexion of the model's upper body and head. Take note of the perspective at play: We see the model from the back (not just the side) view.

The bend of the model's left leg will provide some helpful negative spaces and a visually interesting outline.

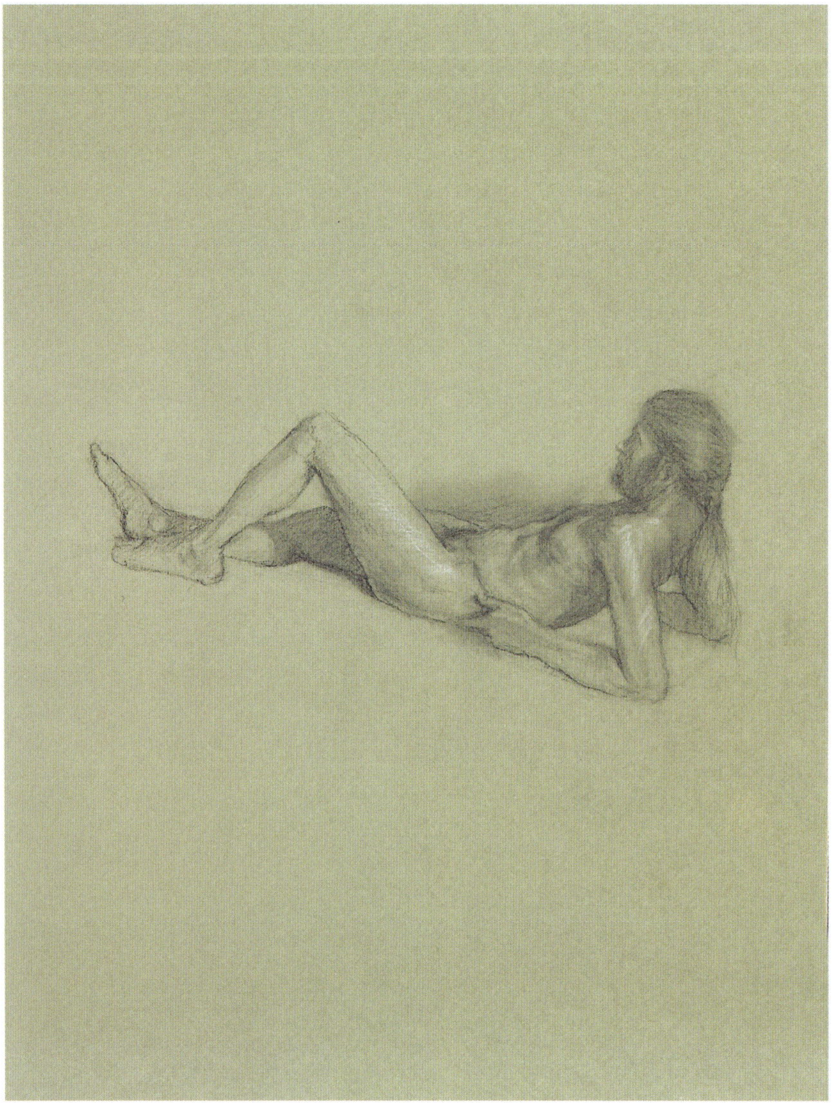

MATERIALS

Surface

green Canson Mi-Teintes 98-lb. (160gsm)

Charcoal Pencils

HB, 2B, 4B and white

Other Supplies

chamois cloth

kneaded eraser

paper towels

Set the Limits and Divide

As with any figure drawing, set the outside limits of the figure first so that you don't run off the page. Subdivide the figure into smaller sections from there.

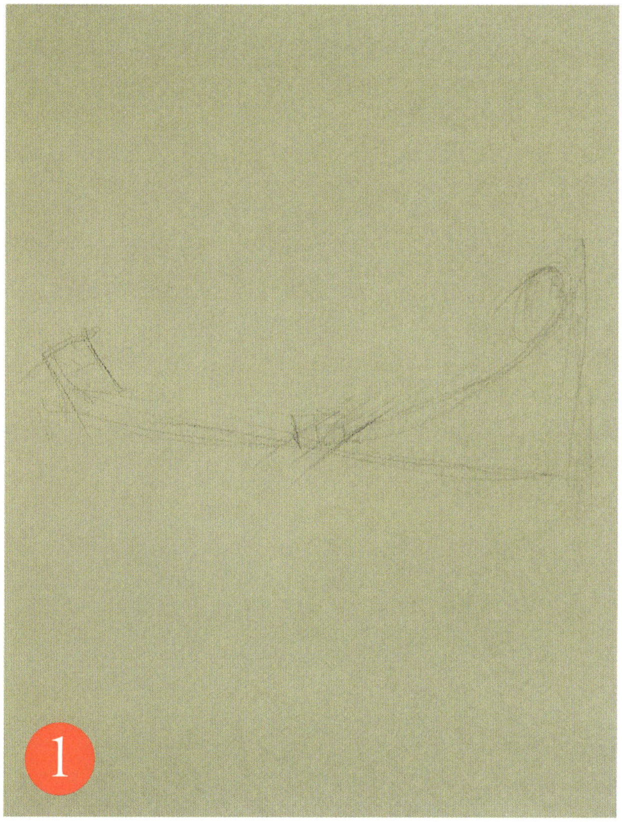

Place the Figure and Brackets

For a reclining figure, set the endpoints and midpoint of the figure immediately. You don't want your drawing to spread off your page.

You can curve the upper bracket if you need to. Just make sure that it's of the same relative length as the lower bracket.

Use an HB charcoal pencil for these steps (unless otherwise specified), keeping the drawing light against the background.

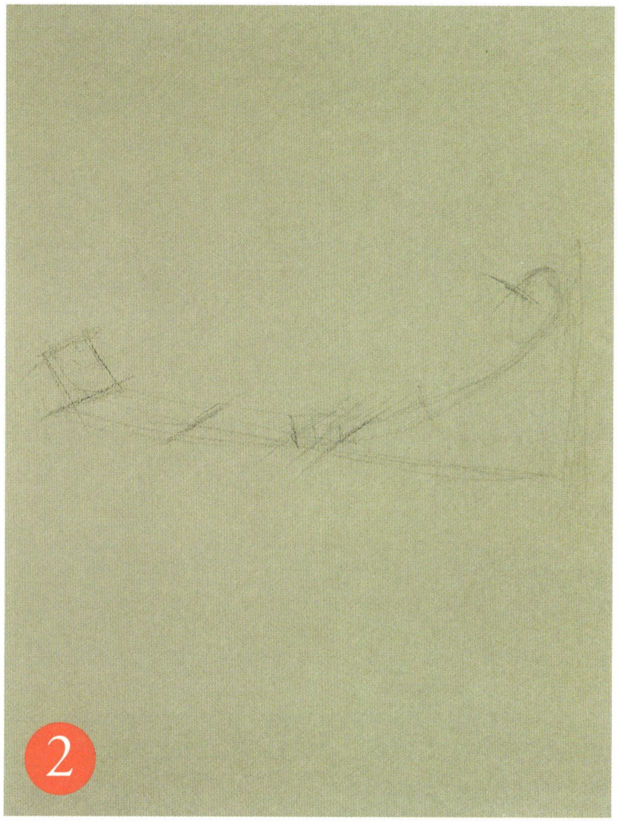

Divide the Brackets and Establish Perspective

Dividing the lower bracket will give us the juncture of the knee joint.

It's never too early to add some lines to establish perspective, giving your figure some width and depth as well as length.

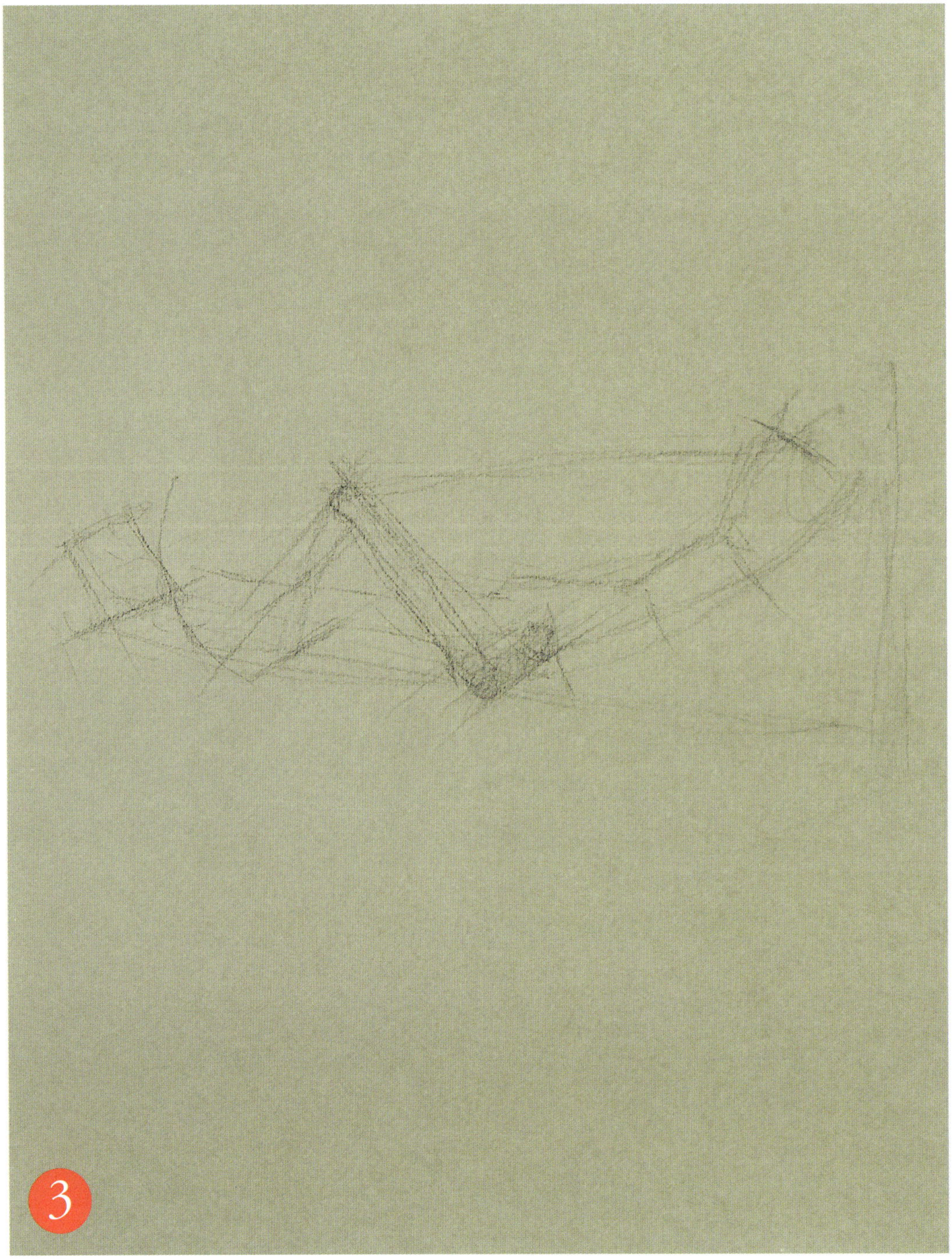

Continue Dividing and Positioning the Figure

With the knee demarcated, we can bend one upward. Dividing the upper bracket again gives us heights for the head and hips.

Double-check your work by comparing the position of the knee on the page to that of the head. Ask yourself what would happen if the model bent all the way forward. Would the width of both knees together equal the width of the head? You can also trace the abstract geometry of negative space created by your figure against the background.

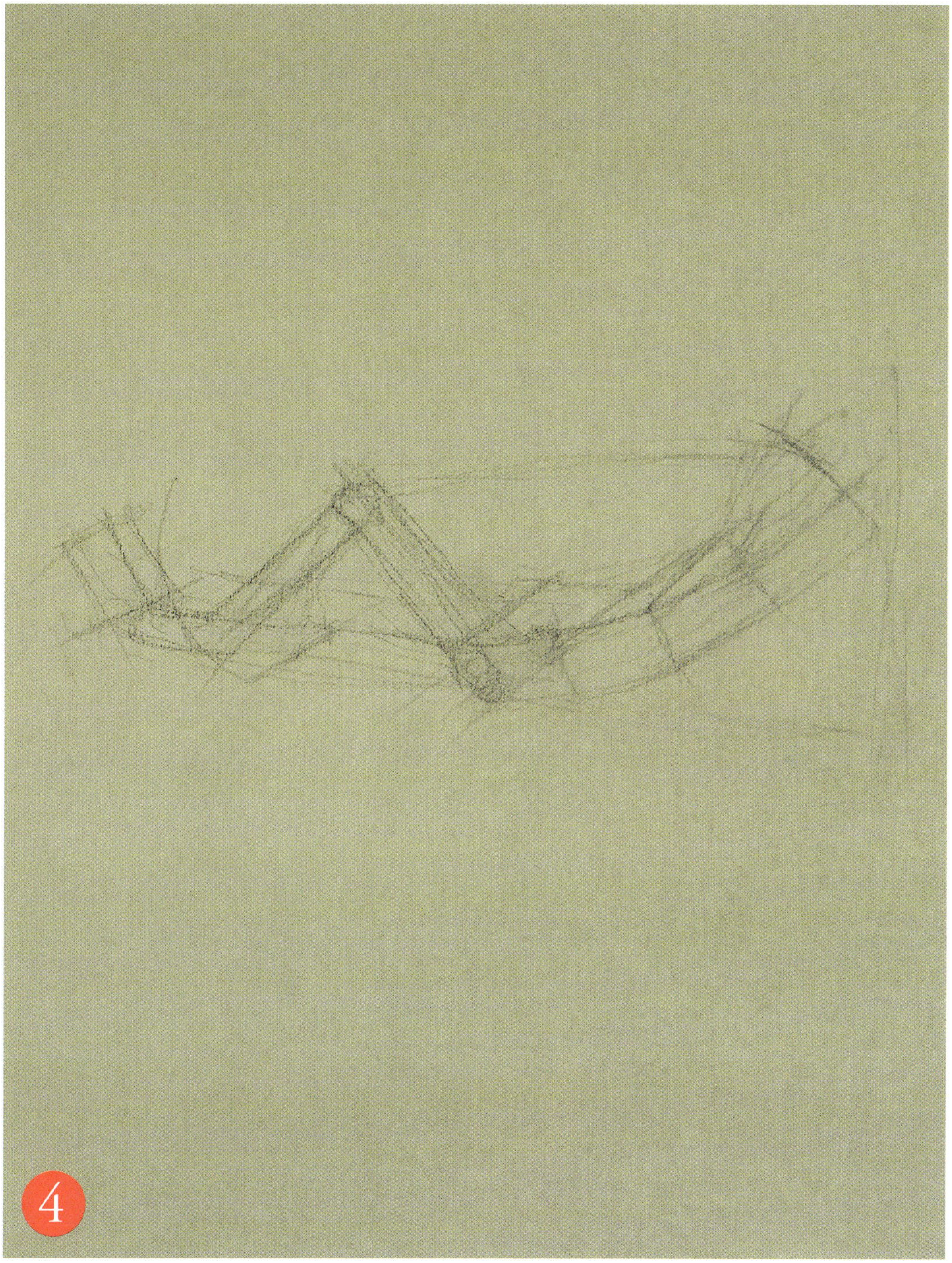

Add Width and Depth to the Figure

Keep working the widths and depths of the body's parts along with its lengths. Would this figure be able to draw his knee up to reach just under his collarbone? Are the knees the same width as the feet?

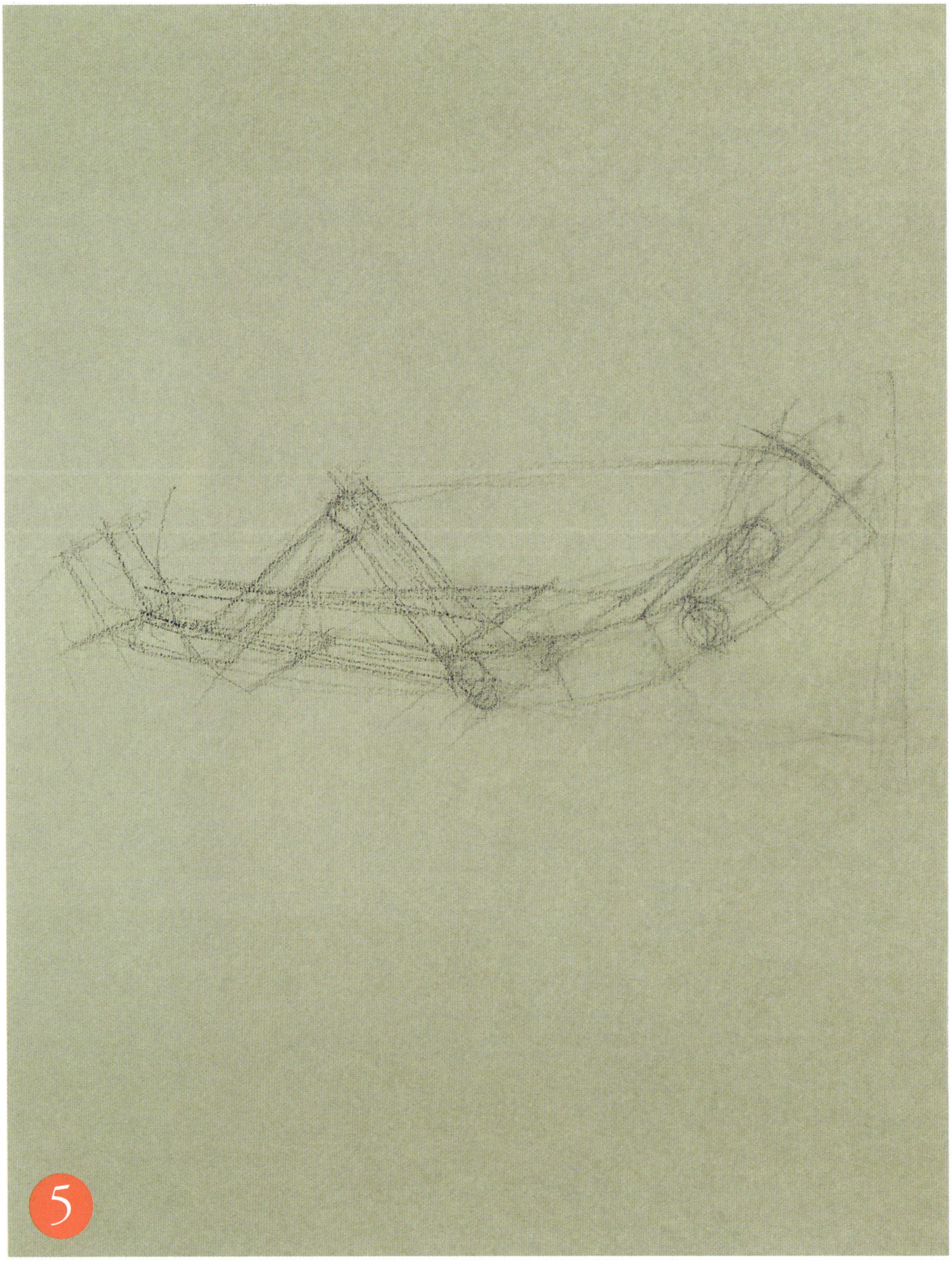

Place the Shoulders

Subdividing the second-to-topmost quadrant of the upper bracket gives us the position of the shoulder line. Here you can place the balls of the shoulders to the outside of the squared-off torso form.

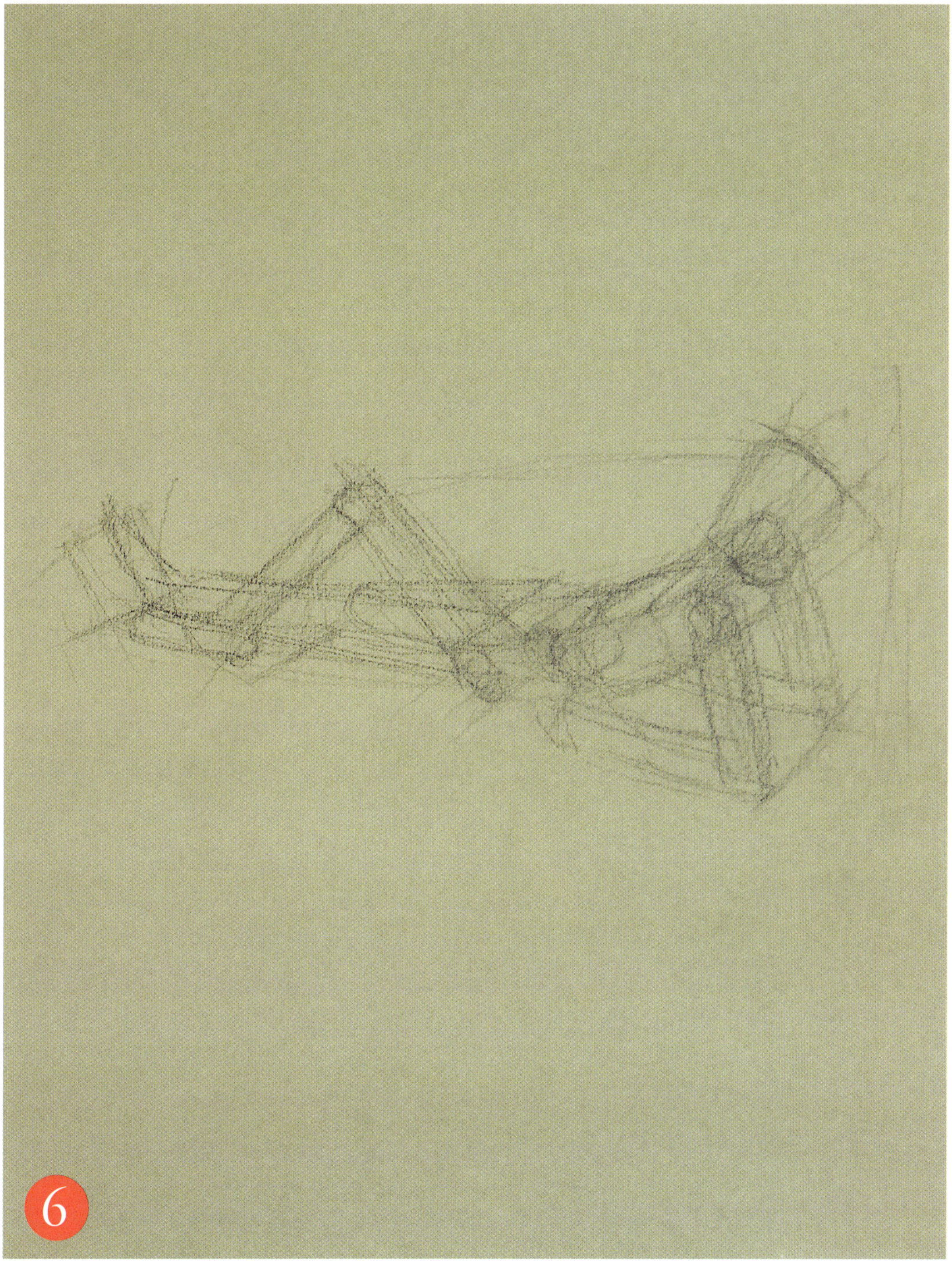

Position the Arms

The elbows, if they were alongside the figure, would fall between the pelvis and the rib cage. Here you can rotate them back to support the figure.

Even in this position, a line connecting the tops of the arms and another line connecting the elbows should form a square (in perspective).

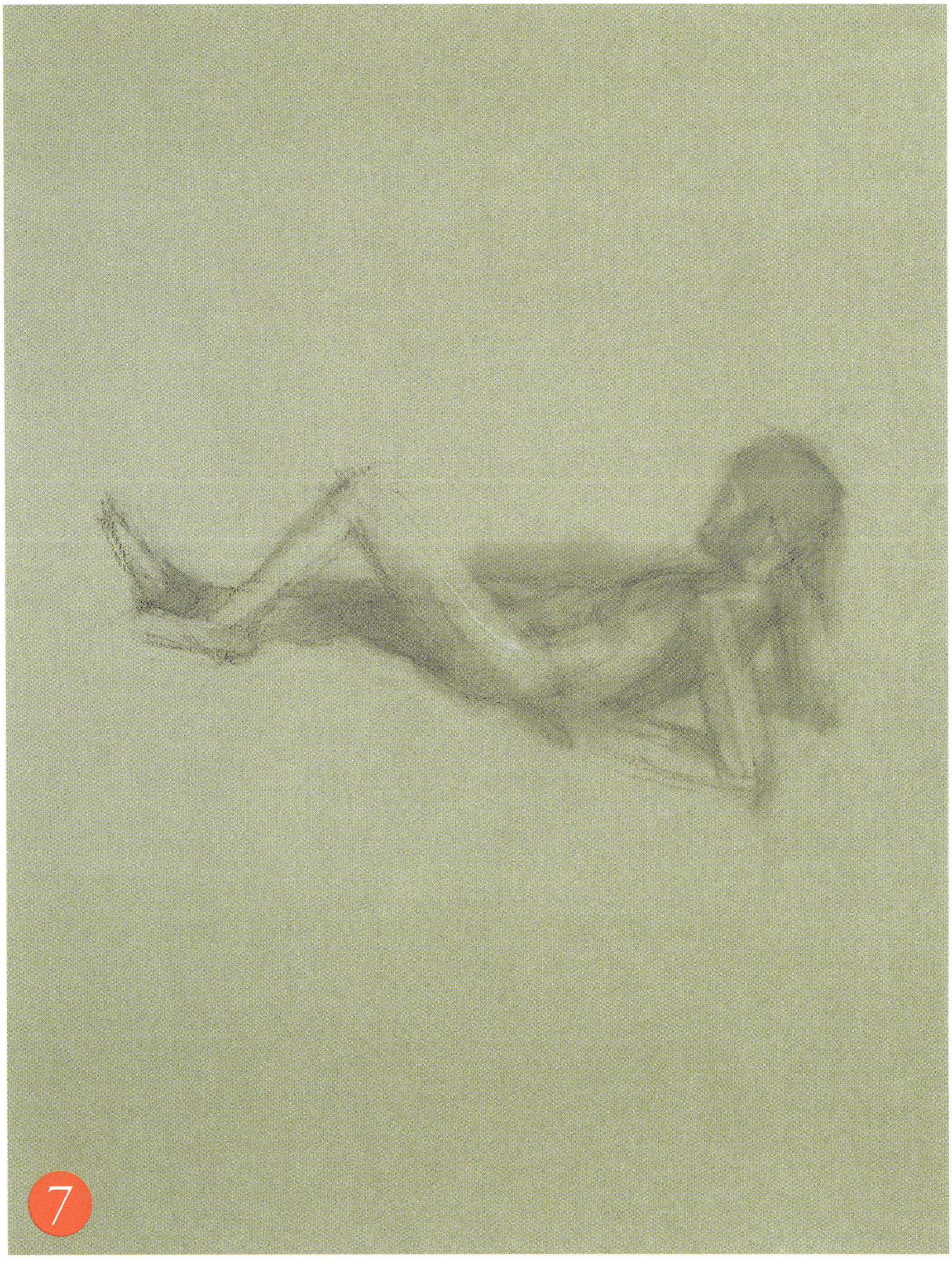

Erase the Guidelines and Start the Highlights

With a "scaffolding" now well established for the figure, we can blur out all our construction lines. The residue of the HB charcoal pencil you used to make the construction lines should be enough to give a sense of illumination. If not, gently tone the area with the HB or a darker grade charcoal pencil, and rub it out again until you achieve the amount of contrast you want in your drawing. Use a kneaded eraser to lighten all the light-receiving planes.

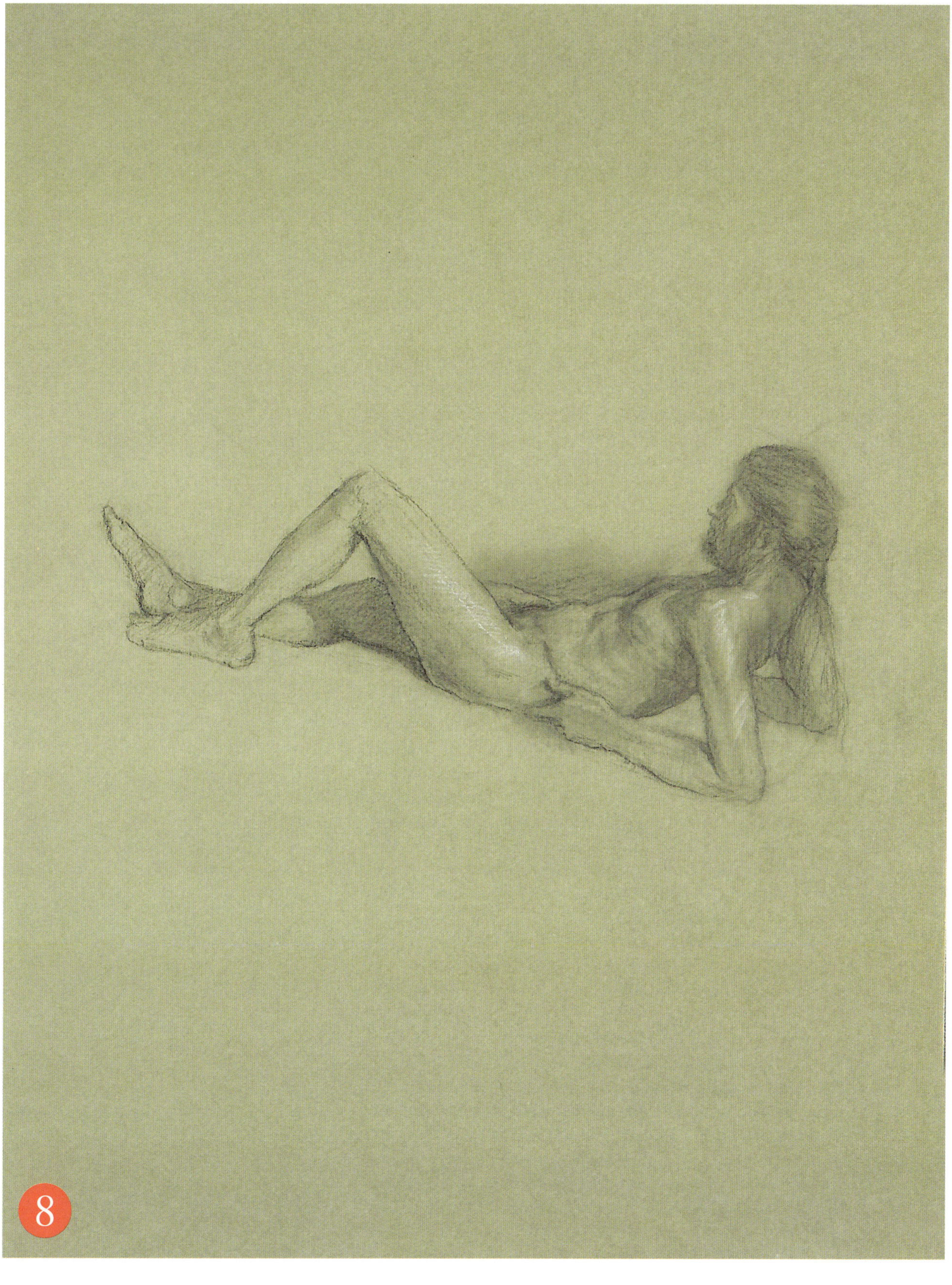

Finish Developing the Drawing

Adjust your drawing to what you see in the model's pose. You are now free to concentrate on all the other challenges and pleasures of drawing—anatomy, modeling, contour, value and so on.

Demonstration

Foreshortened Female

Poses in extreme foreshortening are probably the most difficult ones to do. But remember, foreshortening and perspective are always at play, even in drawings that appear to be relatively simple. By the same token, almost any drawing will present a figure with at least one body part drawn at full length, parallel to the picture plane. These limbs, when drawn clearly, can be leveraged to establish the contrasting direction of the foreshortened body parts and to establish their relative sizes.

MATERIALS

Surface

white Canson Mi-Teintes 98-lb. (160gsm)

Sepia Conté Pencils

HB, 2B and darker color or black

Other Supplies

chamois cloth

kneaded eraser

paper towels

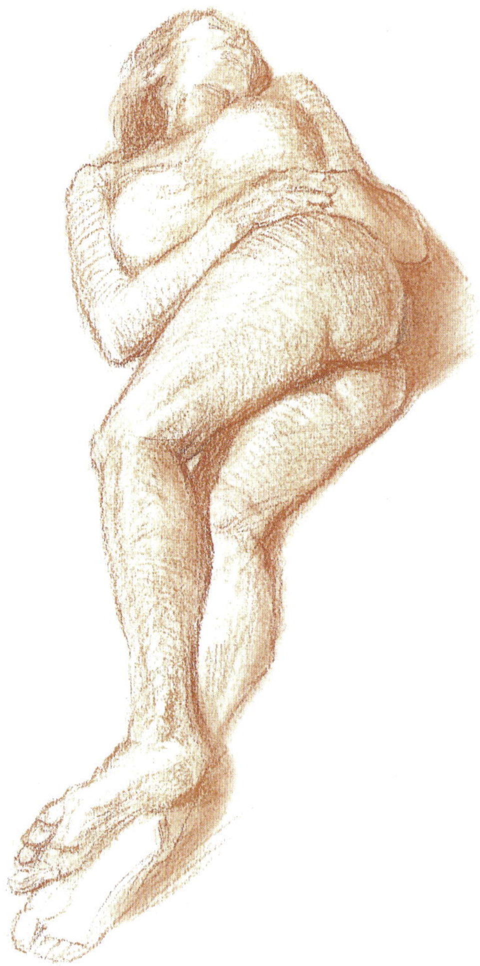

Start With the Big Picture

When rendering a foreshortened pose, start with the big picture. Establish the largest planes and the perspective that they appear in first. Then subdivide from there, using your knowledge of proportion.

Place the Figure on the Page

For a foreshortened figure, start the same way as with any other figure drawing. Use a large gesture to capture the main sweep of the figure. Set your top, bottom and center marks so that you don't run off the page.

Conté, especially colored Conté, is very difficult to erase from the page. So keep your lines light throughout these steps, using the hardest grade you can find (usually an HB) unless otherwise specified.

Divide and Develop the Form

Establish your perspective grid early on. Use Xs where you can to divide planes in half. Divide them in half again as necessary. At the same time, quickly build height and depth for the form by drawing blocks.

3

Divide the Brackets

As always, the lower bracket separates the thigh from the lower leg at the midpoint.

Divide the upper bracket (keeping your perspective) into quadrants to find the proper sizes for the skull and hips.

4

Check the Widths and Depths of the Limbs

Keeping proper widths and depths in the limbs is critical. Remember that the shoulders, hips, knees and feet are all of the same width. Use the same measurement for each foot's height, the knee's depth and so on.

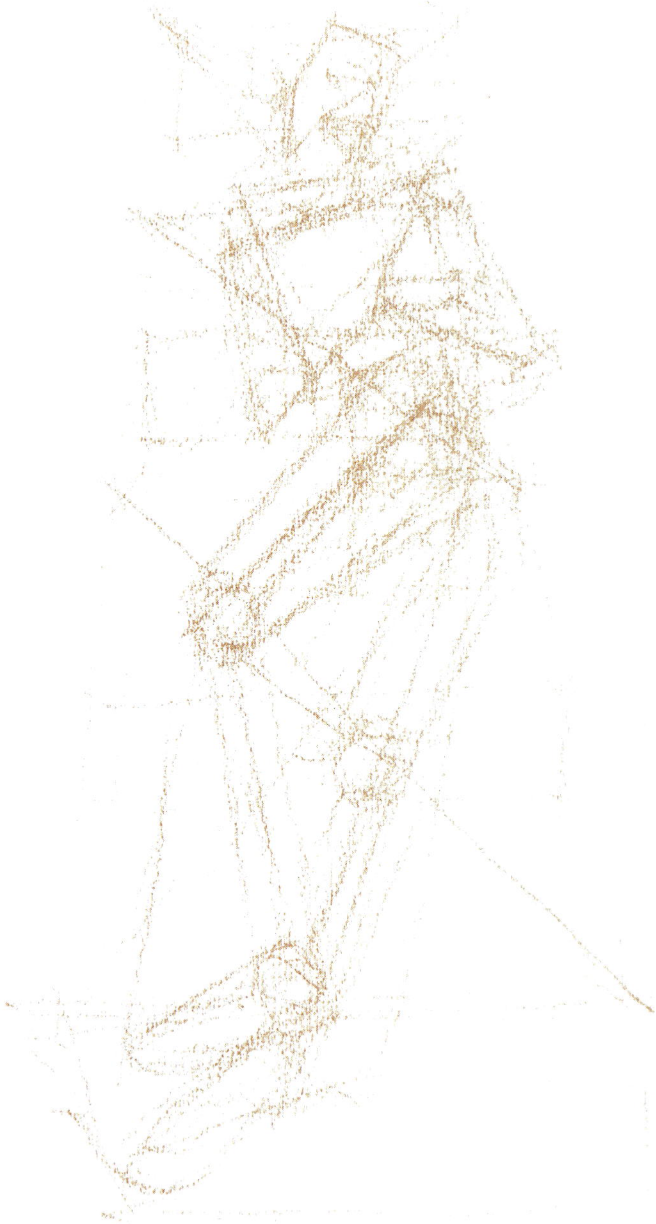

5

Continue Building With Blocks and Check Measurements

Keep expressing the figure using blocks. The blocks will give direction to the various body parts as well as volume.

The width of the feet together should still equate to the width of the head. Use your imagination to manipulate the figure to be certain that the body's proportions still hold. If the figure were to contract her pose all the way into a ball, her knees would reach the shoulder line, and her heels would align with the bottom of her seat.

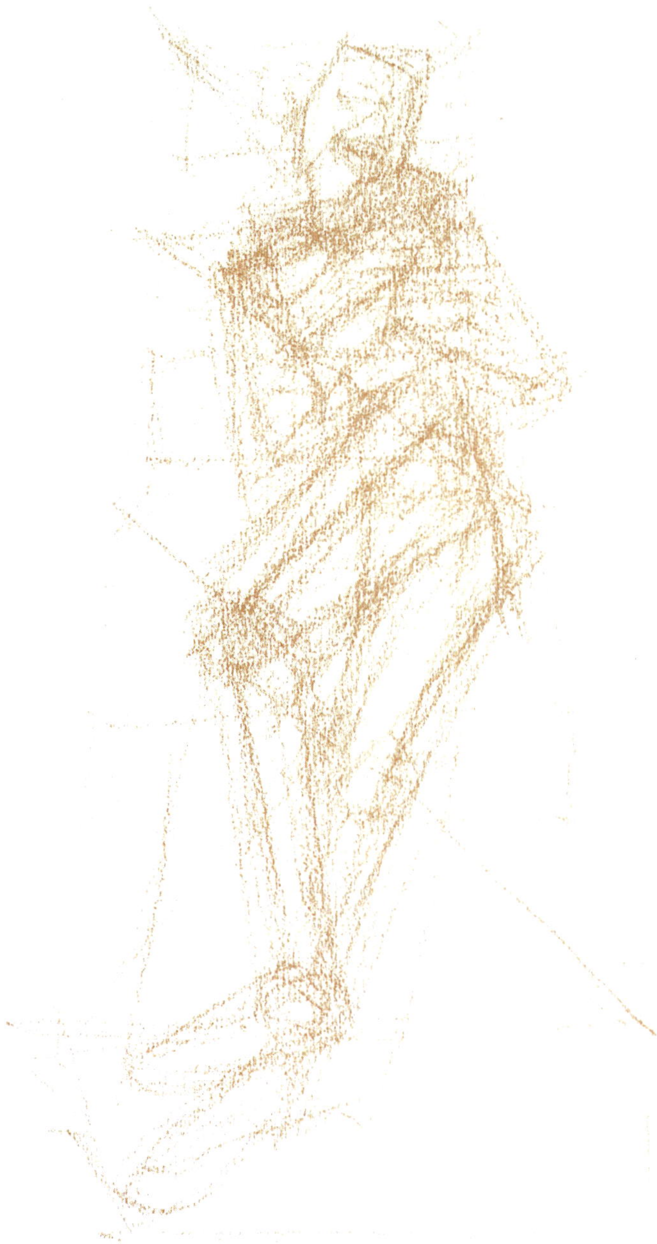

6

Check More Measurements

Continue to double-check the various lengths, widths and depths of the body parts against one another. Make sure that the hands could cover the knees and that the fingers could point to the shoulders.

Divide the head, top to bottom, into thirds to find the proper position of the brow, nose and base of the skull.

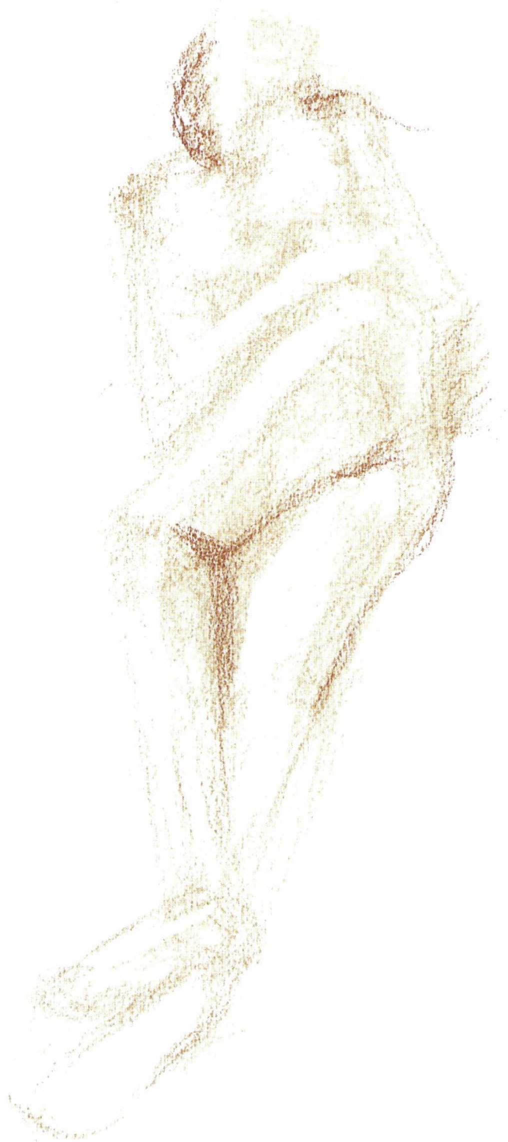

7

Add the Cast Shadows

When working on white paper, the lightness of the paper will have to serve as your lightest light. Where the parts of the figure are turned toward the light, keep the areas broadly lit and clear of any pencil markings. Pick values for your darkest darks and add them in for cast shadows.

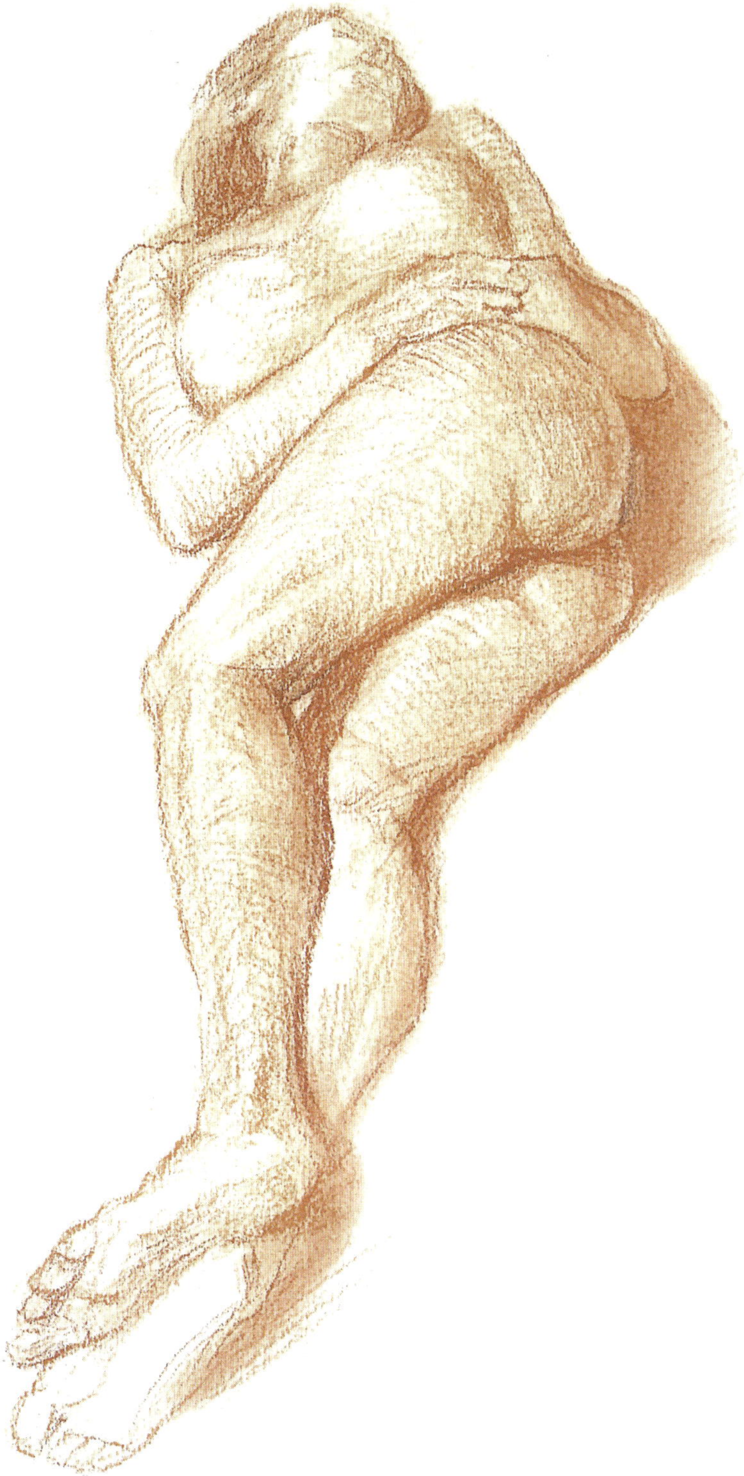

8

Finish Modeling and Adding Contours

Continue to model the form and adjust the contours of your drawing to what the model is presenting. For these tones, use a softer grade of Conté pencil (2B). For your very darkest darks, you can use a bit of a darker colored Conté pencil or even black.

Demonstration

Compact Male

When drawing a compact figure many of the body parts are already laid next to each other or on top of each other, making for easy comparison. To keep the figure in your drawing from looking like a big blob of flesh, carefully separate each body part for the viewer. In addition to exploiting anatomical landmarks, try to represent each limb with a definitive length, width and depth.

MATERIALS

Surface

white Canson Mi-Teintes 98-lb. (160gsm)

Conté Pencils

HB, 2B

Other Supplies

chamois cloth, paper towel or rag

kneaded eraser

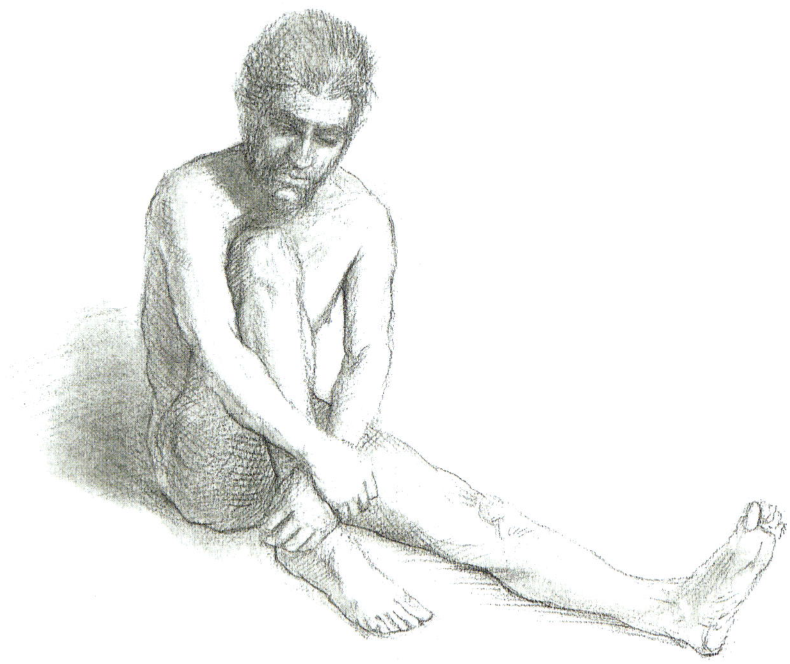

Uniform Limbs

A figure drawn in a compact pose may still have one or more stray limbs extended. Those limbs need to be the same size as the ones that are held tightly together.

1

Place the Figure on the Page

Conté pencil doesn't erase easily, so start your drawing with a hard grade (HB), and lightly indicate the placement of the figure on the page. Continue with the HB Conté pencil unless otherwise indicated.

From the outset, make the extended leg the same length (in perspective) as the height of the upper body bracket.

2

Divide the Upper Bracket

Divide the upper bracket into vertical fourths to find the height of the pelvis at the bottom and the head at the top. Subdividing the second topmost bracket in half will give you the line of the shoulders.

If you were to draw your knees up to your chest, they would come to the shoulder line. So make sure that the same is true of your figure drawing.

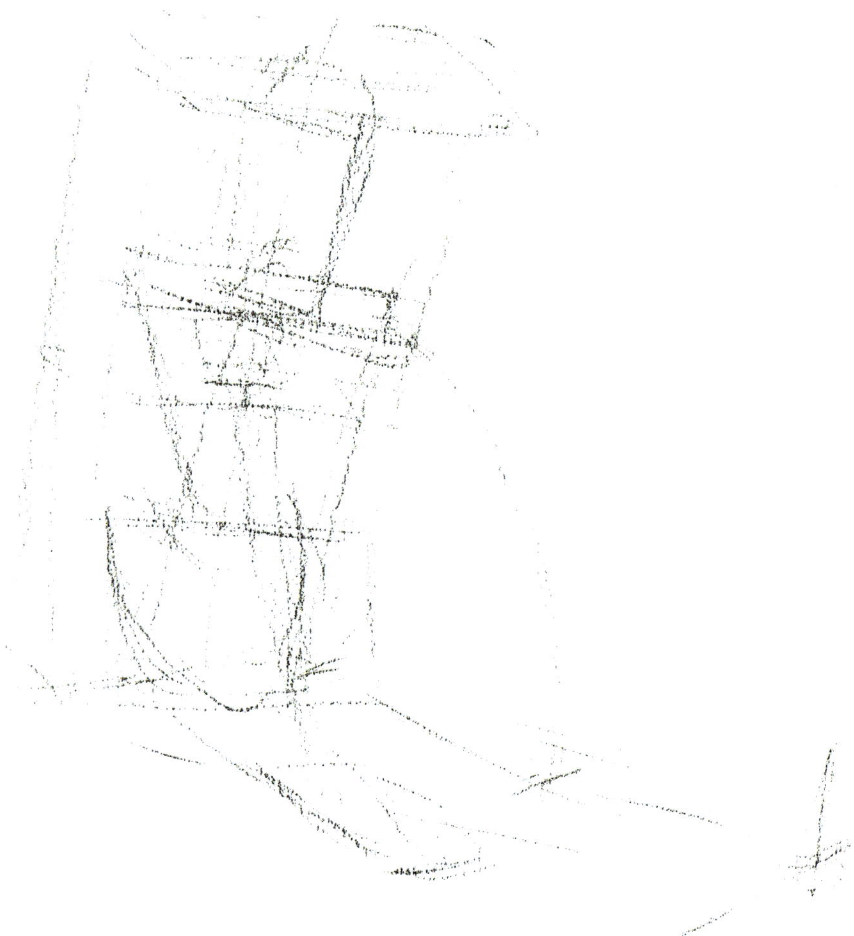

3

Block In the Right Leg and Position the Upper Body

Block in the figure's right leg, making sure that it is the same size as his left leg. You can position the entire upper body inside an imaginary box that already establishes its angle and turn. Set the direction of the shoulders, rib cage and head with light construction lines.

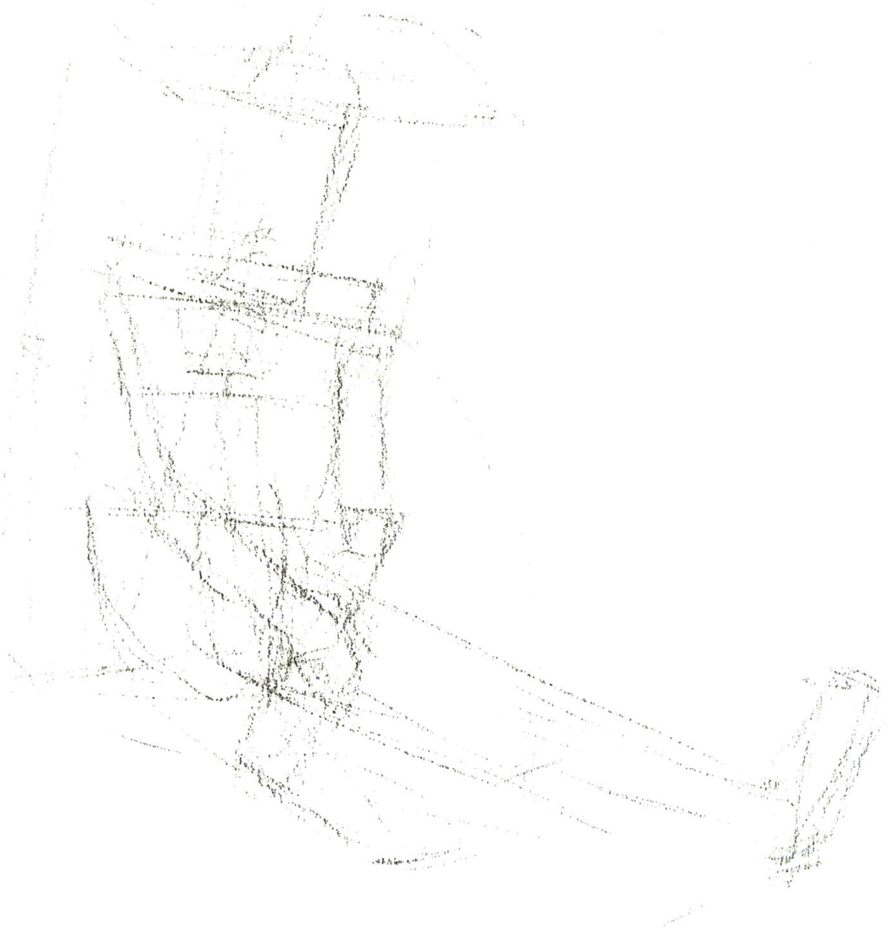

4

Block In the Arms

Begin adding the arms. As always, take the effects of perspective and foreshortening into account. The elbows would just reach the waist if hanging straight downward.

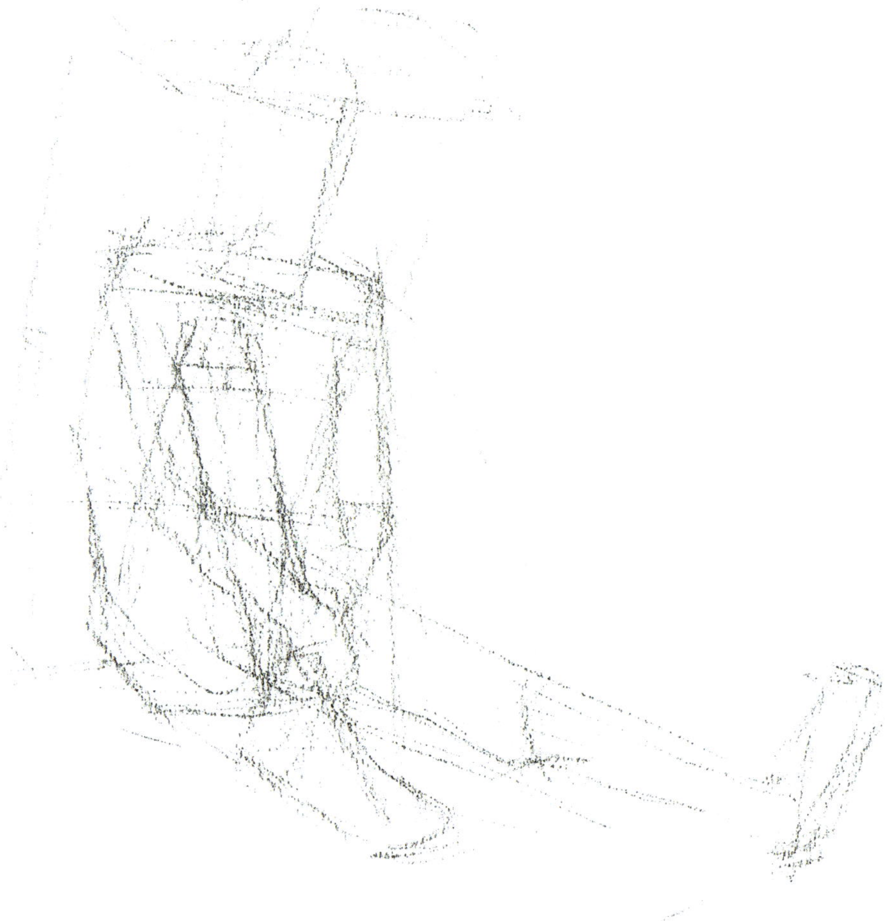

5

Add the Feet

Indicate the height, width and depth of each foot, comparing them with other body parts. Remember that the figure should be able to cover the top surface of his foot with his hand. Equate the width of the feet with the knee and elbow joints.

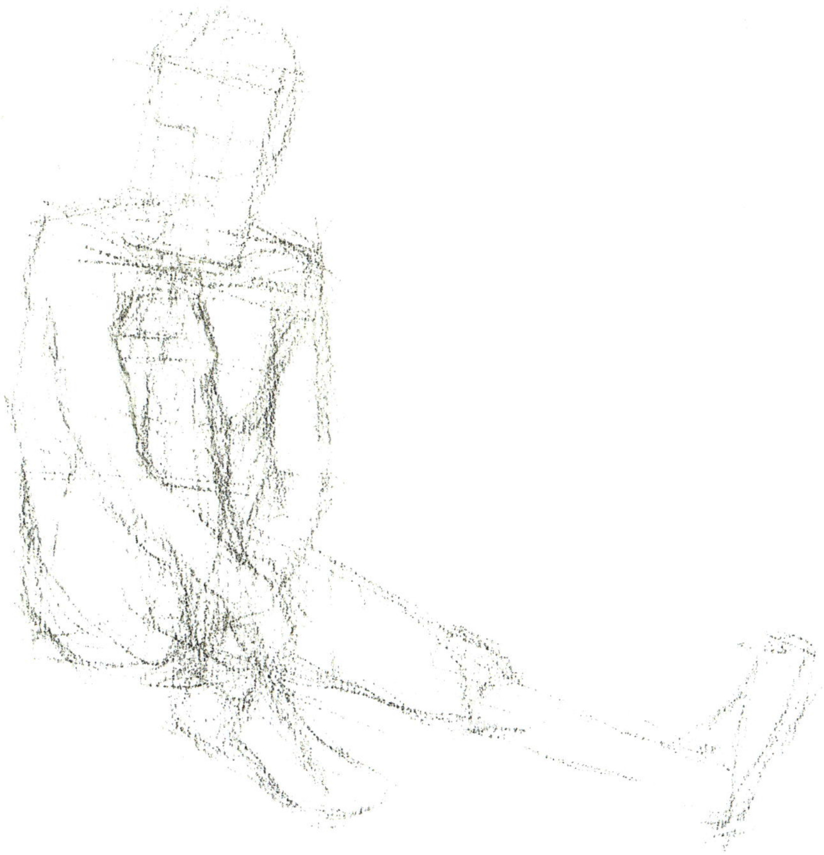

6

Record the Contour Lines

Still working lightly with the HB grade Conté pencil, begin to record the contour lines of the body.

Have the figure move about in your imagination. Ask if he could stand up and forward fold or cross his arms over the top of his head while keeping these proportions.

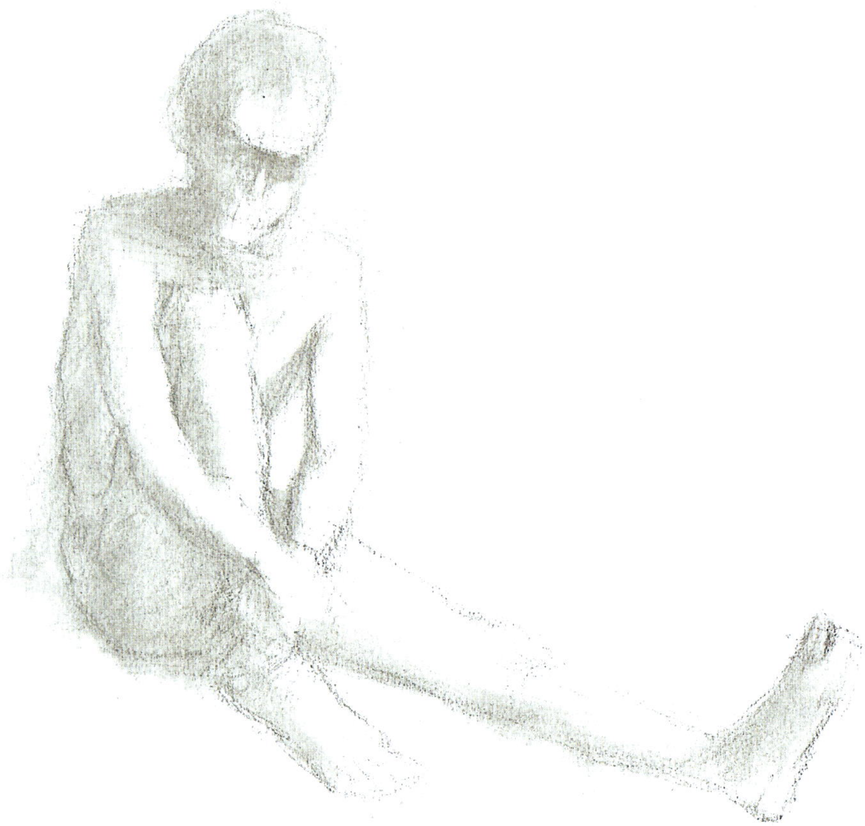

7

Blend the Shaded Areas

With a chamois cloth, rag or paper towel, rub the shaded portion of the figure together, consolidating it into an even tone. With a kneaded eraser, make sure that the lit areas of the figure stay broad and bright.

Use your cloth, pencil or a kneaded eraser as necessary to gently blend the areas between light and dark.

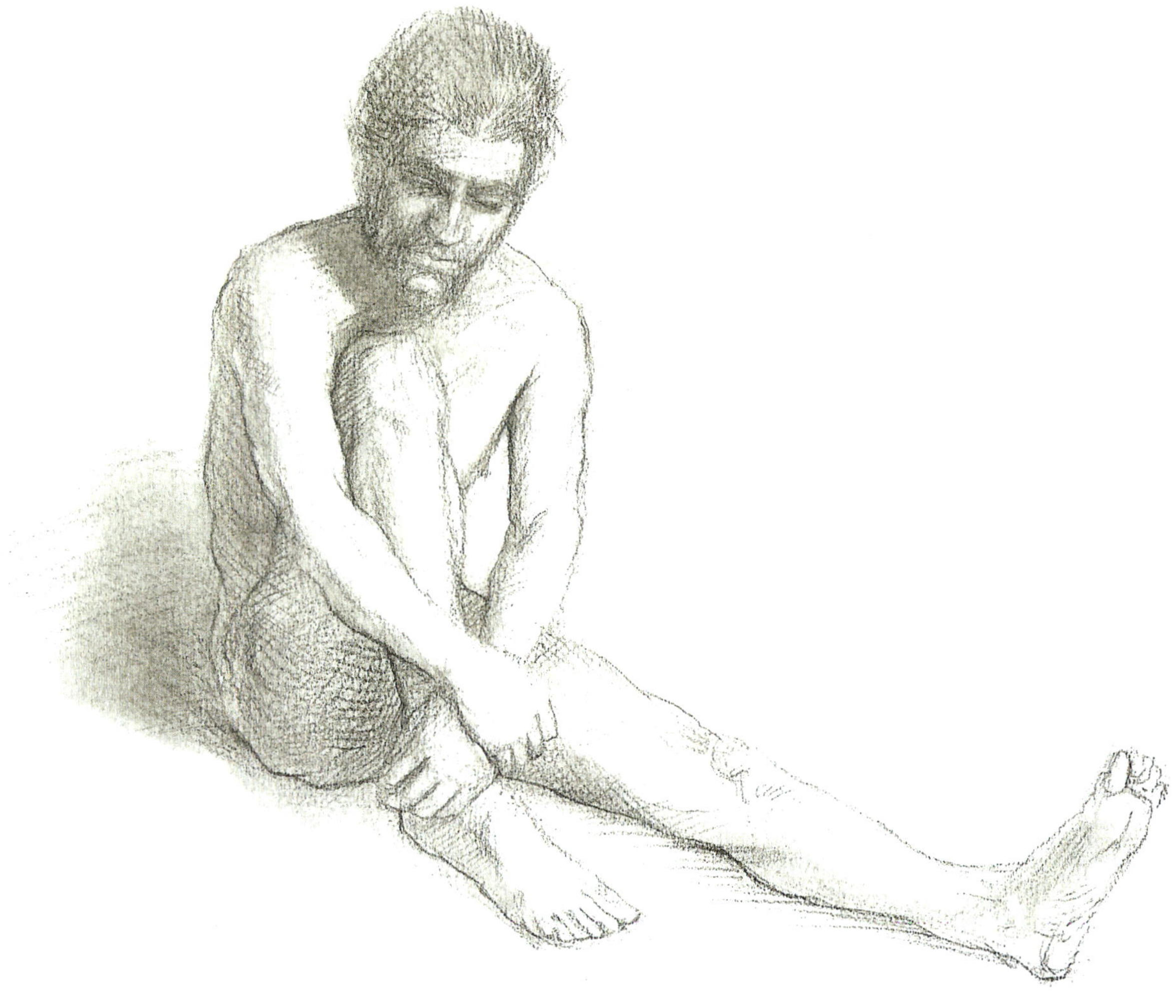

8

Add the Final Details

When you are satisfied with the proportion and blocking of the figure, add contour lines, cast shadows and other details with a softer (2B) Conté pencil. You can also choose to add some contour hatch lines to further darken deeply shadowed areas or to indicate muscle groups.

Demonstration

Compact Female

A compact pose affords a wonderful opportunity to concentrate on the details and subtleties of those parts of the body that are visible. Remember, however, to draw "through" the body, properly setting the position of all the limbs, visible or not. That will help to keep the contour lines fixed and to make sense of them to the viewer.

In this pose, the upper body can readily be divided into four quadrants, the same as if the model were standing. Finding the relative sizes of the lower limbs and arms remains the challenge.

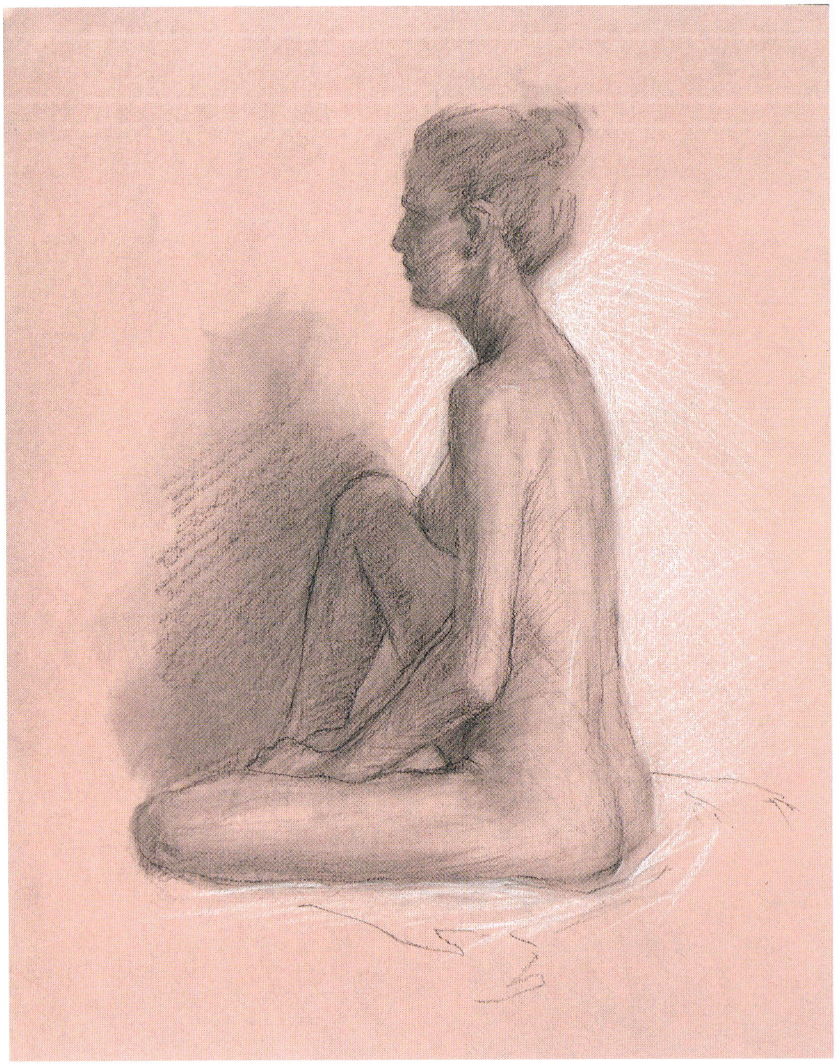

Working in Perspective

With fewer parts of the body visible, setting the proper perspective and position of those that are visible will be critical to making the drawing work.

MATERIALS

Surface

pink Canson Mi-Teintes 98-lb. (160gsm)

Charcoal Pencils

B, HB, 2B, 4B and white

Other Supplies

chamois cloth or rag

kneaded eraser

paper towels

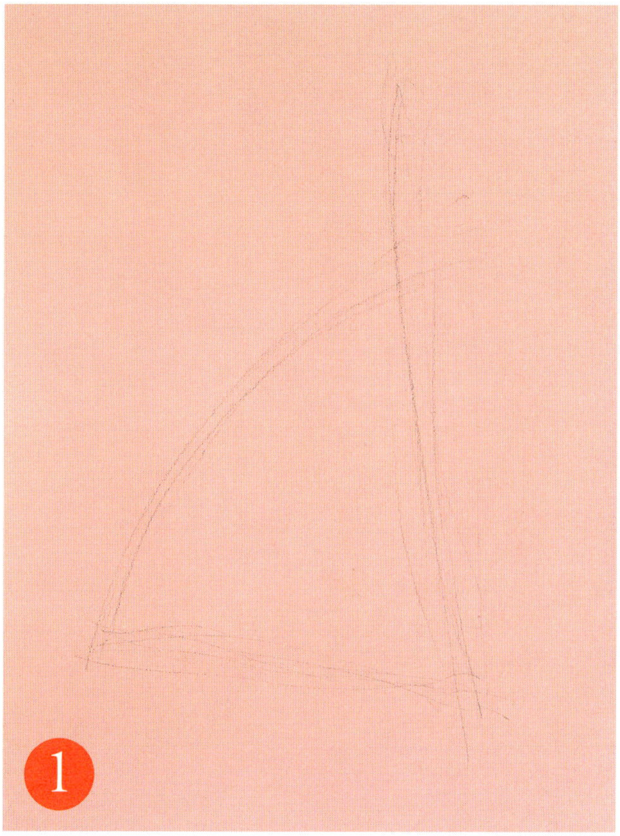

Place the Figure on the Page

When drawing a compact figure, slight distances on the page may show up as significant errors, so be careful when setting the limits and largest proportions of your drawing from the outset.

Using an HB charcoal pencil, set the limits of where you want the figure to appear on the page. Draw the angle of the upper bracket and the thigh, rotating the latter in your mind, to find where the end of the knee will fall.

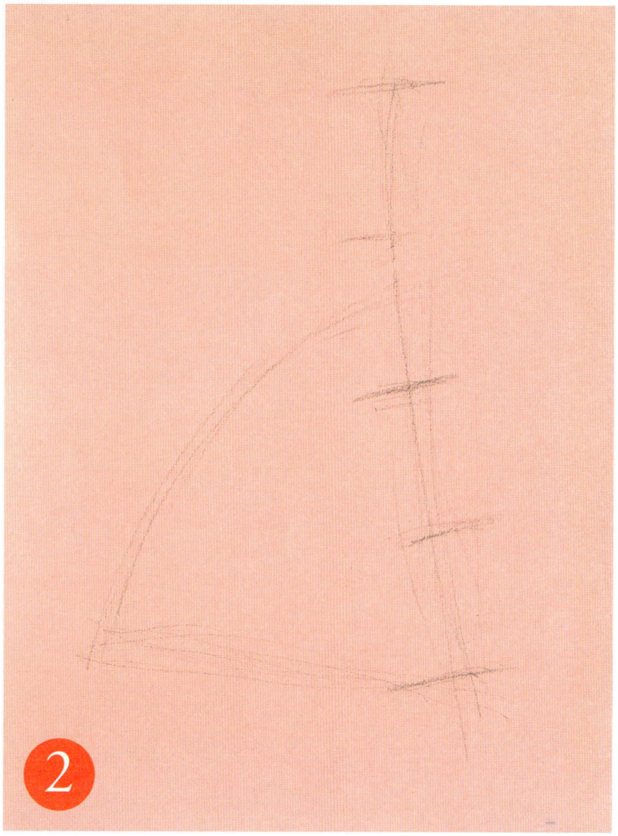

Divide the Brackets

In this instance, the top bracket has its base on the ground plane. Continuing with an HB charcoal pencil, subdivide the next-to-topmost bracket to find the line of the shoulders, and be sure that the thigh will be able to swing up to it.

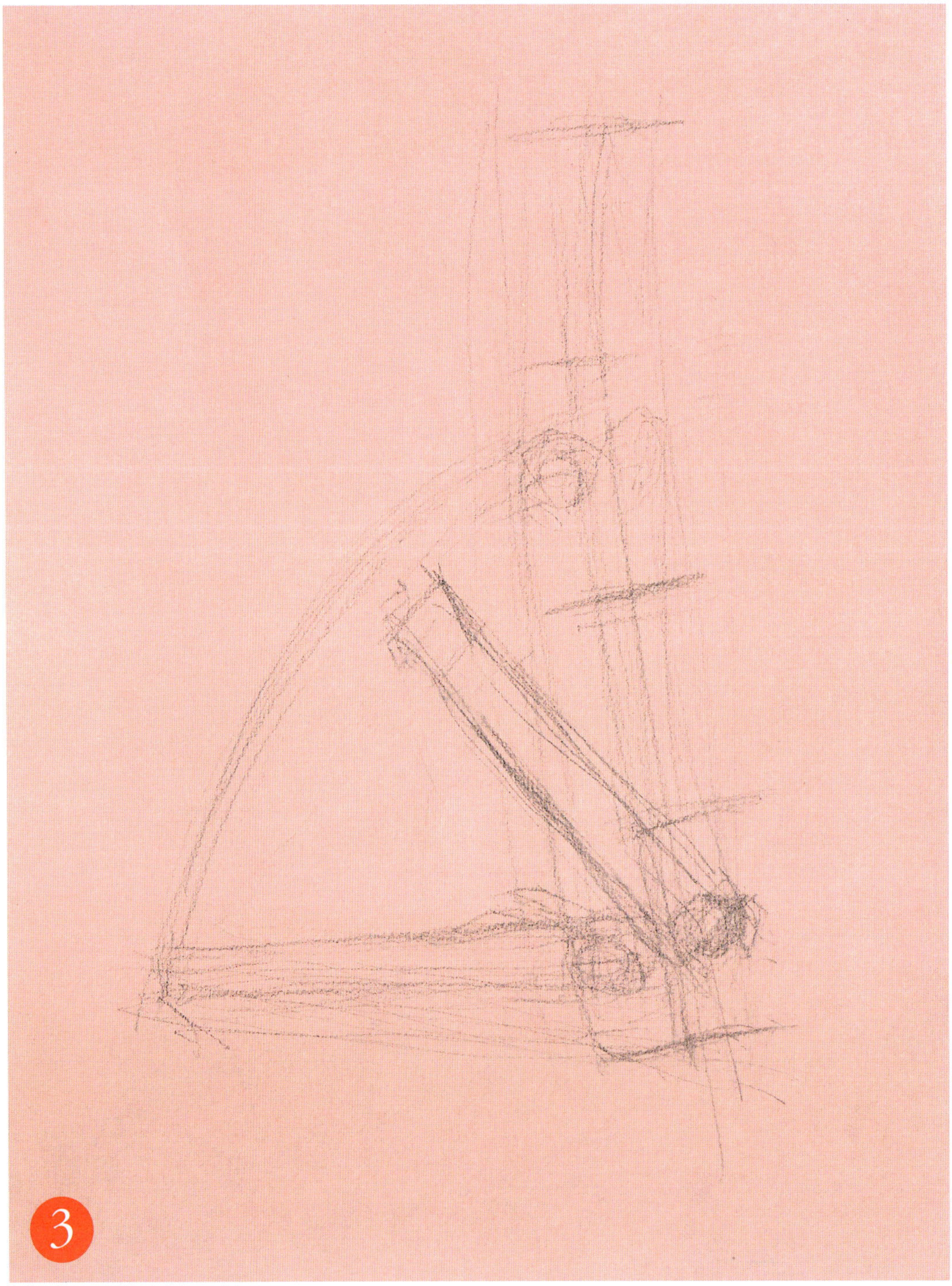

Define the Torso

Don't neglect your perspective lines and block construction for your figure even when it's being seen at a close angle.

Continuing with an HB charcoal pencil, square one of the quadrants (in perspective) to find the width of the hips, and run those lines upwards to help set a general width for the torso.

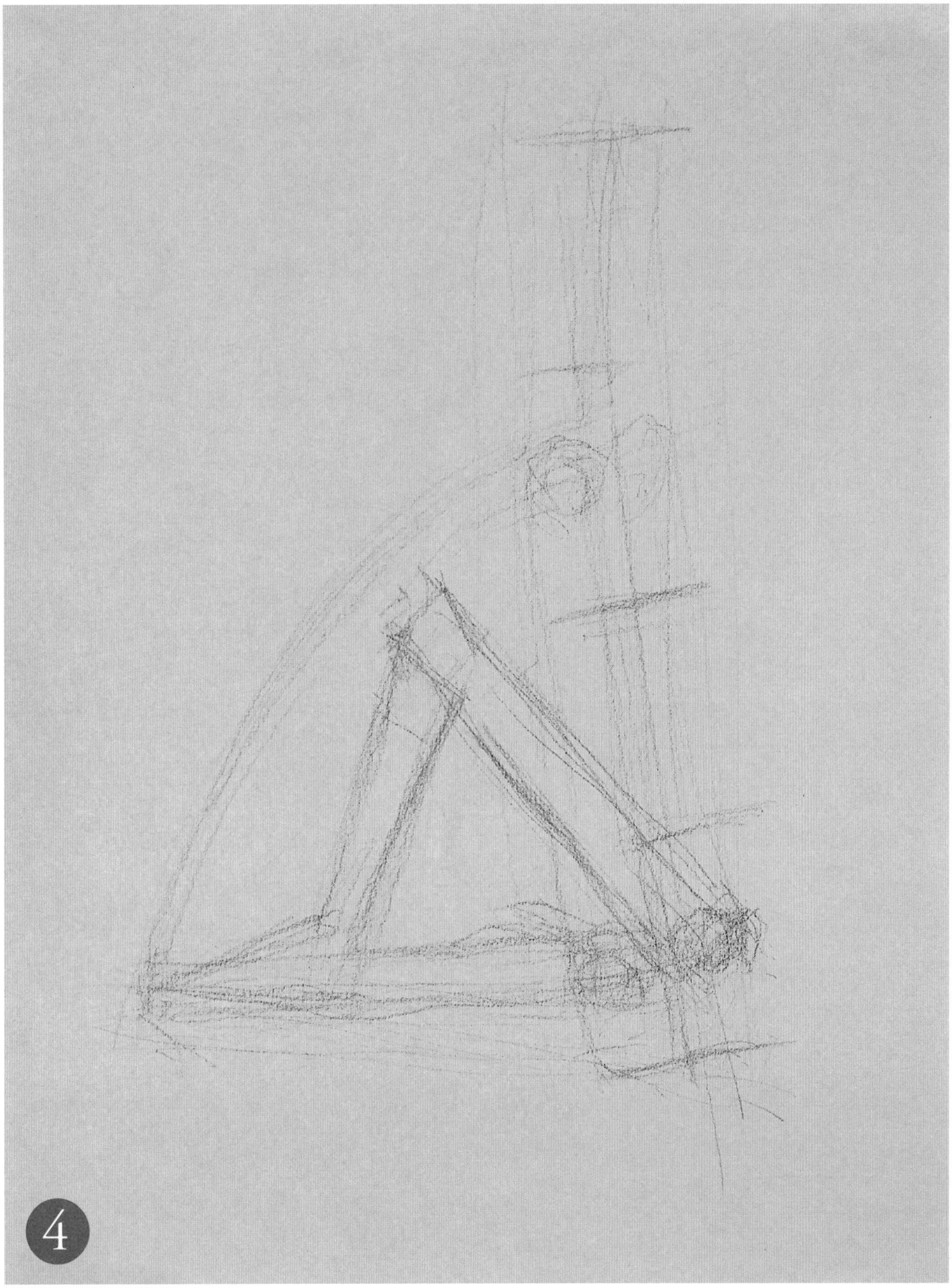

Place the Knees, Foot and Hidden Body Parts

Continuing with an HB charcoal pencil, position both knees properly in the perspective space, knowing that either thigh should be a half bracket in length. The foot (without the heel) should be a quarter bracket in length.

Draw through the figure to account for all the body parts, even those that are hidden from view.

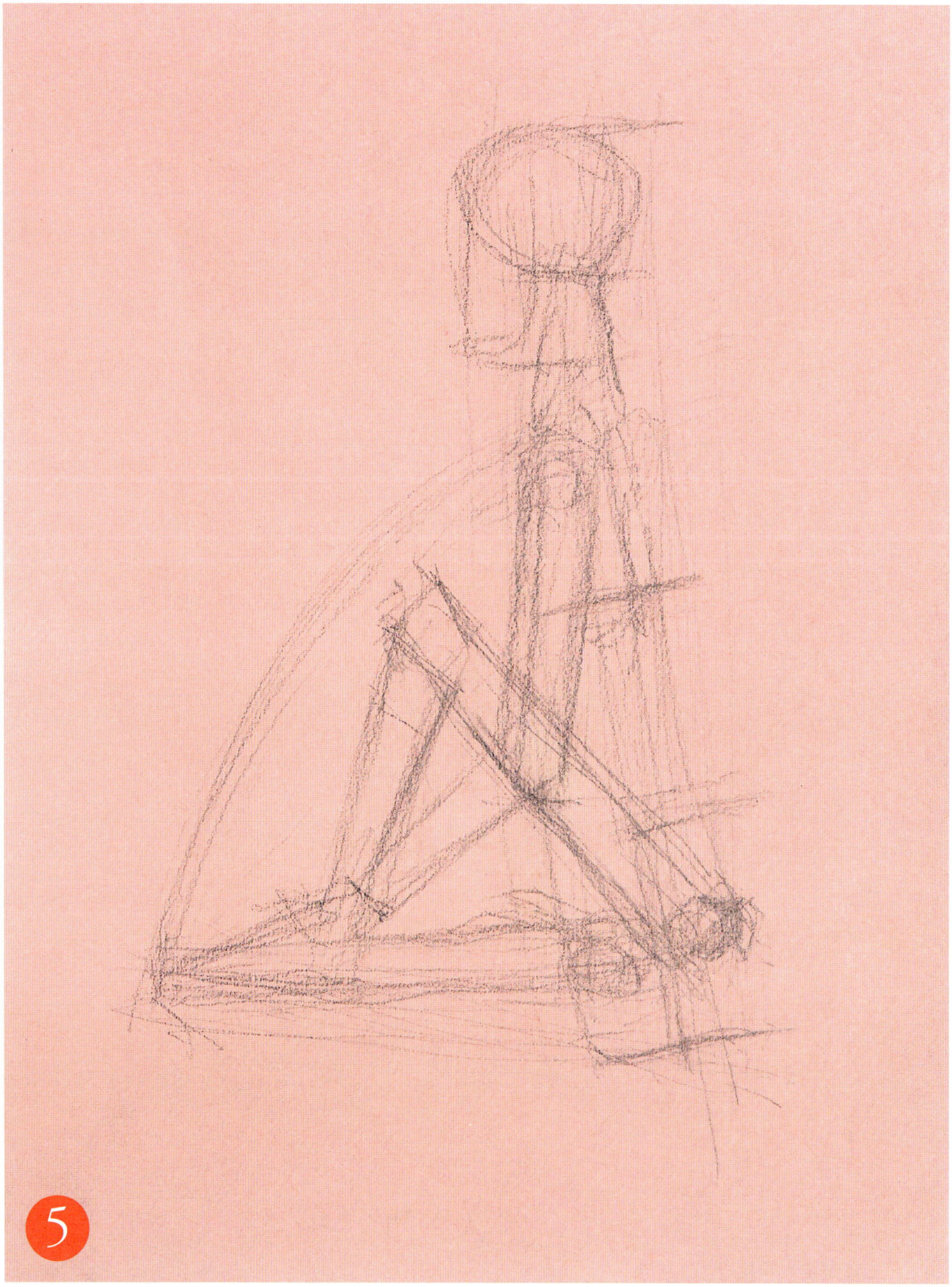

Form the Hips and Skull and Set the Width for the Limbs

Continuing with an HB charcoal pencil, block in forms for the hips and skull, letting the base of the cranium fall on the lower one-third plane of the head.

The widths of the knees, shoulders, feet and hands should be consistent. Don't let the limbs get too thick between these bony ends.

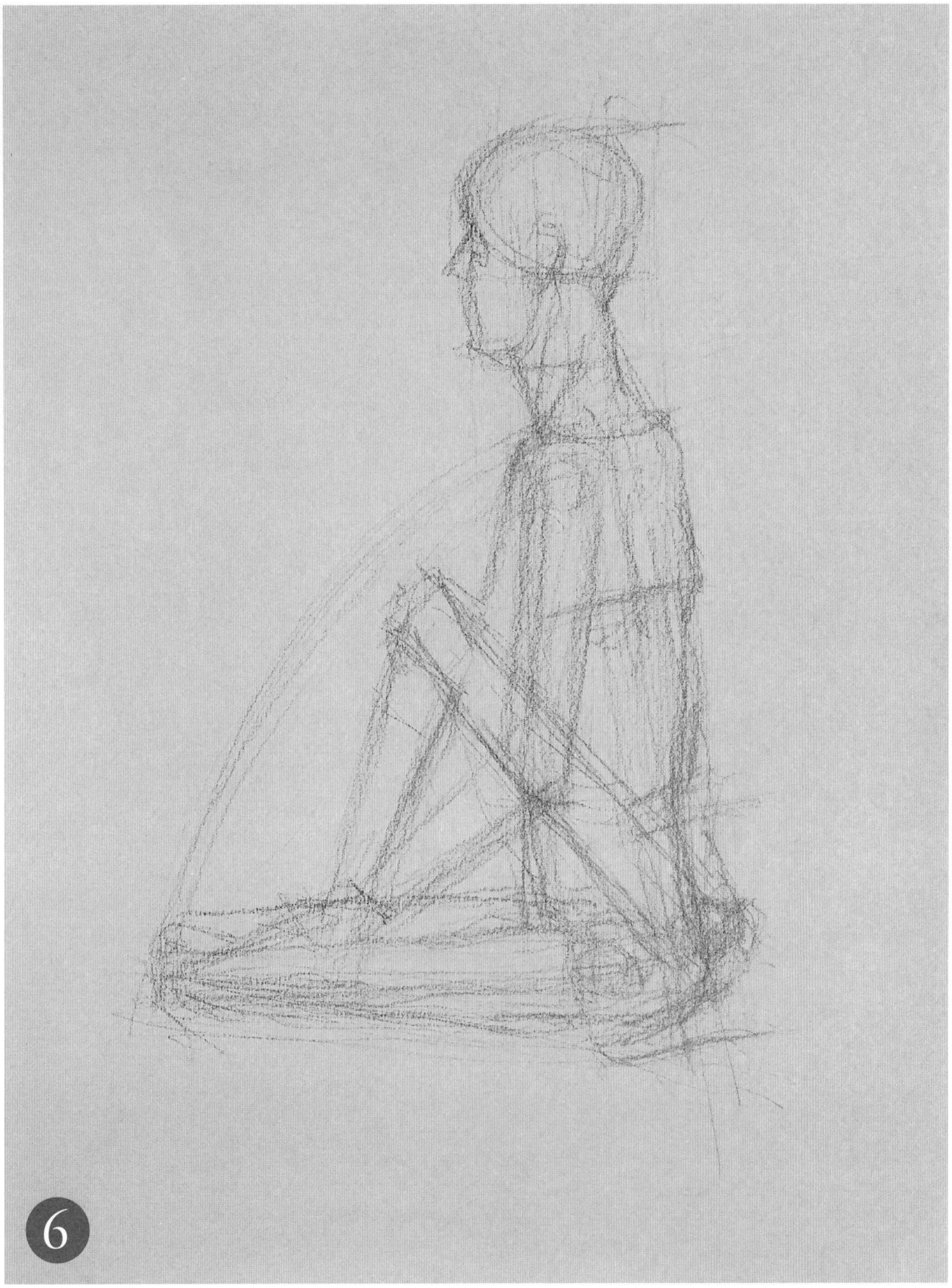

Continue Forming the Body Parts

Continuing with an HB charcoal pencil, let the model better inform the structure of the body parts, but don't lose sight of the perspective that's always at play.

The torso should maintain a consistent depth from the head to the seat, following a zigzag rhythm from front to back.

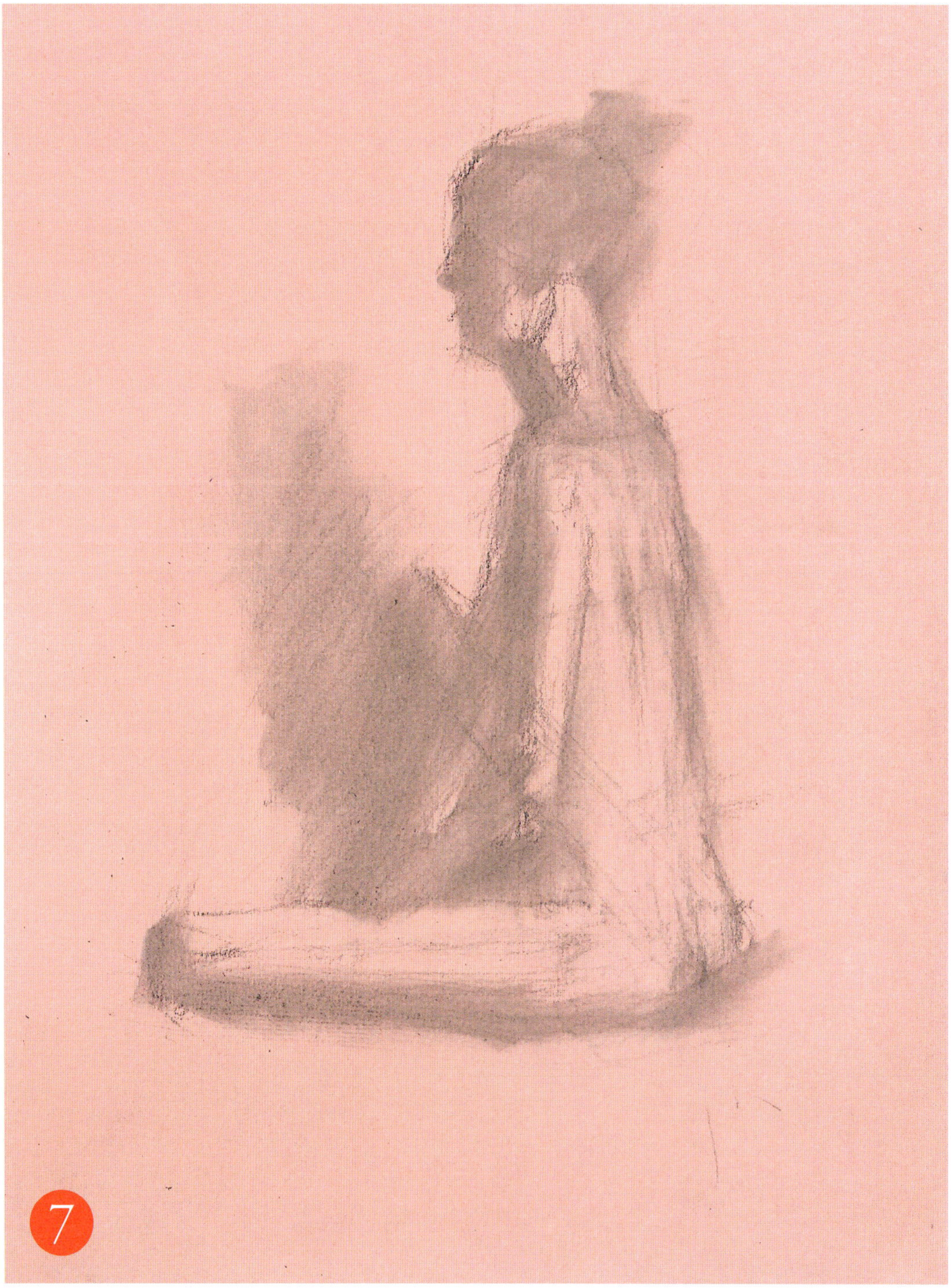

Begin Shading

With the correct proportion and structure in place, you can now start to combine your dark and light areas, rubbing the darks with a rag or chamois, and uniting the lights with a kneaded eraser. If there is not enough contrast of tone, you can darken the shadow area with a softer (B or 2B) charcoal pencil. But first, place at least one highlight point with a white charcoal pencil. Since this will be the whitest white in your drawing, you know that your figure will "live" within this value range.

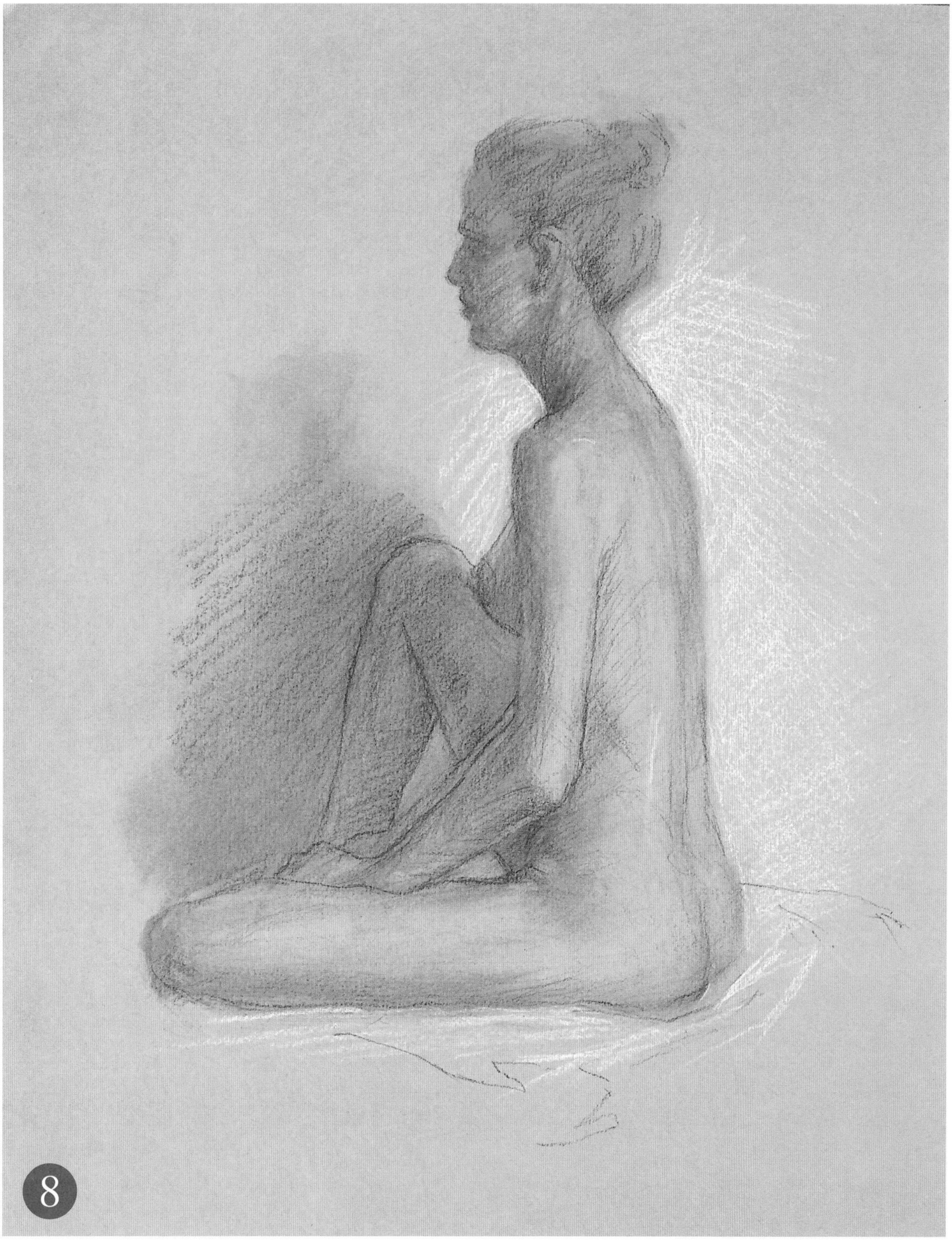

Finish Adding Contours and Highlights

Let your knowledge of the anatomical structure of the figure govern the contour lines you add to your drawing.

Add highlights as necessary with a white charcoal pencil to help your drawing pop.

Demonstration

Action Male

Human beings, even in sleep, do not keep perfectly still. They breathe, they move their limbs, they move through space. While it is an indispensable practice to draw from a model in a fixed pose, eventually, if your art is to grow, you will need to draw figures in poses that are imagined or impossible to hold. (As a matter of fact, eventually all the figures you draw or paint will be imaginary. They will just be represented to the viewer with input or inspiration gained from the model.)

In this case it's not possible for any model to twist that much at the waist. I drew this figure by cobbling together several different poses and unifying the results.

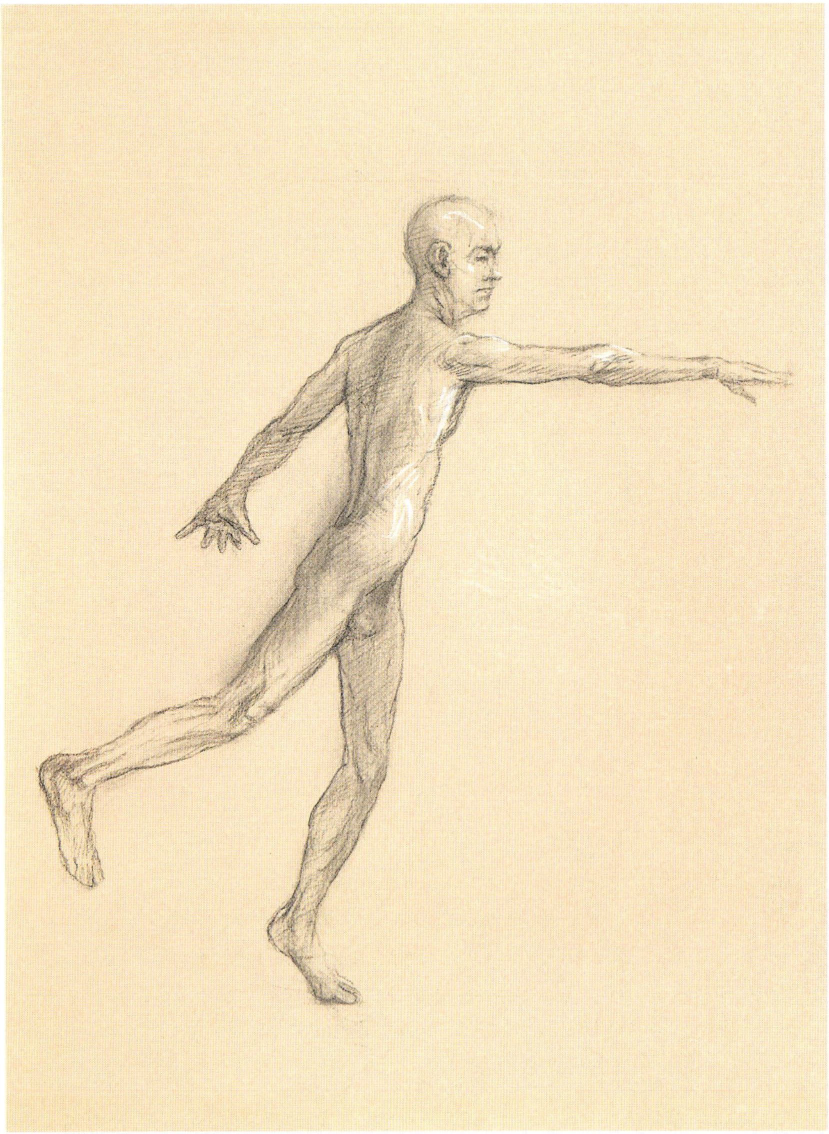

MATERIALS

Surface

tan Canson Mi-Teintes 98-lb. (160gsm)

Charcoal Pencils

HB, 2B, 4B and white

Other Supplies

chamois cloth

kneaded eraser

paper towels

Combining Poses

For this pose, the model took several positions that were then added together into one pose.

1

Begin With a Gesture Drawing

Start off the gesture from the model, your imagination or a combination of the two. Using an HB charcoal pencil to keep your gesture lines light, find a pose and placement on the page that you like. Continue using an HB charcoal pencil unless otherwise specified.

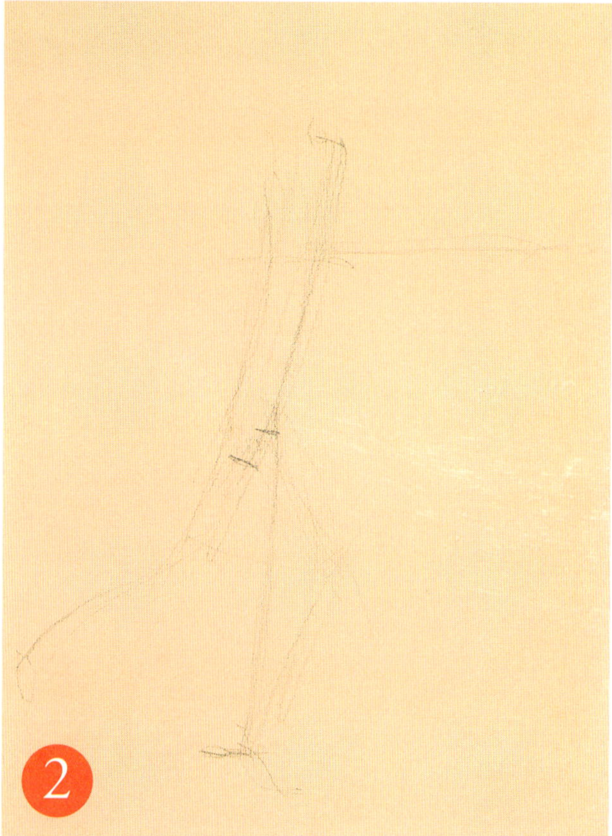

2

Add the Brackets and Place the Figure

Add the upper and lower brackets. Bend the lower bracket in half at the knee joints once you're sure that each half is the correct length.

Make sure none of the limbs will fall off the page. Two outstretched arms would be equal to the figure's height, so give yourself enough room.

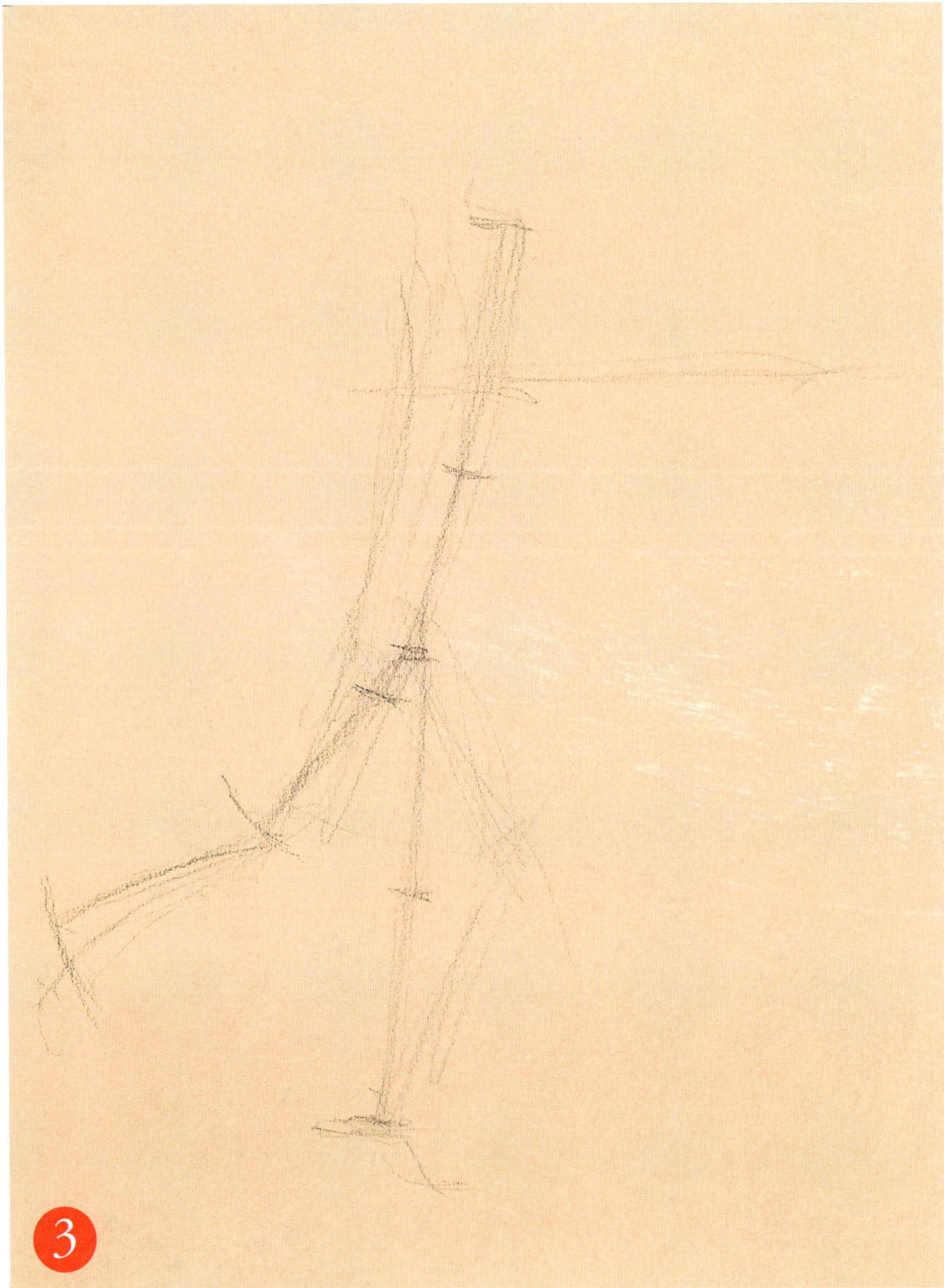

Develop the Torso and Legs

Divide the upper bracket into two. Start to sketch the torso as a block in three dimensions.

Because you know their proper proportions, you can change the position of the feet and legs at any time.

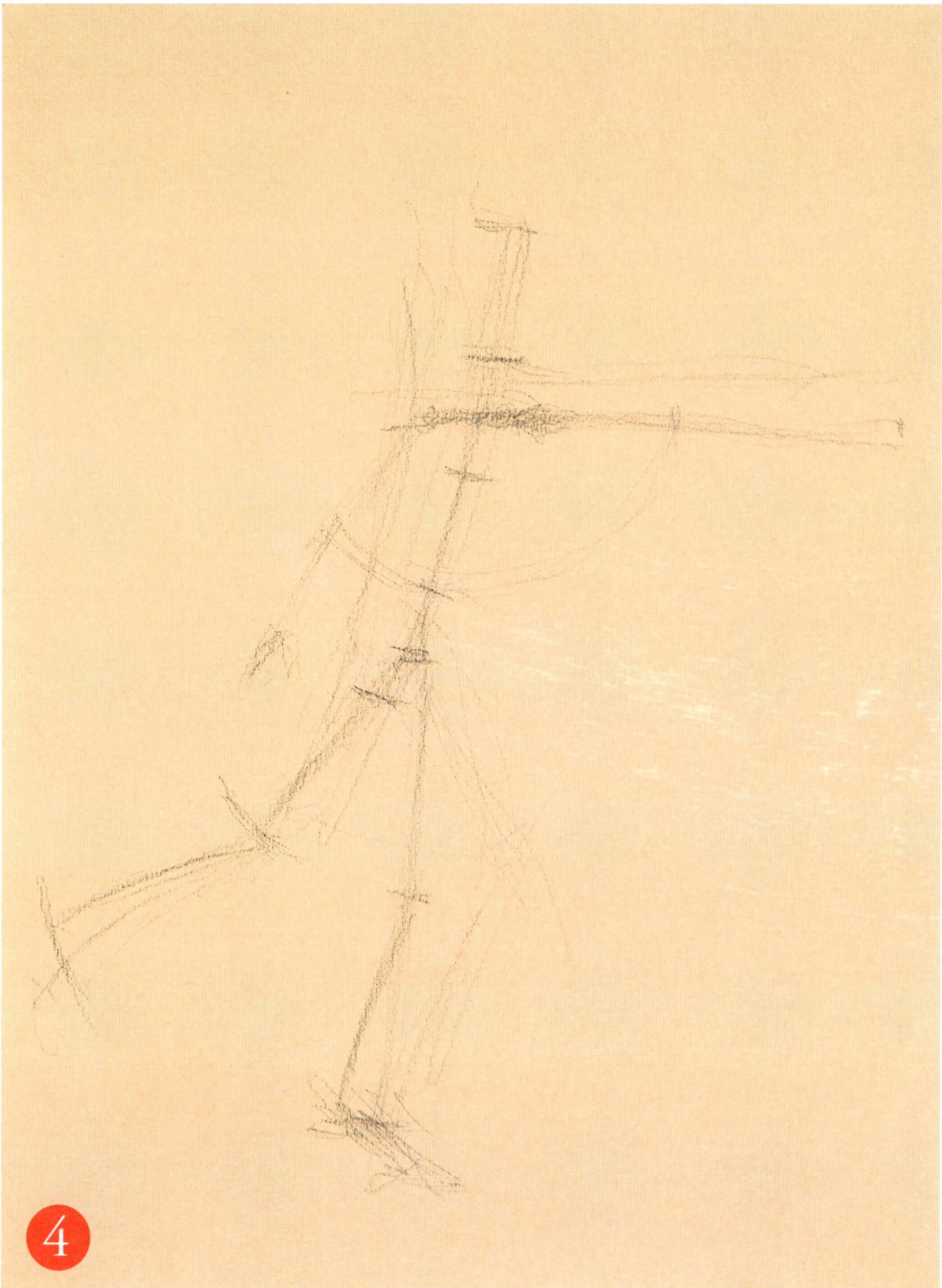

Continue Placing the Body Parts

Divide the upper bracket to find the placement for the head, hips and shoulder line.

Sketch in the limbs on the far side of the body. (In this case, the left arm is in a position that the model can't, in reality, hold.) Make sure that the elbows would align with the waist if they were relaxed.

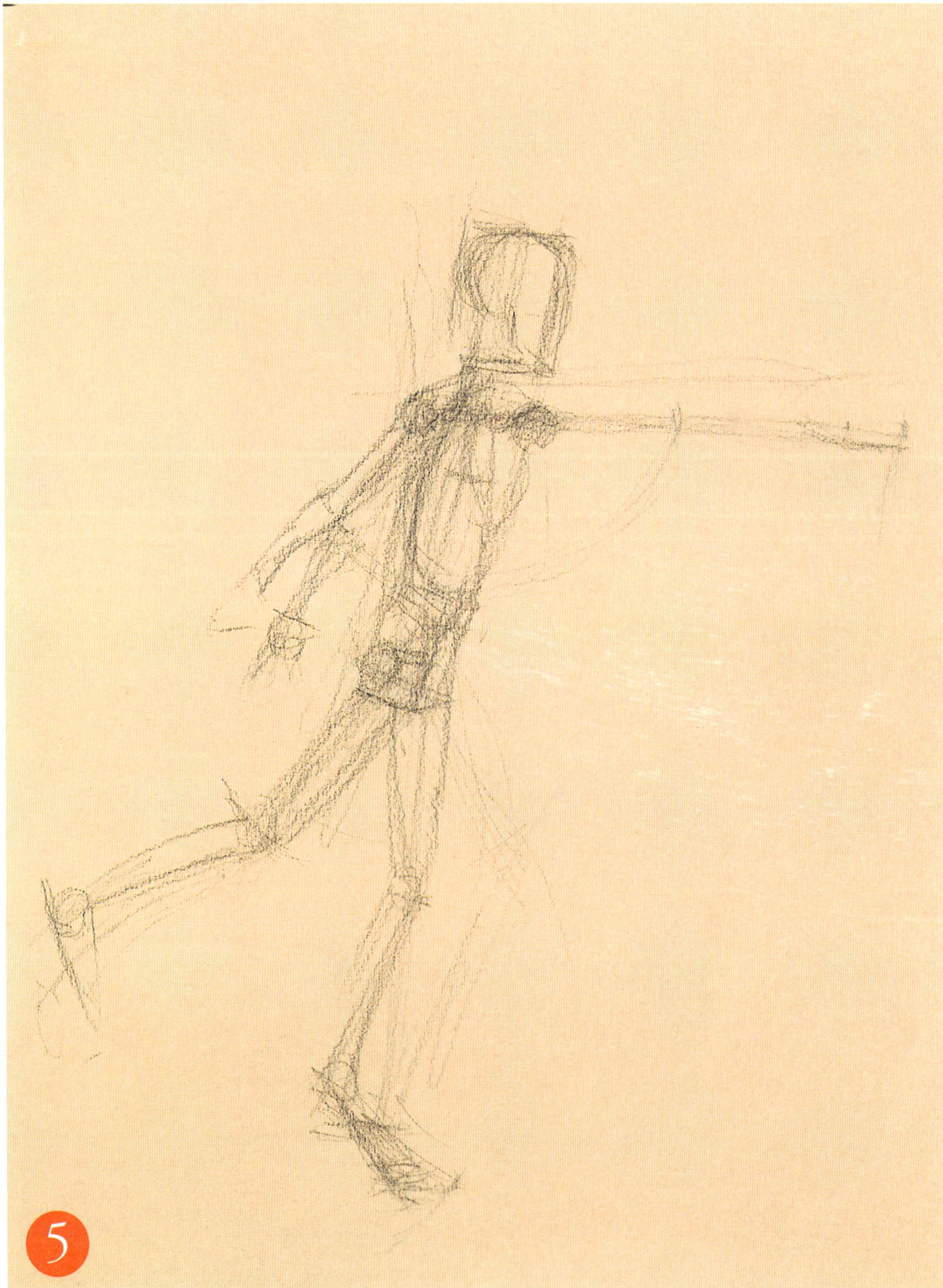

Measure the Width of the Limbs

Establish the correct thicknesses for the limbs. The width and depth of the knees should be equal. They should also be the same size as the balls of the shoulders and hips. You can use the same circle shapes to find the position of the ankle joints.

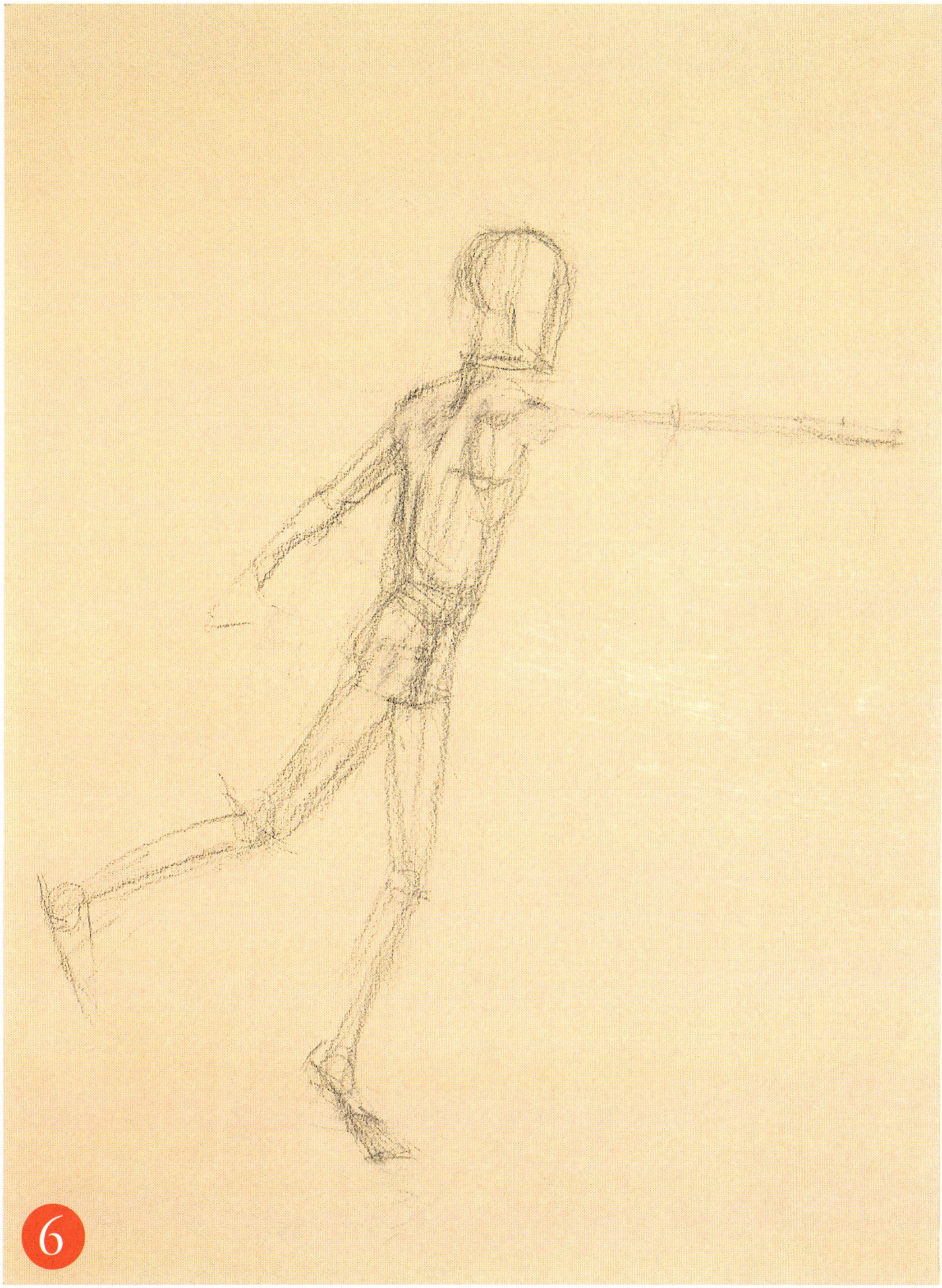

Measure the Arms

The distance from the near end of the upper arm bone to the elbow should be the same as from the elbow to the first knuckle line. One-fourth of that measurement, added onto the end of the forearm, will give you the position of the pinky.

Keep checking if the figure could draw his knees to his chest and so on with the various measurements.

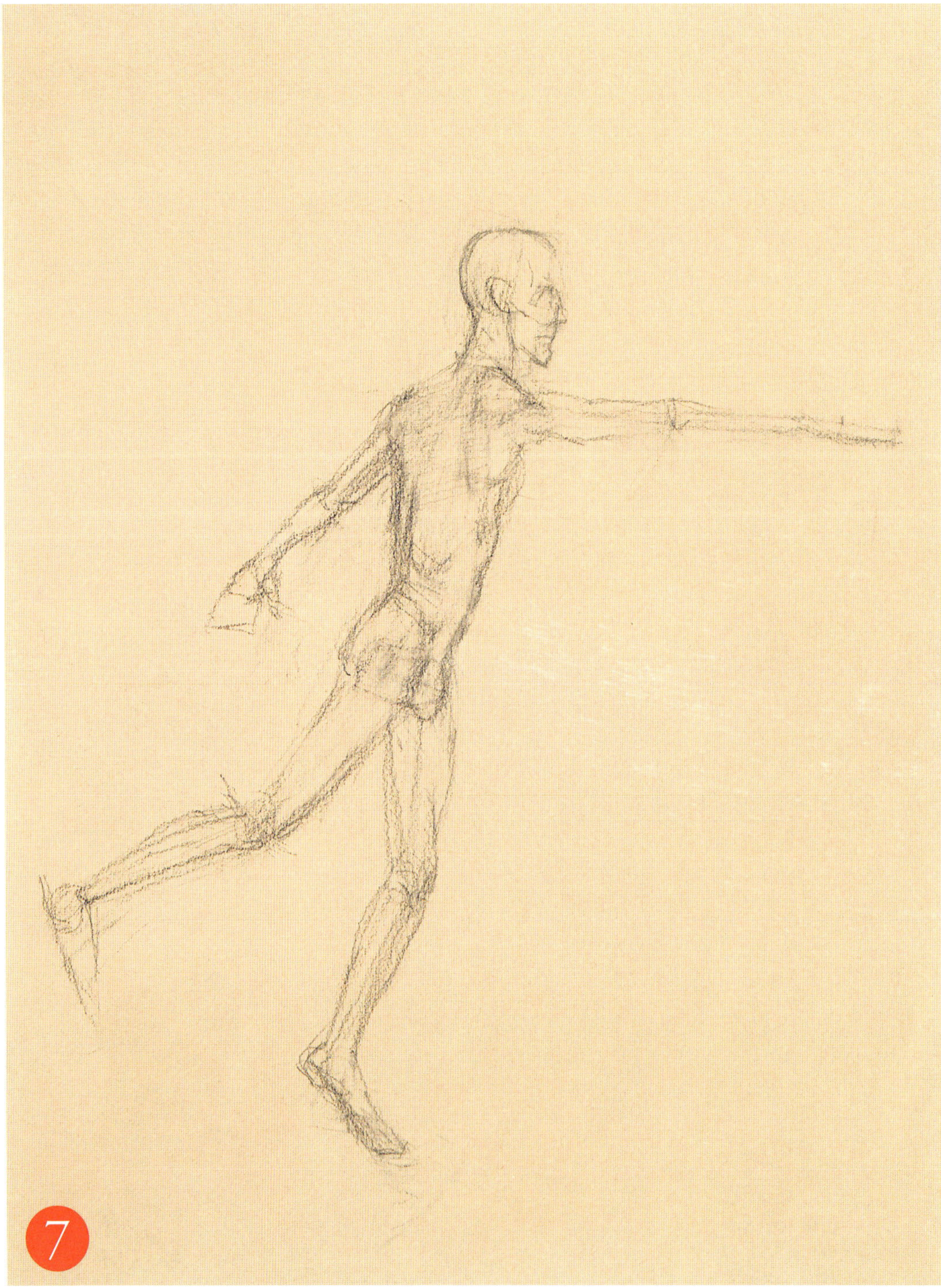

Draw the Far Limbs and Check Proportions

Continue to work from the model, drawing the far limbs in perspective. Keep checking your comparative proportions. The width of the palm of the hand should equal the depth of the knee. The hand should be able to just cover the portion of the foot in front of the ankle.

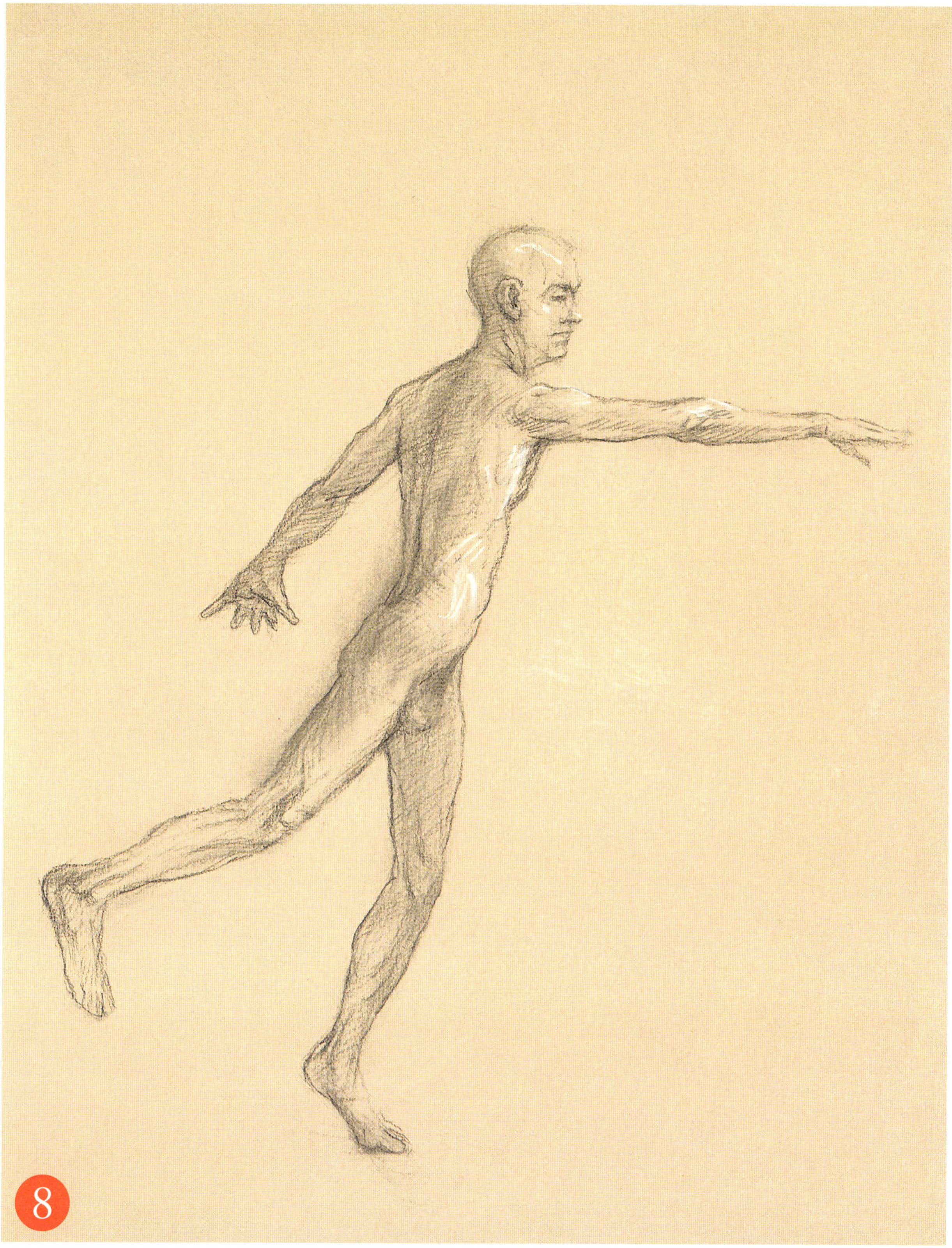

8

Finish Drawing the Pose and the Lighting

You can have the model hold part of the pose at a time if the pose would be impossible to hold in its entirety. Keep the drawing convincing by maintaining a consistent lighting scheme on the different parts of the figure. Use a softer (2B or even 4B) charcoal pencil to add contour lines, hatching and cast shadows. Use a sharp white charcoal pencil to add highlights. Keep them within the clean lighted areas you create with a kneaded eraser.

SKETCHBOOK EXERCISES

Whether you're working in your studio or in a class or even sketching the people you see in public spaces, explore ways that you can use your knowledge of proportion to capture poses quickly.

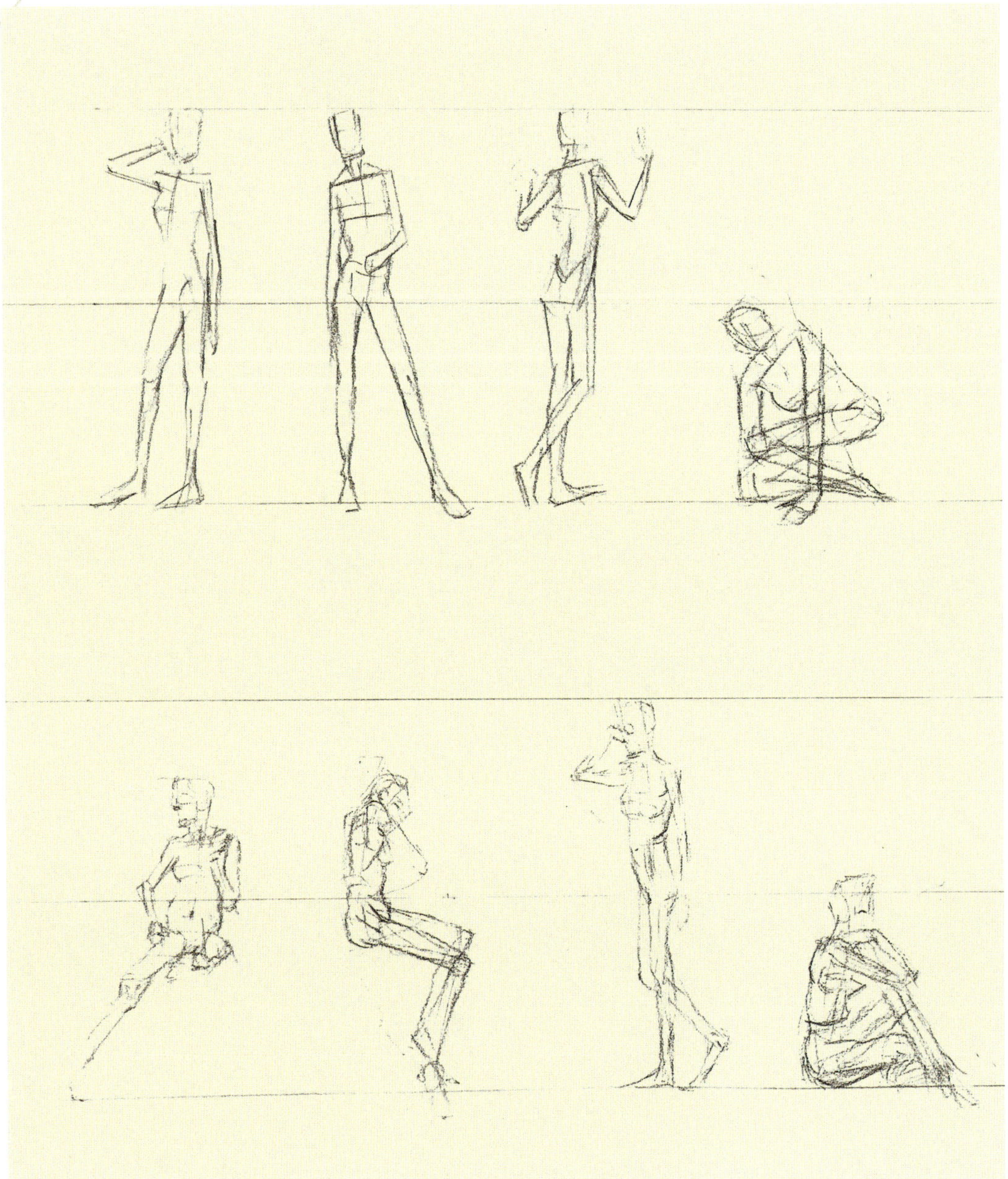

Gesture Exercise

Here's an interesting exercise you can do with a model who is doing gestures (minute-long poses that are often dramatic or unusual). Pre-mark your paper with sets of rules that have a middle line dividing each set in half, top-to-bottom. Do your gesture drawings, making the figure the same size each time. Use the middle rule as a quick way to pinpoint where the center of the body would be if the figure were standing straight up.

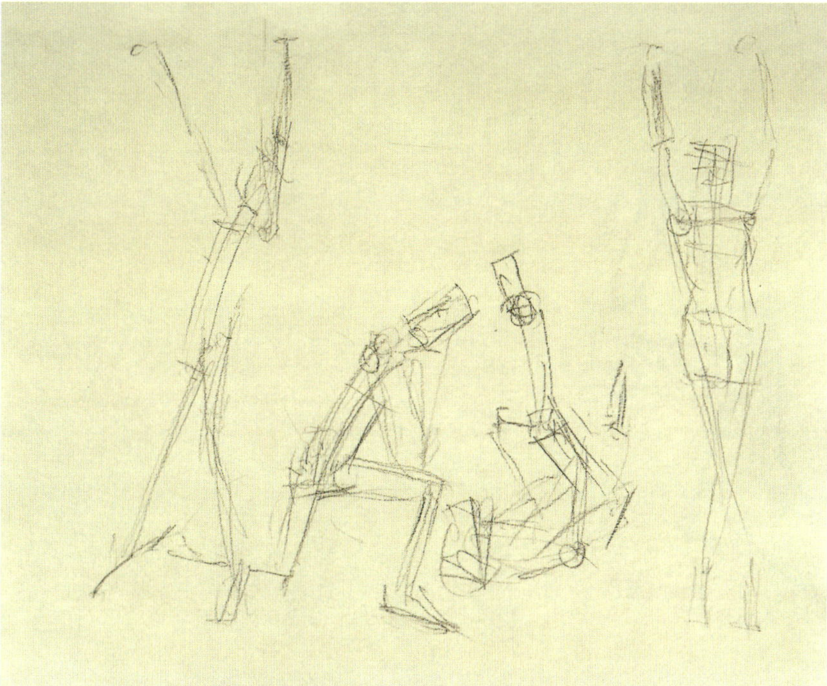

2-Minute Successive Poses Exercise

This single drawing comes from observing a single model during a drawing session. For this exercise, see if you can draw the model in successive poses (here, 2 minutes apiece) in the same scale and in the same space. This will train your ability to draw the model in the correct proportion and will help you see if you can render the figure in the same perspective space. I created this drawing with a soft grade (2B) charcoal pencil on green-gray paper.

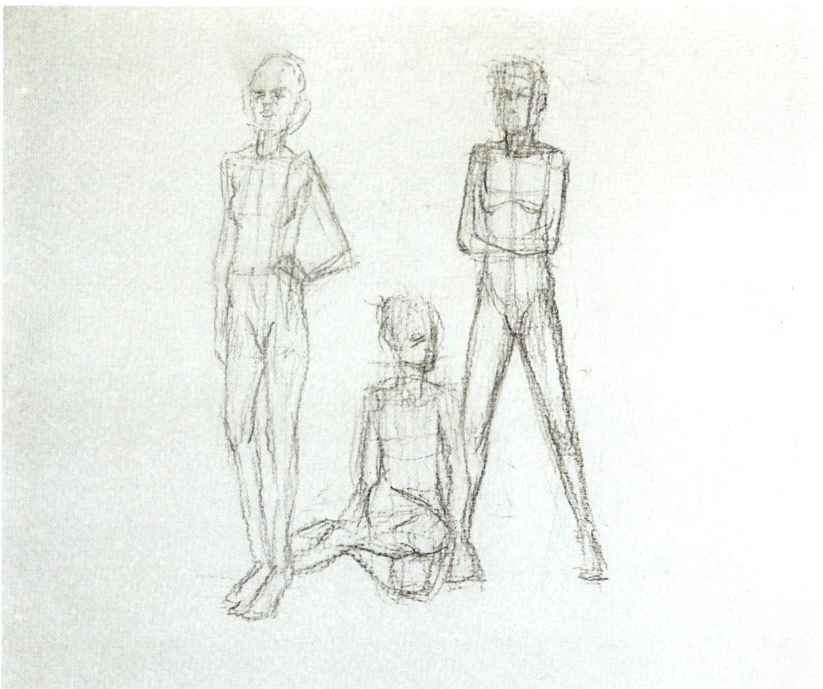

5-Minute Successive Poses Exercise

I created this drawing using a process similar to the previous successive poses exercise, except that each pose lasted for a longer time, 5 minutes apiece. Notice how one of your figures can overlap another to help unify the spacial environment they share. See what kind of a composition you can put together using the model's different poses.

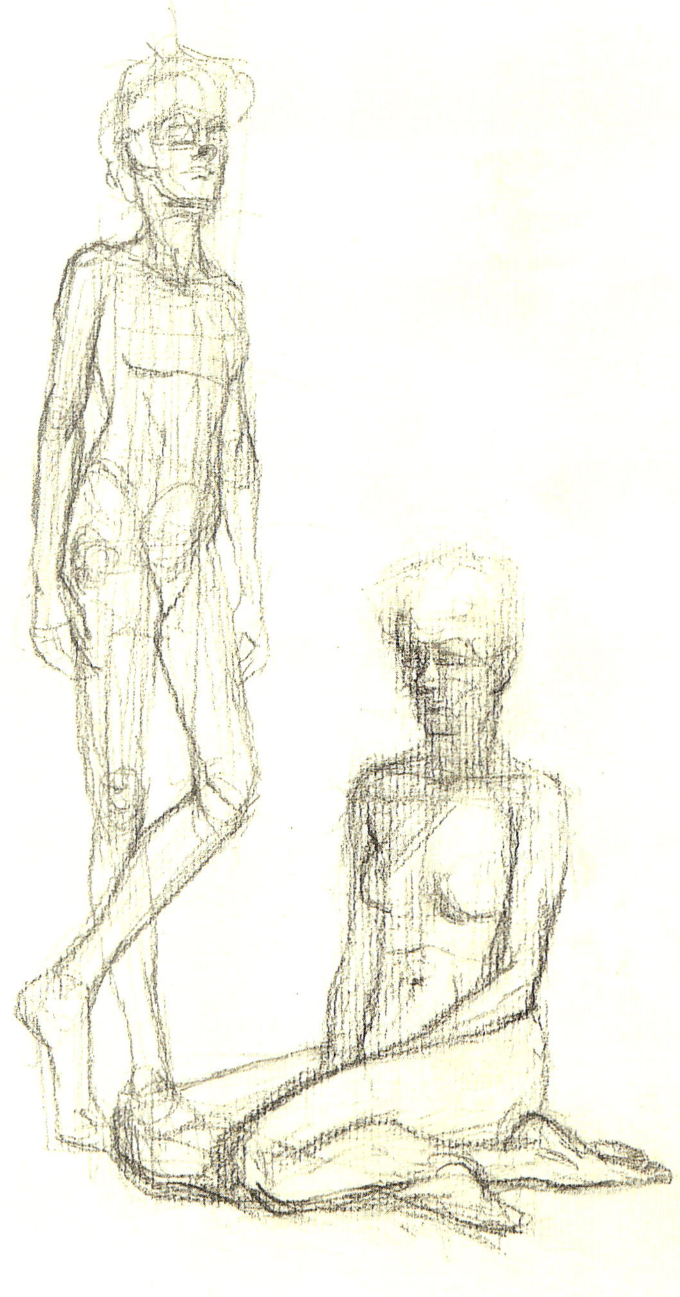

10-Minute Successive Poses Exercise

Here I drew the same model in two 10-minute poses. Try to relate the sizes of the body parts to each other. For the second pose (in this case, it was the seated figure), you can borrow the height, width or depth of the body part from the first drawn figure. Remember to foreshorten the appropriate limbs, as the perspective of the drawing will dictate. Once again, try to make all the figures in your drawing the same scale and to live in the same pictorial space.

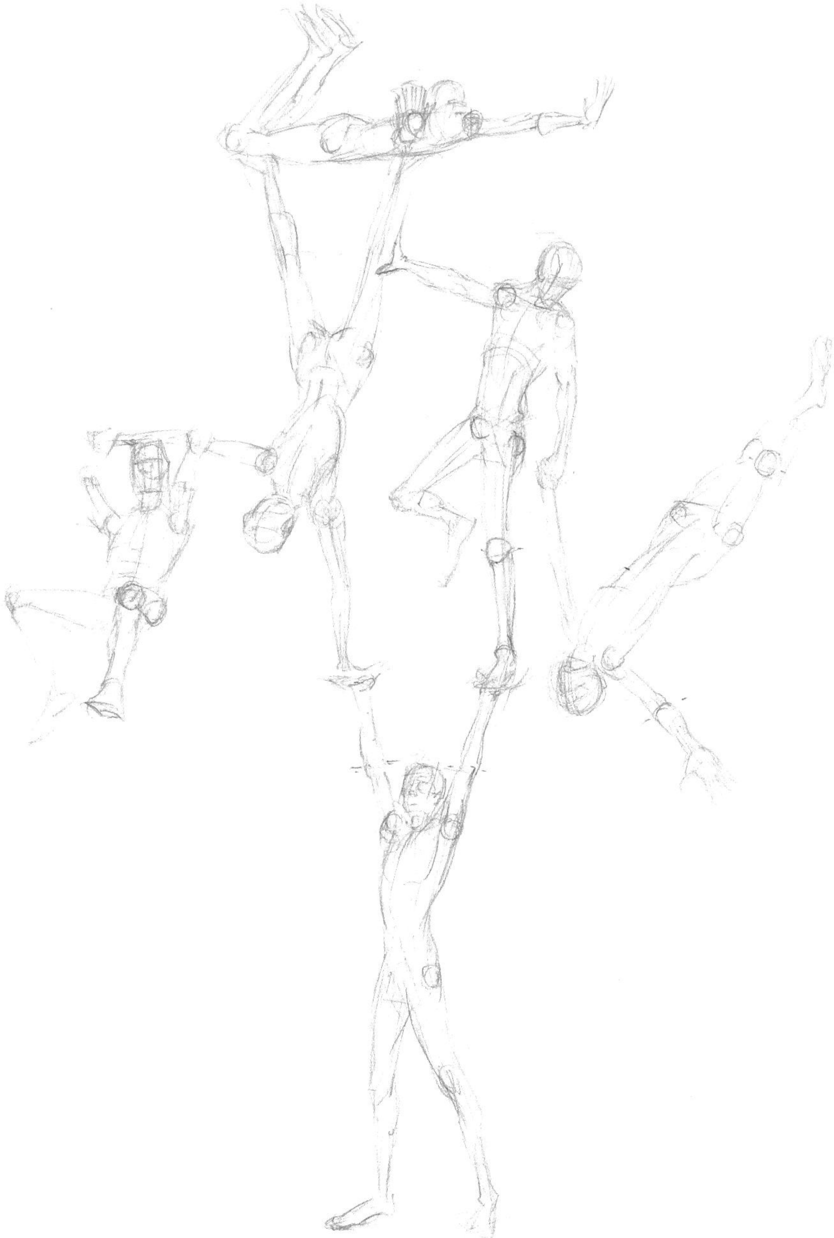

Drawing From the Imagination Exercise

I created this whimsy or fantasy drawing using nothing but an HB lead mechanical pencil and a sheet of plain drawing paper. Obviously, no model or group of models posed for this drawing. It is straight from the imagination. When you create multifigure compositions, it would be impractical to pose a group of several models together while you search for a good solution for your finished artwork. So even if the anatomy isn't perfect and the line work is loose, having a solid sense of figure proportion can free your imagination and your figures to let loose and fly.

INDEX

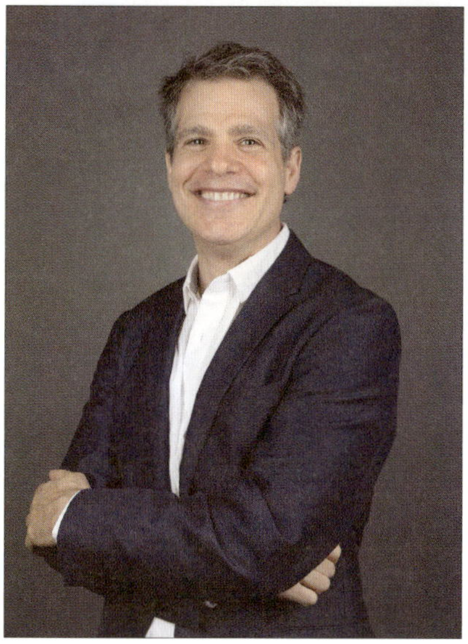

Photo by Louis Santore

ABOUT THE AUTHOR

Michael Massen is a sculptor, painter and draftsperson. He lives in New York City, where he made his living for years as an art director and graphic designer.

Mr. Massen holds a BA from Wesleyan University and an MFA in painting from the New York Academy of Art.

He is the author of *The Artist's Guide to Drawing the Clothed Figure* published by Watson-Guptill Publications.

Mr. Massen teaches regular workshops in figure drawing at the Art Students League of New York in addition to other venues. Visit his website at **michaelmassen.com**.

ACKNOWLEDGMENTS

My deepest thanks and appreciation go to Mary Bostic, Amy Jones, Brittany VanSnepson, Jamie DeAnne, Sarah Laichas and Geoff Raker at North Light Books, and thanks, especially, to the many models who posed for the illustrations and whose professionalism made this book possible.

DEDICATION

For Miriam and Nina and Richard,
and Jerry and Jean and Molly.

 Published by North Light Books, an imprint of F+W Media, Inc., 10151 Carver Road, Suite 200, Blue Ash, Ohio, 45242. (800) 289-0963. First Edition.

a content + ecommerce company

Other fine North Light Books are available from your favorite bookstore, art supply store or online supplier. Visit our website at fwcommunity.com.

20 19 18 17 16 5 4 3 2 1

Distributed in Canada by Fraser Direct
100 Armstrong Avenue
Georgetown, ON, Canada L7G 5S4
Tel: (905) 877-4411

Distributed in the U.K. and Europe
by F&W Media International LTD
Brunel House, Forde Close, Newton Abbot, TQ12 4PU, UK
Tel: (+44) 1626 323200, Fax: (+44) 1626 323319
Email: enquiries@fwmedia.com

Distributed in Australia by Capricorn Link
P.O. Box 704, S. Windsor NSW, 2756 Australia
Tel: (02) 4560-1600; Fax: (02) 4577 5288
Email: books@capricornlink.com.au

ISBN-13: 978-1-4403-3756-7

Edited by Mary Burzlaff Bostic
Production edited by Brittany VanSnepson
Designed by Jamie DeAnne
Production coordinated by Jennifer Bass